The Royal Artillery at War With Napoleon

The Royal Artillery at War With Napoleon
During the Peninsular War and at Waterloo, 1808-15

ILLUSTRATED

Francis Duncan

Edited by
John H. Lewis

*The Royal Artillery at War With Napoleon
During the Peninsular War and at Waterloo, 1808-15*
by Francis Duncan
Edited by John H. Lewis

ILLUSTRATED

FIRST EDTION

Leonaur is an imprint of Oakpast Ltd

Copyright in this form © 2020 Oakpast Ltd

ISBN: 978-1-78282-890-7 (hardcover)
ISBN: 978-1-78282-891-4 (softcover)

http://www.leonaur.com

Publisher's Notes

The views expressed in this book are not necessarily those of the publisher.

Contents

The Development of the Royal Horse Artillery	7
Peninsular War—Roliça, Vimiera, Corunna	24
Walcheren	53
Passage of the Douro, and Talavera	73
Busaco and Torres Vedras	93
Barossa, Badajoz, and Albuera	113
Ciudad Rodrigo and Badajoz	141
Salamanca and Burgos	157
Vittoria and San Sebastian	175
Conclusion of the Peninsular War	211
Waterloo	230
Appendix	264

CHAPTER 1

The Development of the Royal Horse Artillery

"The Royal Horse Artillery was formed as an additional corps to the regiment of Artillery on the 1st February, 1793." Remarkable for its brevity, this early reference of the formation of the Royal Horse Artillery is also remarkable for its inaccuracy. It was *not* an additional corps to the Royal Artillery, but from the very commencement an essential, integral part of it.

The Driver Corps, formed in 1794, *was* an additional corps to the Royal Artillery; but its officers were, until after Waterloo, drawn from a different source, and its men were never artillerymen. The Royal Horse Artillery, on the other hand, was invariably officered by the Royal Artillery, and was recruited from its ranks. Of the wisdom, or otherwise, of this policy, it will be necessary to treat hereafter; but of the fact there can be no doubt. Yet again, in the brief record quoted above, are compressed other inaccuracies. The Horse Artillery did not spring into existence, as a corps, on 1st February, 1793, as the words would imply. Two troops were authorised in January of that year, but not for twelve years of straggling augmentations of staff-officers and troops, can it be said to have attained its proper maturity.

It is fortunate that an officer of the regiment has been found, at once so capable and so patient in tracing out the circumstances which impressed on the world the necessity of this arm, as the author of the papers on 'The Mobility of Field Artillery, Past and Present.' According to this writer, England was the last among the leading nations in Royal Europe to adopt the use of Horse Artillery. (Captain H. W. I., Hime, Royal Artillery, Proceedings R. A. Institution.) As early as 1788, the subject had strongly attracted the attention of the Master-General of the Ordnance; but, unfortunately, he referred it to a committee. The period of gestation, so to speak, in committees on military subjects is very great; in this particular instance the winter of 1792 had arrived without any result from their labours.

The introduction of Horse Artillery into the Prussian service dates from 1759; and in 1792 this arm was introduced into the French and Swedish armies. In other European countries improvement had been made in Field Artillery, without, however, adopting the system of *mounted detachments*; but this latter is the distinctive mark of Horse Artillery. It has been asserted, and on good authority, that Horse Artillery was used in India prior even to its adoption by Frederick the Great—and dating as far back as 1756. If the existence of an artillery without mobility was sufficient to impress on the authorities in that country a sense of the necessity of some improvements, the argument was not wanting.

In an engagement between the English and French troops near Trichinopoly in 1753, "the English, *for more expedition*, marched without any field-pieces;" and when the infantry advanced against the French in an action fought shortly afterwards, "the *artillery, in the hurry, could not keep up with the battalion*." (*History of the Military Transactions of the British Nation in Hindostan,* vol. 1) The advantage of a more mobile artillery must certainly have been apparent after such melancholy exhibitions.

It has already been mentioned in this work that rapidity of movement, more especially under fire, was rendered hopeless by the frequent employment of peasants to act as drivers to the batteries. The formation of the Royal Horse Artillery did not free the Field Batteries from this evil. A quaint circumstance in proof of this is narrated by the author already mentioned (Hime).

In 1798, the Commandant of Woolwich inspected some guns manned by gunners of the 8th Battalion, R.A. The guns were each drawn by three horses in single file, which were driven by contract drivers on foot, hired for the occasion, dressed in white smocks with blue collars and cuffs, and armed with long carter's whips of the ordinary farm pattern. When this formidable array had been reviewed, the commandant, General Lloyd, and the garrison adjutant, expressed their joint opinion that field artillery movements could not be performed quicker. (*Aide-Mémoire to the Military Sciences,* art 'Ordnance'.)

The increase of mobility over that old system—of which the above is a real, although, perhaps, exceptional illustration—which followed the introduction of Horse Artillery can best be shown by another and later instance. At the Battle of Fuentes d'Onor, Bull's troop of Horse Artillery—later D Battery, B Brigade—was surrounded and cut off by the French cavalry. It was at the time under the command of the 2nd Captain, Norman Ramsay.

Guns thus dealt with are almost always lost, and consequently the army ceased to think of Ramsay and his men, except as prisoners. Presently, however, a great commotion was observed among the French squadrons; men and officers closed in confusion towards one point, where a thick dust was rising, and where loud cries and the sparkling of blades and flashing of pistols indicated some extraordinary occurrence.... Suddenly the multitude became violently agitated; an English shout pealed high and clear; the mass was rent asunder, and Norman Ramsay burst forth, sword in hand, at the head of his troop, his horses, breathing fire, stretched like greyhounds along the plain; the guns bounded behind them like things of no weight, and the mounted gunners followed close, with heads bent low, and pointed weapons, in desperate career. (Gleig. Napier)

Between the crawling peasant-driven team on Woolwich parade, and this glowing description of a Horse Artillery battery but a very few years later, there is a contrast, which shows at a glance the immense stride in the direction of mobility, which had followed the introduction of that branch of the regiment to whose story this chapter is devoted. Much of this improvement was due to the fostering care of the master-general, and of the deputy-adjutant-general, afterwards Sir John Macleod; much also was due to the encouragement of general officers, who found to their amazement a force of artillery, which could conform to their most rapid movements; and not a little was due to the practical school of experience opened in the Peninsula; but, to their honour be it stated, the rapid progress towards the standard of perfection attained by the Royal Horse Artillery was mainly due to the labours and the devotion of the officers belonging to it.

While the committee, appointed to decide the question of Horse Artillery in connection with our service, was—according to wont—babbling harmlessly and fruitlessly in the fourth year of its existence, a virtual rupture took place between England and France. The Duke of

Norman Ramsay at the Battle of Fuentes d'Onor

Richmond, then master-general, immediately took the matter himself in hand; and of three schemes, very dissimilar, over which the committee had been debating, he selected the following, as the basis of the organisation of a troop of Royal Horse Artillery.

Detail.	Horses.	Drivers.	Ammunition.	Distribution of detachments.					Civil List.	Remarks.
				Captains.	Lieuts.	N.-C. O.'s.	Gunners.	Drummers.		
5½-inch howitzers (2)	8	4}	160	1	1	2	20	..	..	{4 men held the horses in action.
Waggons (2) . .	8	4}								
3-prs. (2) . . .	8	4}	480	1	1	2	20	..	..	Ditto.
Waggons (2) . .	8	4}								
6-prs., Col. Williams' (2)	4	2}	160	..	1	2	20	..	..	Ditto.
Tumbrils (2) . .	4	2}								
Horses for detachments	66	..	..	..	..	..	..	..	..	
2 Sergeants, Sergt.-Major, and Clerk of Stores . . .	2	..	..	..	..	2	..	..	..	
Drummers to have bugle horns, and act as orderly men.	2	..	..	..	..	..	..	2	..	
1 forge cart . . .	3	1	..	..	..	..	..	..	..	
1 waggon for Artificers' Stores . .	3	1	..	..	..	..	..	..	..	
Officers' horses not included . . .	..	..	..	..	..	..	..	..	..	
CIVIL LIST.										
1 Commissiary of horse	1	..	..	..	..	..	..	..	1	
2 Conductors of horse	2	..	..	..	..	..	..	..	2	
1 Collar-maker . .	1	..	..	..	..	..	..	..	1	
1 Wheeler . . .	1	..	..	..	..	..	..	..	1	
1 Blacksmith . .	1	..	..	..	..	..	..	..	1	
1 Farrier. . . .	1	..	..	..	..	..	..	..	1	
Total	123	22	800	2	3	8	60	2	7	

The formation of the first two troops, A and B, took place at Woolwich, having been ordered in January 1793. The captains were R. Lawson, afterwards so distinguished in Egypt, and the brigade-major of the regiment, J. Macleod afterwards deputy-adjutant-general. In these—as in the other troops subsequently formed—great care was taken to appoint none but officers of well-known ability. This fact, combined with the permission given to the Horse Artillery to select the best recruits joining the regiment, had the immediate effect of causing the new branch to be looked on as a *corps d'élite*: as, indeed,

MOUNTED OFFICER R.H.A.

OFFICER R.H.A.

was the case in every other country in Europe, except Austria. Whether this has proved a benefit, or otherwise, to the corps, will hereafter be considered. The *esprit* generally to be found in a *corps d'élite* was fanned by other and minor considerations. It must be remembered that the gunners of Field Artillery other than Horse Artillery, and of Garrison Artillery, were, and still are, interchangeable. But in the Horse Artillery:

> The men were magnificently dressed, they were amply paid, and they were not haunted by the constant dread of being suddenly and forcibly torn from the Field Artillery service, which they loved, and thrust into the Garrison Artillery service, which was strange to them. (Hime.)

Only 4 guns per troop were granted at first; and the establishment consisted, in addition to the officers, of 8 non-commissioned officers, 49 gunners, and 35 drivers. On the formation of C and D Troops, on 1st November, 1793, the armament of each troop was raised to 6 guns, and the establishment per troop was 14 non-commissioned officers, 85 gunners, 45 drivers, and 187 horses. (R. H. A. Records.)

The officers appointed to command the new troops were, E. Howorth, afterwards Sir E. Howorth, who subsequently commanded the artillery at Talavera, Busaco, and Fuentes d'Onor, and J. M. Hadden, who afterwards became Surveyor-General of the Ordnance.

The reader will continue to observe the selection always made of able officers to command the troops of Horse Artillery. In 1794, E and F Troops were formed, and the command given respectively to Captain W. Cuppage, an officer who afterwards held for twenty-six years the appointment of Inspector of the Royal Carriage Department, and to Captain J. Butler, an officer who afterwards became Lieutenant-Governor of the Royal Military College at Sandhurst.

In 1794, the number of guns per troop was augmented to 8; and this remained the establishment until 1804, in which year the number was reduced to 6; at which it continued until the reductions after the Battle of Waterloo. In 1794, when the number of guns was raised to 8, the following was the establishment: 15 non-commissioned officers, 97 gunners, 71 drivers, 246 horses per troop. This was reduced in the following year very considerably, and became 15 non-commissioned officers, 85 gunners, 51 drivers, and 170 horses.

The next variation in the establishment was caused by the formation, in Ireland, of G Troop, from detachments serving in that country. The command of the new troop was given to Captain—afterwards

ROYAL ARTILLERY DRIVERS

Sir—G. B. Fisher, an officer who in 1827 was appointed Commandant of Woolwich. For two years after the formation of G Troop, the establishment of the troops was as follows: 8 guns, 16 non-commissioned officers, 96 gunners, 58 drivers, and 190 horses. An augmentation of 1 non-commissioned officer and 1 gunner per troop took place in 1803.

In 1804, the number of guns per troop having being reduced to 6, H Troop was formed at Woolwich, and the command given to Captain A. Macdonald, a smart officer, who subsequently had the good fortune to command the Horse Artillery of the Cavalry Division at Waterloo. On the reduction to 6 guns, the strength of each troop was, 14 non-commissioned officers, 75 gunners, 46 drivers, and 142 horses.

In 1805, an augmentation of four troops took place—I, K, L, and M; and the commands were given respectively to Captain W. Millar, an officer who subsequently became Inspector of Artillery, and Director-General of the Field Train Department; to Captain C. Godfrey, an officer who went on half-pay a few years later, in 1811; to Captain N. Foy, who died in 1817; and to Captain the Hon W. H. Gardner, who died as a Colonel-Commandant in 1856.

For the few years following this augmentation, the establishment remained virtually the same; but, in January 1813, 194 officers, non-commissioned officers, and men were added to act as Rocket Detachments, and also as a depot to supply the troops on service. A depot for the Royal Horse Artillery has existed under various names, and in somewhat chequered circumstances. It commenced—as stated above—in 1813; it existed for many years in the form of an Adjutant's Detachment at Woolwich.

In 1814, the various Rocket Detachments were combined, those at home becoming the 1st, and those abroad the 2nd, Rocket Troop. The officers appointed to command these were Captain W. Gr. Elliott, an officer who retired from the Regiment in 1828, and Captain afterwards Sir E. C. Whinyates, an officer whose ability, zeal, and services have hardly been surpassed in the Regiment. He ultimately—after a long and active career—became Commandant of Woolwich, where his kindly manners were long remembered. He commanded the Rocket Troop at Waterloo, where he was severely wounded.

Among the many heart-breaking reductions which exasperate the artillery student, perhaps none are more distressing, than the reduction of the 2nd Rocket Troop in 1816. The 1st Rocket Troop had never been out of England; the 2nd had done good service at Leipsic and Waterloo. Neither of them had had a long existence; but one had had

MOUNTED ROCKET TROOPER

ROCKET TROOPS

a stirring, glorious history. On the 16th May, 1815, the following order had been issued:—

> His Royal Highness the Prince Regent, in the name and on the behalf of His Majesty, has been pleased to command that *the Rocket Troop of Royal Artillery, which was present at the Battle of Leipsic*, be permitted to wear the word 'Leipsic' on their appointments, in commemoration of their services on that occasion.

And to the same troop the reward fell, given to those who had been at the Battle of Waterloo. Yet, when the pruning-knife came to be used, the troop which had earned these honours was selected for reduction; and, as if adding insult to injury, the word 'Leipsic' came actually to be worn by the surviving troop, which had never been on active service at all! On its reduction, the officers of the 2nd Rocket Troop were transferred to the corps of Royal Artillery Drivers.

Up to this point, we have traced the growth, *numerically*, of the Royal Horse Artillery. The conclusion of hostilities after Waterloo led to very extensive reductions. In 1816, besides the 2nd Rocket Troop, D, K, L, and M Troops were reduced, with the consequent changes of designation in the surviving troops. From a total, of all ranks, amounting to 2675, in 1815, and 2621 horses, the Horse Artillery fell in 1816 to 1181 men and 959 horses. Of the six troops in France with the Army of Occupation, the following was the establishment per troop, each troop having 6 guns:—

> 5 officers, 14 non-commissioned officers, 85 gunners, 56 drivers, 168 horses.
>
> The troops on home service were allowed only 4 guns, and an establishment of 5 officers, 11 non-commissioned officers, 56 gunners, 24 drivers, 102 horses.

But this was merely a beginning. In 1819, B and G Troops were reduced; the troops in France were brought on the Home Establishment, and the number of guns per troop reduced to 2. The strength was then 5 officers, 10 non-commissioned officers, 47 gunners, 18 drivers, 36 horses, per troop; and the total strength of the Royal Horse Artillery did not exceed 616 of all ranks, and 317 horses. (The Duke of Wellington, being at this time Master-General of the Ordnance, invariably selected the artillery for reductions rather than the cavalry and infantry.)

At this miserable establishment the troops remained for some years.

At the creation of the RHA, it was directed that recruits might be taken who were 5 feet 6¾ inches in height: but before six months had passed, the standard was raised, at the urgent request of the captains, to 5 feet 8 inches. (Maj.-Gen. Brome to the Duke of Richmond, 6/9/1793.) There was often difficulty in obtaining a sufficient number of suitable recruits, and even when the troops were complete, it was customary to attach to each, when in the field, a few of the Driver Corps, with additional horses or mules. Extra pay was granted from the first to the officers, non-commissioned officers, and gunners of Horse Artillery. (Lefroy.)

The exact relative *status* of the new branch of the service was speedily settled. On 21st February, 1797, the Board of Ordnance granted the same allowance for forage to the officers, as was allowed to officers of cavalry; and so early had it been decided that the Horse Artillery should take the right of all cavalry, that, as will be seen by the following letter, the master-general would not in 1804 allow the point to be disputed.

D.A. Gen. R.A., to Colonel Cuppage

Woolwich, June 9, 1804.

Dear Colonel,

I submitted to the master general your letter of the 5th instant, relating to a conversation which took place with General Sir David Dundas, when the Horse Artillery marched past with the cavalry, on the king's birthday, in which Sir David, though the Horse Artillery then led, expressed doubts as to the precedence and rank of the Horse Artillery on such future occasions.

Lord Chatham not being aware upon what circumstances Sir David's doubts have arisen, and not considering the communication from you in any other light than as a wish to know how far, as commanding officer of artillery, you are justifiable in making a claim to the right for the Horse Artillery when paraded with cavalry, his Lordship has desired me simply to say that he considers the privilege so well established by practice, as well as opinion, that he is unwilling to suppose it can be disputed.

His Majesty has never seen the Horse Artillery in any other place: they were encamped on the right of all the cavalry (of the Blues) at Windsor: and in all parades of ceremony and honour, placed on

the right of the cavalry.
I am, dear colonel,
Your obedient servant,

J. Macleod.

Both by custom and regulation this precedence continued to belong to the Royal Horse Artillery until July 1869, when it was ordered that the Household Cavalry, *when the sovereign, should be present,* should have the precedence awarded to a body guard.

It was laid down as a rule, that no officer should be appointed to the Horse Brigade, who had not been on foreign service: but as this rule was occasionally broken, it was decided in July 1805 that any officers who had been appointed to the Horse Artillery, prior to having been on foreign service should "(to avoid any officers being confined to one species of duty) be liable after three or four years' service in the Horse Brigade to be exchanged again into the battalions, so that they may take their share of duty on foreign service, and obtain that experience which is necessary to an artillery officer, as he advances in the regiment."

The changes in the dress of the Horse Artillery may be gathered from the following statistics. An order dated 1st November, 1806, lays down the following rules for the dress of officers:—

> Except at dress parades the blue regimental overalls are to be worn till dinner-time in place of the blue pantaloons, which is to be the afternoon dress when at home. At all parades, whether mounted or dismounted, and during the day, the black velvet stock is to be worn, with an inch of shirt collar over it: no other white to be shown. In the evenings, it is requested that black silk handkerchiefs may be substituted with the same proportion of shirt collar over them. When officers are dressed for a ball, evening party, or dine out, they are to wear the jacket open, white pantaloons, plain white waistcoat (with sash over it), light sword, regulation sword-knot, black belt, with cocked-hat and feather. In common a white leather sword-knot is to be worn. Spurs with horizontal rowels to be worn at all times. (General Orders and R.H.A. Records, and MS Notes of General Belson, R.A., 1812.)

Prior to 1812, gaiters and knee-boots had been worn: but on the 14th January in that year his Royal Highness the Prince Regent issued the following order:—

19

The officers of the Royal Horse Artillery are to wear jackets similar to the private men, with an aiguillette. In parade dress, they are to wear white leather pantaloons, and Hussar boots, with gold binding. On ordinary duties or on march, they are to wear overalls of a colour similar to the private men's, and a short *surtout*, which is calculated to be worn likewise as a *pelisse* on service. When attending a drawing-room or *levée*, they may appear in long coats, with lapels and aiguillettes, the same as are worn with the jacket, but without lace on the seams: or in the Regimental jacket, as they may prefer. The officers of the Horse Artillery are likewise to wear cocked-hats, with the star loop, with their *dress* regimentals.

A more important thing, however, than the dress has been the armament of the Royal Horse Artillery. Its greatest deeds have been wrought with the 6-pounder; but that was not its invariable weapon. One troop, as we shall see hereafter, went on service with 12-pounders; on the eve of Waterloo, owing to the want of guns of position, three troops received 9-pounders, instead of the 6-pounders which they had brought from England.

During the Peninsular Campaign, the armament of a troop was as follows:—2 9-pounders, or 2 heavy 6-pounders; 1 heavy 5½-inch howitzer; 3 light 6-pounders; 6 ammunition waggons; 3 reserve waggons, and 4 other carriages. (Lefroy.) Compared with the simplicity of later Horse Artillery armament, the presence of three different guns in the same troop, with the consequent necessity of a variety of ammunition, seems a very complicated and undesirable arrangement. This was frequently felt at the time; and at the change of armament made before Waterloo, a foreshadowing of the modern harmony of weapons might be detected in the arming of I Troop—Bull's—with 5½-inch howitzers only. And right noble was the service done by that troop on the 18th of June.

There can on be no greater mistake than to put rivalry or comparisons, or to expect the same results from the employment of Horse Artillery as of Brigade (*i.e.* Field) Artillery. Though *one and the same arm*, they are equipped and intended for totally distinct purposes. The necessary quick movements of the Horse Artillery could not be attained by 9-pounders; the telling effect of 9-pounders could not be expected from Horse Artillery. One is intended to act with cavalry, and, from the nature of its equipment and the lightness of its metal, is

A LIGHT 6-PDR ON ITS TRAVELLING CARRIAGE

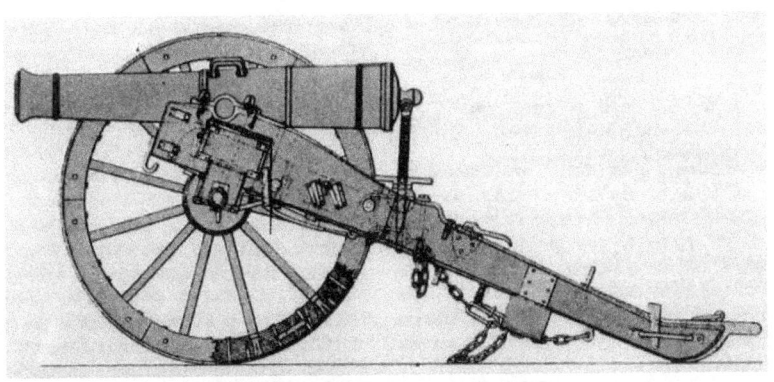

BRTISH 9-PDR GUN AND CARRIAGE

expected to maintain at all times, and under all circumstances, of bad roads, of rough, hilly, or broken ground, the same pace as cavalry; and, in short, to bring artillery into action wherever cavalry can act .

I can name two instances in which, while acting with cavalry, any other than Horse Artillery would have been perfectly useless. One, the affair of Morales, in Spain; the other, the movement from Quatre Bras to the position of Waterloo. Both were specially movements of Horse Artillery, and both tried the wind and speed of our horses. In the latter movement particularly, through a deep cross country, any artillery differently equipped would have inevitably fallen into the hands of the enemy. In all light movements of the Infantry of an army, Horse Artillery is as indispensably necessary and as exclusively effective, as it is with cavalry.

I have myself, in cases of reconnoissance, been withdrawn from the cavalry for the moment, to cover movements in which heavier artillery could bear no part. .... On the other hand, if Horse Artillery has its distinct advantages over heavier guns, so likewise the latter have their distinct purposes, for which the employment of Horse Artillery would be wholly inapplicable and inadequate. .... I have known Brigade Artillery as perfect, in its way, as Horse Artillery; but no more comparison can be drawn between them than "between cavalry and infantry." (Report on the Artillery by Sir R. Gardiner, 31 March, 1848.)

******

Note.—The extra rate of pay to non-commissioned officers and gunners of the Royal Horse Artillery is based on the following general order, dated 21 January, 1793:

> The master-general directs that an allowance of twopence per day, in addition to their regimental pay, shall be made to each non-commissioned officer and gunner of the brigade of Horse Artillery, when and so long as he continues mounted, and having the care and management of an horse, in consideration of the extraordinary and constant attention required of such persons for the due performance of this particular service, which must deprive them of the occasional advantages arising from their being employed in works for which additional pay is given.
>
> The dismounted non-commissioned officers and gunners of this brigade not being in the same circumstances,

nor deprived of their share in the works, will not be entitled to the said allowance; nor will the drivers of this Brigade, as they are to be enlisted merely for that special service, and will have but little of other duties to learn or perform.

Note 2.—The style of horse considered suitable for Horse Artillery at first, may be ascertained from the following instructions, dated Woolwich, March 1810:

The horses to be from four to six years old (when bought), to be short-legged, open-chested, and broad-winded; not to exceed 15 hands 2 inches, nor—four years old—under 15 hands ½ inch; to have good bone and action, the colours to be bay, brown, and dark chestnut.

The price allowed, after a month's trial, was thirty guineas.

CHAPTER 2

Peninsular War—Roliça, Vimiera, Corunna

The history of the Royal Artillery between 1808 and 1814 is concentrated in the Peninsular campaigns—with the one exception of the Expedition to Walcheren. As the war in Spain drew to a close, the Second American War, which had in the meantime arisen, increased in importance, reaching its culminating point in 1814.

It is proposed in this chapter to treat of that section of the wars in the Peninsula, which terminated in the battle and evacuation at Corunna. After a diversion on the subject of the Walcheren Expedition, the Peninsular narrative will be resumed, and be continued uninterruptedly to its close.

The reader will be aware that in the spring of 1808 the Spaniards rose as one man to resist the schemes of Napoleon, who had placed his brother Joseph on the throne of Spain. The English Government, always ready to assist any country which defied the French emperor, placed a force of 9000 men under the command of Sir Arthur Wellesley, who sailed for Portugal on the 12th July, to co-operate with the Spanish forces. This force was subsequently increased to nearly 30,000; but the conflicting instructions given by Government, and the utter ignorance of the real state of affairs in Spain, prevented the possibility of harmony of action among the English forces, and had ultimately much to do with the abrupt and mistaken Convention of Cintra. Portugal had recently suffered dismemberment at the hands of Napoleon as a penalty for its friendship with England; the English expedition had therefore a double motive—the delivery of Portugal, and co-operation with the Spaniards.

How terrible the errors of the English Government were in organising this Expedition can only be realised by a study of the celebrated and standard history of the war; and such a study is necessary to enable one fully to realise the marvellous genius of Wellington, and his determined vigour. (Napier vol.1.) It is sufficient for the purpose of this work to show that, if the Royal Artillery shared the glories of Wellington, they also from the very first shared his difficulties—which were certainly not lessened in their treatment by the Board of Ordnance. The conflicting instructions given by Government to Sir Arthur Wellesley were matched by the total absence of any information from the board to Colonel Robe, who had been appointed to command the artillery of the expedition.

A man full of zeal—one of the best practical artillerymen whom the regiment has ever produced—he naturally sought by every means in his power to ensure the completeness in every respect of the equipment of the force under his control. How completely he was foiled by the masterly silence of the board will be seen by the following letters written by him after his arrival in Portugal. That, in spite of all his difficulties, he succeeded in earning the warm commendations of a chief, who was rarely guilty of many words of praise, is merely another instance of the truth of the saying of the following writer:

> The student who reads the history of the Royal Artillery can hardly fail to be struck by proof after proof that the progress of the regiment has been due to the energy and manly courage of individual officers within its ranks in spite of the withering cold of officialism. . . . So, it must be, and ever will be. Boards and clerks will bind chains in peace round the men of talent, who will either break them when a crisis comes, or die in the effort to do so. (*Times*, 13 Jan. 1873)

The correspondence was as follows:—

Lieut.-Col. Robe to Brig.-Gen. Macleod
Kingston Transport,
Mondego Bay,
July 30, 1808.

. . . I shall therefore take the liberty of mentioning to you some points which it may be essential should on future occasions be put right on the embarkation of artillery. . . . It appears to me necessary that the officer appointed to command artillery on any expedition should know something more of the nature of the service intended than I did, and that he should not be made to take upon trust that everything necessary for his service will be found on board his ships. Our equipment is not yet arrived at the state of perfection to render such a mode efficient; and if it is practised, the commanding officer of artillery will find, as I have, that his brigades will be wanting in articles extremely necessary, and be very short indeed in stores intended for repair or for keeping them in good order. He will perhaps find also, as I have, that intrenching tools, and even platforms, are sent with the Engineer's department for a species of service for which he has not a gun, nor a mortar, nor a round of ammunition. I do not make this a matter of complaint to you.

I complain not of anything, because I can go no further than use to the best of my ability the means put into my power; but I confess it would have been much more satisfactory to me had I been permitted an opportunity of stating before I embarked what might have been sent with me for the real benefit of the service, and I don't think it would have occasioned an hour's delay to the embarkation, or have added a shilling of expense to the country, because the essential articles, if not supplied, *must* be purchased. I have so often mentioned *horses* that I ought perhaps to apologise for again recurring to that subject; and perhaps it may be said that I have no reason to mention them, having the horses of the Irish Commissariat ordered to be turned over to me on landing.

Fortunate, indeed, I think myself to have even *them*. I know not what figure we should have cut without them; but when you learn that they are acknowledged to be *cast horses from the cavalry* turned over to the commissariat, you will readily think that we are not likely to make a very capital figure with them. I have been also fortunate enough to obtain with them a promise of shoes from that branch, sufficient, with the *one hundred sets* supplied to me, to shoe them on first going off. Future service must be supplied as it can, and I shall not let it go unsupplied....

This letter was written by Colonel Robe before he had realised the whole of his wants, and how admirably the Honourable Board had succeeded in proving their ability "How not to do it." The truth dawned on him very soon, and his language of remonstrance became stronger. His next letter to Brig.-Gen. Macleod is dated the 7th August, 1808, from the camp above Lavos, Mondego Bay, and contains the following passages:—

> I now deem it my duty (which were I to neglect I should be highly culpable) to point out to you in the strongest manner the impolicy of sending artillery to a foreign country without horses. Even the horses we have now, old, blind, and casts from the cavalry as they are, we find superior to what we can obtain from the country. The latter are good of their kind, but small, and not of sufficient weight for our carriages. Three hundred good horses would have cost the country no more for transport than as many bad ones, and what we shall do for the brigade now to be landed remains to be decided. ... I must also mention the proportion of general stores which you, sir, know artillery cannot do without, and which ought to be sent out with every embarkation.
>
> Had I been made acquainted with what was to have been embarked, I should not have gone on board ship till the proper proportion had been furnished. *I did everything in my power to obtain the information from the board, and was referred to Mr. ——, who himself at the time was not furnished with any information.* I did at hazard request Mr. Spencer to put on board one hundred sets of horse-shoes and some nails, thinking them an addition to what would be provided for us. *These are all I have had for the horses of three brigades*; and had I not obtained some more from the commissary-general, belonging to the horses delivered to us, the horses must have taken the field *barefoot*. I have made demands for some, and for such things as are most immediately required, and what may be wanted in the meantime must be purchased here.
>
> I write this to you officially, and must not be considered as individually complaining or making difficulties. My people of all classes exert themselves, and I am determined to get on; but I know that, engaged in a department where much is expected, I am doing my country greater service by pointing out what may render that department as complete as it is supposed to be, than if I were to remain for ever silent on the subject.

Then followed the battles of Roliça and Vimiera, to be alluded to hereafter, and merely mentioned here to show that before the date of his next letter Colonel Robe had been able to form a very practical opinion of the board's shortcomings. Writing after Vimiera, on the night of the 21st August, 1808, he says to Brig.-Gen. Macleod:

> My men are staunch, and the admiration of the army; and had they been properly supplied with horses and with stores, as artillery *should have* embarked from England, Europe would not have produced a more efficient artillery. I shall have occasion to write to you and to the board on the latter subjects, as soon as I can obtain time; but give me leave to say now that never more will I leave England taking my provision of artillery upon trust, and coming upon an army burthened with cast horses, or no horses at all, or with brigades unsupplied with any one store to make repair, and scarce a shoe to put on horses when I could beg them. This may be strong; but I have reason to use the expressions after suffering the inconveniences occasioned by the want of these supplies.

On the 1st September, 1808, Colonel Robe pointed out to Colonel Harding, who had arrived to take command of the artillery in Portugal, that:

> Not less than two hundred and fifty horses would be required to render that artillery efficient for taking the field for a length of service. Those received originally from the Irish Commissariat were old cast horses of cavalry, and many of them blind. They now fall off very fast.

The reader will be eager to see how the board explained its shortcomings, and what reparation it proposed to make to the brave officer, who had gained honour for his corps in spite of official blunders. For calm, cool assumption, perhaps the reply sent by the board to Colonel Robe is unsurpassed. It bears date the 6th October, 1808, after the news of the English successes, and the gallantry of the artillery under Colonel Robe, had reached England, and after Colonel Robe had been twice specially mentioned by Sir A. Wellesley in his despatches. It was written, let the reader remember, on behalf of a board whose errors were not confined to those quoted above; which had actually sent guns without their ammunition, and ammunition which would have been useless, had not Colonel Robe succeeded in borrowing suitable guns from the navy.

It was addressed to an officer who had been straining every nerve, night and day, to remedy the defects due to official ignorance, or to what is much the same, official affectation of omniscience;—to an

An officer, private & driver of the Royal Wagon Train

officer who, in spite of the remonstrances which had been extorted from him by his discovery of the board's incapacity, had never attempted to shelter himself behind the faults of others, but had, instead, toiled to remedy them. Let the reader bear these facts in mind, as he attempts to realise the feelings with which Colonel Robe must have perused the following lines:—

> In reply to the parts of your public correspondence in which you have so very warmly complained of some omissions and deficiencies, particularly in the light brigade of artillery shipped at Plymouth, I am to say that his Lordship has, upon inquiry, ascertained that there *were some irregularities* in the embarkation, and that he has, in consequence, expressed his displeasure through the board to the parties concerned, in a manner to make a lasting impression. His Lordship has, besides, issued such orders, and made such regulations, as must effectually preclude every plea or excuse for irregularity or omission in future.
>
> The master-general, in desiring me to give you the above information, has directed me to add that, although he is willing to ascribe much of the style and many of the expressions in the letters to your known zeal for the service, and the anxiety attending an officer during the moments of preparation for the field, yet his Lordship cannot but regret that, instead of forwarding a complaint, which it would be the wish and the interest of the ordnance to attend to, you should have allowed yourself to arraign, with such improper and unmerited asperity, the conduct of the Ordnance Department in general.

The old, old story! Officialism, on being detected in error, hurriedly, and with attempts at dignity, assumes an air of injured innocence, and neither forgives nor forgets the unhappy soldier who is the means of revealing its shortcomings. What a contrast does Colonel Robe's dignified and soldierlike acknowledgment of this reprimand present! Having first acknowledged the congratulations of the master-general on the conduct of the artillery at Roliça and Vimiera, which he had caused to be read to the men on parade, and entered in all the order-books, thereby, as he wrote, Lisbon, 7 Jan. 1809, "awakening every joyful feeling that could arise in the breasts of soldiers," he proceeded as follows:—

> The latter part of your letter is indeed a great source of grief to me, and has hurt me more than I can express. I had hoped

to have obtained for my whole conduct the approbation of his Lordship the Master-General and the Board of Ordnance. I set out with the most earnest desire to fulfil, to the extent of my abilities, every duty I might be honoured with, and to abide in the strictest manner by their orders, for which purpose I applied for instructions and such information as the very limited time prior to my departure would admit. The shortness of that time, our expected destination (which, as you know, we had reason to believe was far more distant than it proved afterwards to be) certainly produced in me an anxiety that the branch of service entrusted to me should be supplied in the manner most conducive to the end for which it was sent out. (The force had originally been destined for South America.)

This anxiety may have caused a warmth of expression not deemed advisable in public correspondence, however good the intention. And that an unfavourable impression has been received in His Lordship's mind I, with pain, perceive, and submit in the most respectful manner to the animadversion you have received His Lordship's commands to make.... Whatever the warmth of my feelings might have been which impelled me to the remarks that have caused His Lordship's displeasure, I entreat that they may be ascribed to the peculiar situation in which I was placed. My letter to you was written on the ground of, and almost during, the action, and, consequently, that degree of coolness was not attended to which ought to have been manifested.

    The difficulties of the campaign of August 1808 were increased by the insincerity and disunion of the Spaniards, the feebleness of the Portuguese support, and the extraordinary conduct of the English Government in sending general after general with conflicting instructions. The supersession of Sir Arthur Wellesley at a critical moment, uncalled for and undeserved, would have paralysed a less determined commander. To his resolution, his singleness of purpose, and his tact in dealing with the Portuguese authorities, is the fact due that, brief as the campaign was, it was marked by two brilliant engagements, and established already the military reputation of the English troops. The British Army in Portugal, in 1808, was gathered from the four winds of heaven, without harmony either in instructions or management, and destitute of adequate equipment or supplies.

The main body, which sailed from Cork, had been intended for South America; the contingent brought by Sir John Moore had been sent in the first instance to Sweden, on an errand rendered fruitless by the obstinacy of the Swedish monarch; and the rest of the army was gathered in instalments from Gibraltar, Madeira, and various parts of England. The annexed table, prepared from the embarkation returns, shows the method in which the artillery portion of the army was collected:—at first destitute of horses, and, later, embarked with so much precipitation, that in many instances the horses died from long confinement on board ship; and in others it was found that animals had been hurriedly purchased, and embarked afflicted with fatal and infectious diseases, which spread rapidly among those which were healthy. The horses which were purchased in the country were small, and unfitted for artillery work.

The roads round Lisbon, and in the district traversed by Sir A. Wellesley's force, were of the worst description; and Colonel Robe and his successor, Colonel Harding, wrote to the board, expressing their thankfulness that, for the three brigades engaged at Roliça and Vimiera they had been able to procure *oxen* to draw the guns, with horses as leaders! The remonstrances of Colonel Robe and his successors succeeded in procuring from England, as the annexed table will show, a suitable supply of horses as the year advanced; but the honours gained by the corps had been earned before these arrived (*see table following*).

In addition to the companies (Captain Geary's and Captain Raynsford's) which embarked with Colonel Robe to form part of Sir A. Wellesley's force, 161 of the King's German Artillery were also detailed. (Later 3 Battery, 2 Brigade and 7 Battery, 17 Brigade.) The services of this corps during the Peninsular and Waterloo campaigns were of the highest order. The headquarters of the corps were at this time at Porchester, and the strength in 1808 was as follows:—

Field officers, 4; staff officers, 6; staff sergeants, 3. Two troops of Horse Artillery, consisting in all of 372 officers and men, and 186 horses. (Muster Rolls of K. G. Artillery, 1808.)

Four marching companies, in all 714 officers and men—with 67 horses.

One of these companies was stationed in the Mediterranean.

An addition to Colonel Robe's force of a doubtful value was received from Gibraltar. Lieut.-Colonel George Ramsey was ordered from Gibraltar with three companies to meet the artillery expected

RETURN of the OFFICERS and MEN of the ROYAL ARTILLERY, and of OFFICERS' or DRAUGHT HORSES, or others under the ORDNANCE, which were sent from various Stations to Spain or Portugal during the Year 1808, with the Dates of their respective Embarkations.

	Date of Embarkation.	ROYAL ARTILLERY.					R. A. DRIVER CORPS.						General Total.	Horses.
		Officers.	N.C. Officers.	Gunners.	Drummers.	Total.	Officers.	N.C. Officers.	Drivers.	Trumpeters.	Artificer.	Total.		
Embarked with Sir A. Wellesley	June, 1808	10	27	204	4	245	2	18	143	2	10	175	420	..
Embarked with General Spencer from Gibraltar for Cadiz	June 13, 1808	3	6	53	1	63	..	1	13	..	..	14	77	..
Embarked with Sir J. Moore for Sweden, and then for Spain	April 30, 1808	24	62	406	8	500	3	18	276	2	30	329	829	360
Embarked with Generals Ackland and Anstruther	July 23, 1808	10	29	187	4	230	3	13	178	2	14	210	440	300
Embarked from Gibraltar by order of Sir H. Dalrymple	Aug. 13, 1808	8	27	186	3	224	..	..	..	..	..	..	224	..
Embarked from Madeira for Portugal with General Beresford	Aug. 17, 1808	3	14	94	2	113	..	..	..	..	..	..	113	..
Embarked with Sir D. Baird from Cork	Sept. 23, 1808	8	26	205	3	242	2	20	181	2	16	221	463	300
Embarked with Sir D. Baird from Woolwich	Sept. 22, 1808	10	26	200	2	238	2	20	181	1	15	219	457	300
Embarked from Woolwich; Horse Artillery	Oct. 5, 1808	12	28	160	..	200	..	..	109	2	14	125	325	296
Embarked from Portsmouth: Horse Artillery	Nov. 18, 1808	10	26	161	..	197	..	..	108	2	14	124	321	304
Embarked from Portsmouth	Dec. 8, 1808	2	..	1	..	3	4	28	213	3	19	267	270	600
Total embarked for Portugal or Spain in the year 1808		100	271	1857	27	2255	16	118	1402	16	132	1684	3939	2460

N.B. The return given by Napier in vol. i. p. 590, of his 'History,' neither includes the R. A. drivers, nor the officers and N. C. officers of the R. A. of several of the detachments mentioned above, but merely the gunners. It, however, does include the King's German Artillery, which is not shown in this purely regimental return.

from England, and a *car brigade* of guns, as it was termed, was issued from the Ordnance stores, for the service. Two of the companies, and Colonel Ramsey, were sent back to Gibraltar immediately on their arrival in Cadiz:—only one, Captain Morison's (later 8 Battery, 13 Brigade), being allowed to proceed in charge of the guns. Colonel Ramsey, however, had time to inspect the car brigade which had been issued to him, and his official report on it was not complimentary the store-keepers.

A similar brigade, it would appear, had been sent to Sicily, a few weeks before, (to D.A.G. from Cadiz, 21 July, 1808); and the clerk of stores had hopelessly confused the two. The shafts for the howitzers had been sent with the 6-pounders; seven gun-wheels had been put on board for use with the waggons—although not interchangeable,—and one waggon was entirely useless. The stores were inadequate and unsuitable; and there was neither a commissary, nor an artificer, with the detachment. A little further vacillation on the part of the authorities led to two companies leaving Gibraltar for Portugal immediately after the return of those under Colonel Ramsey; and one of these, Captain Skyring's, had the good fortune to join Colonel Robe in time for the Battle of Vimiera. (Later 1 Battery, 6 Brigade.)

Colonel Robe's force anchored in Mondego Bay on 28th July; and on the following day Sir Arthur Wellesley, who had preceded the army, and had been engaged in diplomatic as well as military duties, arrived, and gave orders for the disembarkation. The French withdrew from the coast, and the inhabitants showed symptoms of co-operation with the English, which were, however, sadly neutralised by the conduct of their rulers; while Sir A. Wellesley pressed forward, on the 9th August, to Leiria, hoping to cover the disembarkation of the additional troops which he now knew were on their way from England, and perhaps at the same time to strike an effective blow, as near to Lisbon as possible, with the force under his command. This would have the effect of inspiring the Portuguese with courage; of asserting the right of the English to control the military operations of the Allies; and of disarranging the plans of the French.

The English Army was augmented at Lavos on the 6th August by General Spencer's contingent; and was divided into six brigades, under Generals Hill, Nightingale, Craufurd, Bowes, Ferguson, and Fane. (G.O. dated Lavos, 7 Aug. 1808.) A demi-battery of artillery was attached to each brigade; howitzers being attached to the 1st, 2nd, 5th, and 6th Brigades, and the 9-pounders being kept in reserve. On the line of march, the artillery always moved in front of the brigades to which they were attached, and the artillery of the reserve followed the Infantry.

The advance of Sir Arthur Wellesley was perfectly successful; he succeeded in cutting the line of communication between Generals Loison and Laborde, and in inducing the French commander-in-chief, Junot, to quit Lisbon, and take the field with the reserve. The timidity and self-interest of the Portuguese leaders robbed him, however, at a critical moment, of several thousand troops; so that in his first engagement with the enemy he had the assistance of no more than 1650 Portuguese. That engagement was the one known as the combat of Roliça—fought on the 17th August, with superior numbers on the side of the English, but against a General, Laborde, who was not only very able, but also occupied a position of great natural strength.

The attack of the English, who, with the Portuguese, numbered 14,000, was made in three columns, the left commanded by General Ferguson—the right composed of the Portuguese—and the centre, consisting of three brigades, commanded by Sir Arthur in person. The Royal Artillery had 18 guns, one half of which came into action to cover the advance of the Infantry. So determined was that advance, and so critical did General Laborde's position become, as the left column, under General Ferguson, closed in upon his right, that he fell back to a new and parallel position, on the heights of Zambugeira. The steep heights, and dense brushwood, which had to be traversed in the advance of the English, rendered the attack of this new position a more difficult and costly one, and the losses of the 9th, 29th, and 82nd Regiments were especially heavy.

The ardour of the troops was, however, irresistible; and Laborde again fell back, handling his troops with the utmost skill. In a very short time, after one or two attempts to make a stand, the French were in full retreat—"leaving three guns on the field of battle, and the road to Torres Vedras open to the victors." (Napier.)

The loss of the French was admitted by themselves to be 600 killed and wounded; but it was probably much greater. Sir Arthur Wellesley, writing on the following day, (*Wellington's Supplementary Despatches*, vol. 6), (said the loss had been reported to be 1500; and Colonel Robe, in his despatch to the Ordnance, said that the loss of the French far exceeded that of the English, which amounted to 479 killed and wounded. The loss of the Royal Artillery on this occasion was, as Colonel Robe wrote (to D.A. Gen., R.A. 18 August, 1808),

The Battle of Roliça

irreparable. Captain Henry Geary, an officer of great promise and experience was killed.

He was, by his own desire, and as senior captain, in charge of guns with the Light Brigade, and was killed while pointing his gun within one or two hundred yards of the enemy. I regret him as an officer, for he was invaluable; and as a friend and old fellow-campaigner, by no means less. His loss to his family cannot be appreciated; but it will always be a comfort that he died as he had lived, in the very act of doing his duty to his country, and a true Christian.

The force of artillery under Colonel Robe's command at Roliça numbered 660 of all ranks. (Napier vol. 1.)

The next engagement between the French and English forces took place under singular circumstances. Sir Arthur Wellesley had been reinforced by the brigades under Generals Ackland and Anstruther—thus bringing his force up to 16,000 men, besides 660 artillery, and 240 cavalry—exclusive of the Portuguese under Colonel Trant. The greatest number which Junot could bring against this army could—it was known—hardly exceed 14,000. Further English reinforcements being known to be on the way, Sir A. Wellesley decided on assuming the offensive.

Unfortunately, Sir H. Burrard, one of the three generals sent out by the English Government to assume the command, arrived on the night of the 20th August, and Sir A. Wellesley was obliged to wait on him for orders. No arguments that he could employ could persuade Sir H. Burrard to attack before the arrival of the expected reinforcements; and Sir Arthur parted from him with feelings of the most bitter disappointment. Fortunately for him, and for the army, Junot, who by this time had reached Torres Vedras, resolved himself to assume the offensive; and to attack the English in their position near the village of Vimiera.

The battle commenced at seven o'clock on the morning of the 21st August, and deserves a special mention in this work. For at Vimiera, for the first time, as Napier and Oust show, did the French realise the difference between the English forces and those with whom they had hitherto been contending;—for the first time did they appreciate those qualities with which they were so soon to be familiar: "the stolid firmness and resolute thrust of the infantry, and the wonderful skill and precision of the artillery." No chronicler of this battle fails to

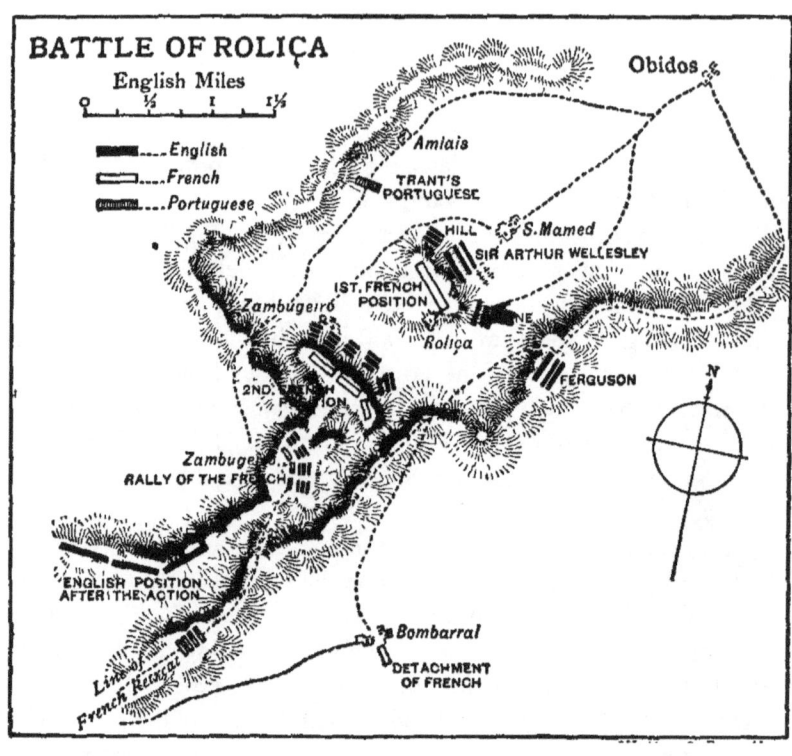

speak of the "murderous fire of Robe's artillery;"—a fire which told with admirable effect at the most critical periods of the engagement. The number of guns present was small—only 18, as at Roliça; but on this occasion all were engaged—the reserve as well as the divisional artillery being brought into play.

The right wing of the English Army consisted of the 1st Brigade, under General Hill; the centre, of the 6th and 7th, under Generals Fane and Anstruther; the left, of the 2nd, 3rd, 4th, and 8th, under Generals Ferguson, Nightingale, Bowes, and Ackland; and the reserve was composed of the 5th Brigade, under General Craufurd.

The attack of the French was made with great gallantry, in spite of many difficulties caused by the broken and wooded nature of the ground, and was directed against the English centre in the first instance, and mainly against General Fane's brigade. That officer, wisely availing himself of a discretionary power granted him, and seeing that the position was a favourable one for the employment of his artillery against the advancing columns, brought up the guns of the reserve at once, and with those of his own division formed a battery, which played on the advancing foe with "such a shower of shell and grape as might have been sufficient to stop any troops" (Cust); and although the French troops *did* reach the summit of the hill on which the English stood, they were, as Napier writes, so "shattered by the terrible fire of Robe's Artillery," that they fell an easy prey to the gallant charges of the 50th Regiment.

At another part of the line, where skirmishing between Anstruther's brigade and the French was going on, the artillery played an equally important part. A column of grenadiers had been sent forward by Kellermann to share in this part of the battle, and:

> Coming at a brisk pace, these choice soldiers beat back the advanced companies of the 43rd Regiment; but to avoid Robe's artillery, which ransacked their left, they dipped a little into the ravine on the right, and were immediately taken on the other flank by the guns of the 4th and 8th Brigades; then, when the narrowness of the way, and the sweep of the round shot, were crushing and disordering their ranks, the 43rd, rallying in one mass, went down upon the very head of the column, and with a short but fierce struggle, drove it back in confusion. (Napier.)

Yet again: in the attack upon General Ferguson's brigade made by Solignac, who expected to find a weak force on the left to op-

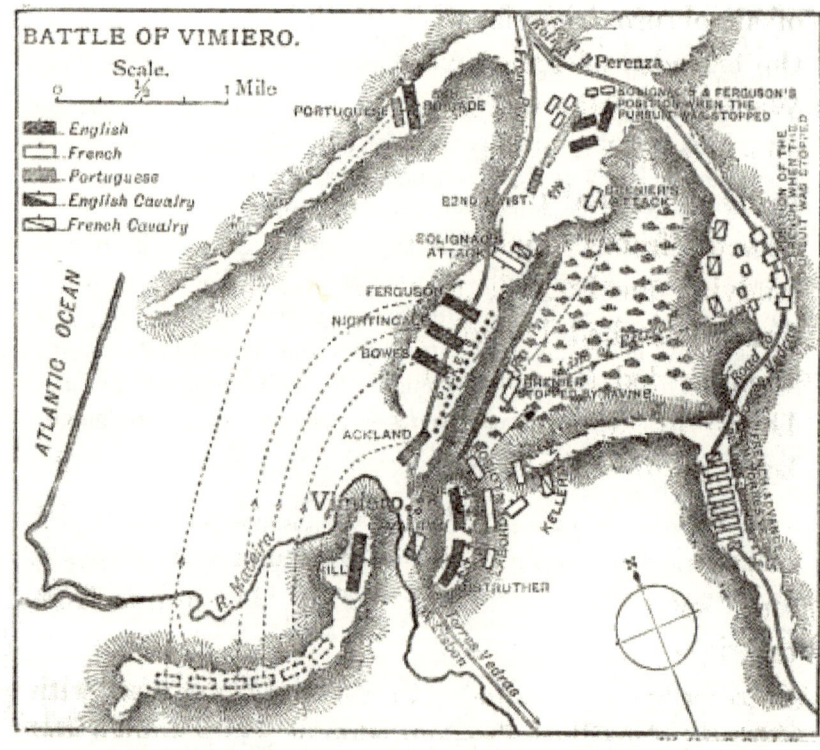

pose him,—but found it strengthened with the same forethought and skill as marked, in days coming on, the tactics of Wellington at Waterloo,—we read of the "powerful artillery which swept away their foremost ranks." As the reader finishes the account of this battle, and reads of the French retreating in confusion, leaving thirteen of their guns on the field, he can scarcely realise that the whole artillery force of Sir A. Wellesley was little more than the captured guns represented. How much of the effect of this force, small as it was, was due to the individual exertions of all ranks may be gathered from the following extract from Colonel Robe's despatch to the Ordnance:—

> Never was man better supported by his officers and soldiers than I have been. I would not change one of them, from the Major to the youngest subaltern, for anything in the world; and only regret my son was not with me. My men are staunch and the admiration of the army.

It may interest the professional reader to know that great part of Colonel Robe's report after Vimiera was occupied with praises of Shrapnel's spherical case, of which he begged large additional supplies. He concludes with a sentence which proves the *entente cordiale* which existed between himself and his superiors.

> Nothing but the unexampled assistance and attention of Sir A. Wellesley, and the general officers, could have brought this artillery into the field in an efficient manner; and I am proud to say they have never yet stopped an hour for us. (Col. Robe to D.-A.-Gen. Vimiera, 21 Aug. 1808.)

Sir H. Burrard, with the chivalrous courtesy which has so often been repeated in the annals of the English Army, did not interfere with Sir A. Wellesley's command during the battle, but at its termination he declined to accede to the proposal of the latter to undertake an energetic pursuit, which would doubtless have ended in an unconditional surrender of the French troops. Of Sir Arthur's bitter disappointment,—of the further complication caused by the arrival of yet another general to supersede Sir H. Burrard—Sir Hew Dalrymple,—of the singular Convention of Cintra, which while it certainly succeeded in procuring the evacuation of Portugal by the French, did so on terms which were very disproportionate to the success of the English arms,—and of the indignation in England which followed the news of this marvellous treaty,—it is beyond the province of this work to treat. The state of affairs in Portugal—the absence of all harmony of plan or action, was such as to call from Sir Arthur Wellesley the expression, "Considering the way in which things are likely to be carried on here, I shall not be sorry to go away." (*Despatches* vol.6.)

The recall of Sir Hew Dalrymple, Sir H. Burrard, and Sir A. Wellesley to England, on account of the Court of Enquiry ordered to investigate the circumstances under which the Convention had been agreed to, left the command of the English forces in Portugal with Sir John Moore. An army of 28,000 men was concentrated at Lisbon under that general. The command of the artillery, which had been considerably reinforced, had been given to Colonel Harding, who endorsed every complaint which had been made by Colonel Robe, but who seems to have been somewhat more of an optimist than that officer; for in one of his letters, describing his field artillery, he wrote that "four oxen and two horses bring along a gun famously." On his arrival at Lisbon, he found that he had to arrange for the proper equipment not merely of his own batteries, but also of the artillery of a force of 4000 Spaniards at Lisbon, whom the Convention had set free, and who, when armed and equipped, marched for Catalonia.

Sir John Moore decided on taking the field in October 1808, but being misinformed as to the state of the roads, he decided on breaking up his army, so as to march by different roads, and to unite at Salamanca with another army under Sir David Baird, which had landed at Corunna. The artillery was ordered to march through the Alemtejo and by Badajos to Talavera, and was arranged by Colonel Harding as follows. (Colonel Harding to D.-A.-Gen.) He himself, Lieut.-Colonel Wood, Major Viney, with the following companies, Thornhill's, Drummond's, Wilmot's, Raynsford's, Craufurd's, Carthew's, and Skyring's, went with the army; the guns being four brigades of light 6-pounders, and one of 9-pounders. He was unable to take a brigade for each company, for lack of horses.

Colonel Robe was left in command at Lisbon, with Major Hartmann and three companies of the King's German Artillery, Captain Bredin's company of the Royal Artillery, and half a company of the same under Captain Lawson. The guns to which these were attached consisted of a 12-pounder brigade, three brigades of light 6-pounders, a few howitzers, and the car brigade of 3-pounders from Gibraltar, mentioned above. The force of artillery with Sir David Baird's army, which had landed at Corunna, was commanded by Colonel Sheldrake, and consisted of four companies and a proportion of drivers. The guns used by this force, and by the Horse Artillery under Colonel George Cookson, which arrived—also at Corunna—on the 8th November, 1808, were as follows:—One 9-pounder brigade and three brigades of light 6-pounders, which moved on to Betanjos: one 9-pounder brigade, and one of light 6-pounders, which remained at Corunna; and one light 6-pounder brigade, and a brigade of mountain artillery, for service with the cavalry, as soon as horses and mules could be obtained. (Colonel Cookson to D.-A.-Gen. Corunna, 9 Nov. 1808.)

Of all the difficulties encountered in the winter campaign of 1808 by the Royal Artillery, the scarcity of horses was the greatest. The table given in a former part of this chapter shows that after the first gross omission in the case of Colonel Robe's force, the Ordnance Department endeavoured, as far as numbers were concerned, to send an adequate supply of horses to ensure that mobility without which field artillery is a sham. But that the simplest precautions as to quality and soundness were overlooked is too evident from the monotonous protests of all the officers who found themselves in a position of responsibility. Colonel Harding, writing from Lisbon, reported that he had obtained permission to sell the artillery horses he had received from England, as useless and worn out, and to purchase those of the French Army, which was then embarking under the provisions of the Convention of Cintra.

Colonel Cookson had not reached the Downs ere he had to report the appearance of glanders among the horses entrusted to him; and Colonel Robe had to report the death, immediately after landing, of 75 out of 300 horses—more than half occasioned by the same complaint. The officer in charge of the drivers attached to the artillery under the command of Colonel Sheldrake, reported that "all his horses were in dreadful order when they embarked, that he had lost many, and that he attributed it in a great measure to the horses being a great many very old." Mules were difficult to obtain—the horses of the country were few and of small size; and in spite of the plaintive appeals from successive officers that "it cost no more to the country to keep a good horse than a bad one," shipload of cripples from England followed shipload, and nothing but superhuman exertions on the part of all on the spot enabled the artillery to move at all.

The desperate state of affairs may be gathered from a report of Colonel Robe's, in which he described the means left to him for horsing the brigades in his charge, after Colonel Harding's force had left Lisbon with Sir John Moore. With 52 field guns, liable to be de-

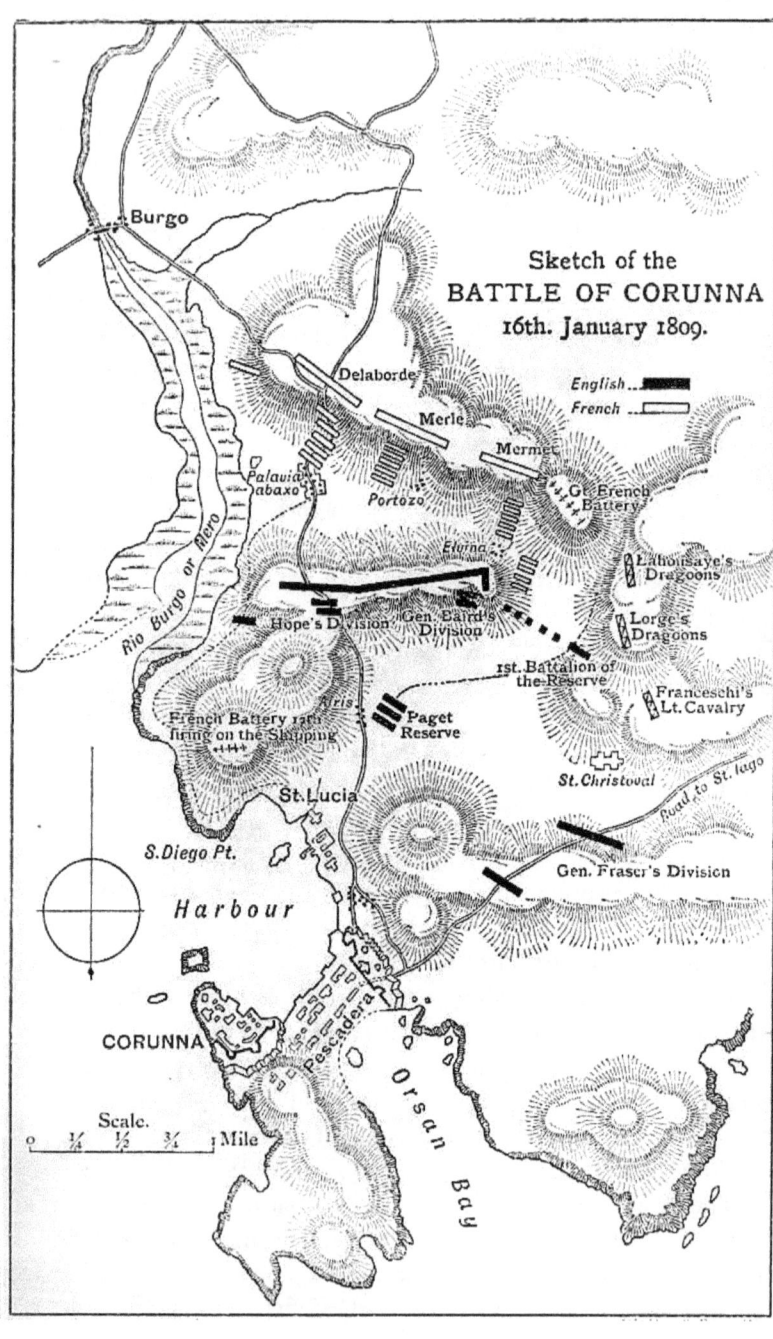

manded at any moment by Colonel Harding, he had only 500 men; but this number was lavish compared with that of his horses. He wrote to D.-A.-Gen. 1 Nov. 1808:

The following is a state of the horses left with me on the departure of the army for Spain:—

	Horses.	Mules.
Effective	15	3
Sick or lame	49	4
	64	7
Since died of general decay, or destroyed for glanders . .	7	1
"Remaining . .	57	6

The sick of these are reported to be in a very bad condition; and nearly the whole of them to be at present unserviceable, from lameness, age, and sore backs.

So great was the scarcity of horses, that when the Horse Artillery landed at Corunna, the officers' horses were taken on repayment—without their consent, and they were left to purchase any animals they could find in the country. That Colonel Robe had good reason to fear a demand being made on his small depot may be seen from the following account of the number of horses, which the state of the roads between Lisbon and Spain had rendered absolutely necessary or the brigades which had marched with Colonel Harding. Every artillery carriage, of whatever description, had 6 horses; the long 6-pounder gun had 8, and the 12-pounder had 10. (Official Return to Sir H. Burrard, Nov. 1, 1808.) Besides this, horses were required for the officers, non-commissioned officers, and for park duties; and the ammunition waggons, for conveyance of such as could not be carried on the limbers, were drawn by a motley collection of horses, mules, and oxen.

Six days after this return was prepared, Colonel Robe's supply had decreased to 40, and the demands from the front were such that he declared no less than a reserve of 600 horses would be required to meet them. (Colonel Robe to D.-A.-Gen. 6 Nov. 1808.)

There is a danger, in perusing the story of the Peninsular War, lest all the reader's admiration should be given to the courage and endurance of the men, or the skill of the leaders. But there were men who would infinitely rather have endured bodily suffering, than the charge which neglect or ignorance at home had thrust upon them. To feel in all its terrible reality the starvation of equipment, without which no adequate results can be expected either from skill or courage;—to know that if that equipment is not in some way forthcoming, the disgrace of failure or consequent disaster will be transferred from those to whom it is due, and will be visited on themselves;—and at the same time to be certain that any responsibility which they may assume is at their own peril, and can only be exercised with a halter round their neck of possible disallowances, reprimands, and suspicion,—all these produce in men a state of mind, beside which danger or bodily hardship seems almost repose. And it was in such a condition that many of England's best soldiers had to live during the war in Spain—enduring more than has formed the theme of song and story—and yet bearing it without sympathy, without acknowledgment.

No one can thoroughly understand Sir John Moore's campaign in Spain without bearing in mind the boasting and lying of the Spanish generals, with whom it was intended that he should co-operate, and the yet more extravagant falsehoods of the Spanish Government. Deluded by these, Sir John Moore, even after he had heard of the surrender of Madrid to Napoleon, pressed on to Majorga in the hope of effecting a junction with the Marquis Romana, and of receiving Sir David Baird's reinforcement from Corunna. With an English Army of 25,000 men he pressed still farther on to Sahagan, where for the first time he heard the whole truth, and realised the strength of the French armies which were being directed against him, under Napoleon himself. With every Spanish general already beaten in detail, Madrid in the hands of the enemy, and greatly superior forces hurrying to meet him, he commenced a retreat which has become famous,—the first step of which is thus described by Colonel Harding to D.-A.-Gen. Majorga, 25 Dec. 1808:—

> We fully expected to have engaged the enemy on the 23rd, about five leagues from Sahagan; the army was in full march at 8 o'clock on the night of the 23rd, and hoped to have fallen in with them early in the morning of the 24th. An intense hard frost, and the whole of the roads one sheet of ice from the snow thawing during the day, was much against the march of artillery, as we had not time to rough all the horses. The march of the troops was stopped an hour after they marched off; some of the troops, particularly Downman's troop, were out till 2 in the morning. The general received some information immediately after the troops marched off, which caused their sudden return.

We now seem to be pointing towards Corunna, and forming depots that way.

Our movements have lately been so intricate and unexpected, that if I had had time to write to you, I could give you little information. . . . Lieutenant-Colonel Cookson has the command of the three brigades on the right of the line, Evelegh's, Bean's, and Wilmot's. Lieutenant-Colonel Wood has charge of those on the left of the line, Downman's, Drummond's, and Carthew's. Four reserve brigades with the park are Raynsford's (9-pounders), Craufurd's, Brandreth's, and Wall's (light 6-pounders) brigades. The park, stores, and ammunition are under Major Thornhill. The depots advanced are under Captain Skyring. There is a brigade of mountain guns somewhere, which I hope will not join us, but return to Corunna. We have lately received 59 prize horses, which, although not good, are a great help to us, from our great loss.

English troops are apt to become demoralised during a retreat; and in the retreat to Corunna, irregularity was increased by the intense cold, suffering, and hardship which the men had to endure. The conduct of the rear-guard and of the cavalry was, however, beyond all praise; and was due in a great degree to the constant presence of Sir John Moore himself, whose skill, firmness, and powers of persuasion never shone more clearly than at this time. But, even when irregularity was greatest, it vanished when an engagement appeared probable: it was at such times as these, that perfect discipline prevailed. The artilleryman reads with pleasure that while 2627 men strayed from the English Army during the retreat, not one belonged to his corps; and that Sir John Moore himself was so struck by this fact and by their general conduct, that he wrote, "The artillery consists of particularly well-behaved men." (Cadell.) These words are the more gratifying as the strength of the artillery was considerable—eleven brigades of guns,—and the duties of the men were very arduous.

Several affairs of small importance took place between the two armies, but the English came in sight of Corunna without any general engagement. The dismay which seized everyone on learning that the transports had not yet arrived may be imagined; fortunately, it was short-lived, as they soon made their appearance.

The story of the artillery at the end of the retreat, and during the Battle of Corunna, may be summarised from Colonel Harding's reports. On the 11th January the army took up a position about five miles from Corunna; but on the 14th, being unable, with their reduced numbers, sufficiently to occupy this ground without danger of being outflanked, they withdrew to a position about three miles nearer the town, leaving their original ground to be occupied by Soult, before the battle. On the 12th all the artillery, except the brigades required for outpost and rear-guard duties, was ordered by Sir John Moore to be embarked; and at the same time a magazine containing 12,000 barrels of powder, situated about four miles from Corunna, was blown up with great skill, under the supervision of Colonel Cookson.

This was not done, however, until some 400 barrels had been carried for the use of the artillery, along dreadful roads, for a distance of four miles, on the shoulders of the artillerymen; while at the same time serviceable arms were issued from the stores to all the troops, in exchange for those which had become useless during the retreat. A supply of ammunition at the rate of 70 rounds per man was also given out. These measures had the double effect of destroying valuable stores which must have inevitably fallen into the hands of the enemy, and of giving an advantage to the English Army in the battle which ensued, which was denied to their opponents, whose arms and ammunition had suffered greatly during the harassing marches of the preceding days.

All the artillerymen, who could be spared from the embarkation of guns and stores on the 14th and 15th, were employed in the destruction of the guns and mortars on the sea front of Corunna (which would otherwise have been used against the English fleet, on the occupation of the town by the French), and also of those mounted on a small island in the bay. Upwards of 50 heavy guns and 20 mortars were dismounted, spiked, and thrown over the precipice, and their carriages and beds destroyed. In this the men were assisted cheerfully by the inhabitants, although, as Napier points out, they were aware that the English Army would ultimately embark, and that they would incur the enemy's anger for having taken part in any military operations. This conduct, so inconsistent with the insufficient defence made by the Spaniards as a nation, drew forth from the historian a remark:

> Of proverbially vivid imagination and quick resentments, the Spaniards feel and act individually, rather than nationally.

The artillery of the outposts, on which the brunt of the action of the 16th fell, was commanded by Major Viney, and consisted of 145 officers and men of the Royal Artillery, and 94 officers and men of the Royal Artillery Drivers. (Official M.S. Return signed by Colonel Harding.) The guns employed were seven light 6-pounders, one 5½-inch howitzer, and four Spanish 8-pounders.

The names of the officers serving under Major Viney's command were as follows: Captains Truscott, Wilmot (later in command of the D Battery, 4th Brigade), Godby, and Greatley; Lieutenants Sinclair and King; and Assistant-Surgeons Price and Hutchison. The officers of the Royal Artillery Drivers were Lieutenants Abercromby and Read.

A slight affair of picquets took place on the 15th; but even as late as noon on the 16th, Sir John Moore told Colonel Harding that he did not think the enemy meant to attack, and therefore he continued the embarkation. Most of the horses and appointments belonging to Downman's and Evelegh's troops of Horse Artillery had been lost during the retreat; and their guns, and those of several of the other brigades, had been placed on board ship; so that many of the artillerymen, who had been present during the retreat, and were under fire on the 16th, were without their guns on that day, and were employed in bringing up ammunition for the army. The artillery of the outposts, although lightly armed, did good service; but the ground was not calculated for the manoeuvring of guns, either on the side of the French or of the English.

On Monday the 16th, at 3 p.m., Soult advanced with all his army in three columns, his cavalry and artillery remaining on the heights to cover his formations. Two divisions of the English Army, under General Hope and Sir David Baird, occupied the most advanced ground on their side, with their left to the Bay of Corunna; a third division, under General Frazer, was posted on some heights to the right—more retired—commanding the approaches to Corunna from the Vigo Road. Captain Gardiner, Brigade-Major to the R.A. wrote to D.-A.-G. 23 June, 1809:

> The action became general about 3 o'clock, and an uninterrupted fire of cannon and musketry was kept up till one hour after dark. They evidently pushed for our right, which was our weakest point, but the firmness of our line was in no way to be shaken. At one time I feared they would outflank us from their numbers; but this was prevented by the movements of the reserve under General Paget. At a little after 6 o'clock Soult retired, leaving us masters of the field, and in possession of a village he occupied in the morning.

This village, Elvina, had been to the Battle of Corunna what Hougomont and La Haye Sainte were afterwards to that of Waterloo. The battle, at various periods of the day, raged fiercely round it. Here Sir David Baird received the wound which compelled him to leave the field; and it was when watching the attack by the English reserve on the French troops in possession of this village late in the day, that Sir John Moore received the wound which proved fatal. Its retention by the English at the close of the day was therefore a distinct proof of victory.

But it was not a victory, as General Hope well said, which could be attended by any very brilliant consequences to Great Britain. (Despatch to Sir D. Baird.) The utmost that could be hoped for was the embarkation of the army without molestation. Thanks to the defeat of the French, their want of ammunition, and the friendly courage of the inhabitants of Corunna, the whole army, with the exception of the rear-guard, was embarked with perfect order during the night of the 16th. The incessant rumble of wheels over the field denoted the gathering of the wounded, and their conveyance in the artillery carts and waggons to the beach. The guns which had been engaged during the day were taken for embarkation to a sandy bay, south-west of Corunna, but, as Colonel Harding wrote:

> The weather would not permit it: the guns were spiked; the carriages destroyed; and the whole thrown over a precipice into deep water.

The rear-guard had been detailed by Sir John Moore himself, to assist the Spaniards in manning the guns on the land front of Corunna—to keep possession of the small island in the bay—and to cover the embarkation of the troops from the citadel. The artillery attached to it was commanded by Major Beevor, assisted by Major Thornhill, Captains Truscott, Beane, Brandreth, and Greatley, and Lieutenants Maling, Wright, and Darby. There were 36 non-commissioned officers and 253 men. The whole of the rear-guard was embarked, but with difficulty, on the evening of the 18th and morning of the 19th. The voyage to England was tempestuous in the extreme. Many officers and men died on the passage; many others, including Colonel Harding himself, only survived their hardships a few months. The whole army landed in England at various ports in such a state of destitution, that the whole nation was shocked, and could not believe it possible that the story of the final success was true. These skeleton regiments, starved and half-clothed, had not the appearance of an army fresh from victory; and for many years the skill displayed in the retreat upon Corunna, and the subsequent success, received little, if any, credit from the people.

So ended Sir John Moore's campaign in Spain;—and with it—his life.

The many letters from the various officers, whose correspondence with the Ordnance is extant, tell in simple words the worth of the leader who fell at Corunna. One writes:

> You have heard of our terrible loss: we not believe he was dead. (Colonel Harding to D.-A.-Gen.)

Another writes:

> General Hope's despatches will acquaint you with our affecting loss. You will imagine how severely I felt it. I saw him after he received the wound, but he was talking with such firmness, that I did not apprehend the danger he was in. (Captain, afterwards Sir, R. Gardiner to D.-A. Gen.)

General Hope's words cannot be too frequently read.

> The fall of Sir John Moore has deprived me of a valuable friend, to whom long experience of his worth had sincerely attached me. But it is chiefly on public grounds that I must lament the blow. It will be the consolation of every one who loved or respected his manly character, that after conducting the army through an arduous retreat with consummate firmness, he has terminated a career of distinguished honour by a death that has given the enemy additional reason to respect the name of a British soldier. Like the immortal Wolfe, he is snatched from his country at an early period of a life spent in her service: like Wolfe, his last moments were gilded by the prospect of success, and cheered by the acclamation of victory: like Wolfe, also, his memory will for ever remain sacred in that country which he sincerely loved, and which he had so faithfully served. (Despatch to Sir D. Baird, 18 Jan. 1809.)

The following return shows the strength of the Royal Artillery left in Portugal, after the evacuation of Spain by Sir John Moore's army. It also shows the number who had returned at various times from the Peninsula, prior to 27th February, 1809, having proceeded thither with the various contingents detailed in the preceding table. (*See table following.*)

TABLE showing the NUMBER of OFFICERS, NON-COMMISSIONED OFFICERS, GUNNERS, and DRUMMERS of the ROYAL ARTILLERY; and also of the OFFICERS, NON-COMMISSIONED OFFICERS, DRIVERS, TRUMPETERS, ARTIFICERS, and HORSES belonging to the Royal Artillery Drivers, relanded from Spain or Portugal before the 27th February, 1809.

	ROYAL ARTILLERY.						ROYAL ARTILLERY DRIVERS.						
	Officers.	N. C. Officers.	Gunners.	Drummers.	Total.	Officers.	N. C. Officers.	Drivers.	Trumpeters.	Artificers.	Total.	General Total.	Horses.
Relanded in Great Britain and Ireland, fit for service	64	178	1,215	16	1,473	14	105	1,116	14	97	1,346	2,819	764
In Portugal, per return of 1st January .	31	84	556	11	682	2	7	219	2	28	258	940	..
Total	95	262	1,771	27	2,155	16	112	1,335	16	125	1,604	3,759	764

N.B. There had been purchased, or otherwise obtained, in Portugal, and still remained effective, 146 horses and 78 mules; but as they had not been sent from England they are not included in the above table.

CHAPTER 3

Walcheren

To an artilleryman the Walcheren Expedition has an interest which well repays him for turning his eyes and thoughts from the Peninsula to this strange island in the Northern Sea. Here no less than seventeen troops and companies of his corps were present; and so important was their duty considered, that the Master-General, Lord Chatham, who was also commander-in-chief of the forces employed, requested the deputy-adjutant-general, Brigadier Macleod, himself to accompany the army in command of the artillery. And on this island, so baneful to our troops, and yet so beautiful, a singular historical question connected with the regiment was settled, which will receive detailed notice in this chapter.

Forming the right bank of the West Scheldt at its mouth, the islands of South Beveland and Walcheren, now united by a railway embankment, present to the traveller the most singular appearance. Rich and fertile beyond measure, they are yet only saved from submersion by the sea by means of costly dykes, kept efficient by incessant labour. In most places the island of Walcheren, especially, is many feet below the level of the sea; and even its highest points, the towns of Middleburg and Flushing, have frequently suffered great injury from the inroads of the ocean. One such inundation had occurred in 1808, and tended to make the autumn of 1809 exceptionally unhealthy. Dykes now not merely surround the island itself, but also the individual villages and farmhouses on its surface, giving a curious fortified appearance to the whole.

Flushing and Antwerp, in the hands of Napoleon, strongly fortified, and offering protection and anchorage to his fleets, were a strong and perpetual menace to England, and gave an appearance of probability to his threats of invasion, both in the eyes of the English people and their Government. One of the strongest arguments against the Walcheren Expedition has always been that it was a dissipation of England's military resources, which, if concentrated on the Peninsular campaign, would have produced infinitely greater results. But it is easy to argue thus with the wisdom which follows the fact.

The danger which was involved in the fortifications of Antwerp and Flushing was very present to the English people; and immunity in that respect seemed then more desirable than victory at a distance, even although that victory might, in the end, have been a more serious blow at Napoleon's power. And the importance of Flushing, armed as it was, may be now better realised by imagining it in the hands of a powerful Continental dynasty,—not dismantled and disarmed, as it has been since the siege to be treated of in this chapter,—but with batteries sufficiently strong to protect the anchorage in front, and with a fleet riding there, within a few hours of the English coast. Were such a thing ever to occur again—and it is by no means impossible—Englishmen would perhaps confess that there was more wisdom in the Expedition of 1809, which rendered Flushing harmless, than has generally been allowed.

★★★★★★

The Infantry force with the expedition numbered 33,096
The Cavalry   "   "   "   "   "   3,015
Sir J. T. Jones, from whose work these numbers are taken, gives only the *field* and not also the *siege* artillery companies

★★★★★★

Much of the unpopularity attending it, and all the incompleteness of execution, were due to a want of harmony between the naval and military commanders, which has never yet been satisfactorily explained, but which undoubtedly was the main cause of the first part of the scheme—the capture of Flushing—being the only part that was executed. Lord Chatham would appear to have been much to blame in the matter; but there has been a mystery connected with it all, which cannot be cleared up. Of that nobleman's military incapacity there is, however, no doubt; nor is the reader surprised to find that his name disappeared, soon after this Expedition, from the list of the Masters-General of the Ordnance.

The troop of Horse Artillery which accompanied the force was that commanded by Captain A. Macdonald, and was later D Battery, A Brigade. The sixteen companies will be found enumerated in the various tables of the battalions. General Macleod took Captain—afterwards Sir Robert—Gardiner as his brigade-major; and it is from the private diaries of these officers that the main regimental incidents connected with this expedition have been obtained. Captain Drummond was the general's *aide-de-camp*. (Sir J. T. Jones's *Sieges*.) The field officers who accompanied the artillery were Colonel Terrot, Lieut.-Colonels Dixon, Franklin, Cookson, and Wood, and Majors Griffiths, Dixon, and Waller. The immense battering train included 70 guns and 74 mortars; and we learn that not merely was a large supply of Congreve's rockets taken for employment as siege weapons, but also that every man in the Regiment who had been trained to the use of rockets was ordered to embark with the army. (A.-A.-Gen. to Colonel Neville, 18 July, 1809.)

The name of nearly every artillery officer with the expedition will appear in the course of the narrative. In the meantime, the following numerical return of the force under General Macleod's command will be found worthy of perusal. (*See table following.*)

The Second Division of the army, which General Macleod accompanied, sailed from the Downs on Saturday, the 29th July, 1809, and anchored the same evening in the Stein Diep. On the following day they weighed anchor, and moved into the Room Pot, where they found the First Division, and where orders were at once given for the troops to land in light marching order.

At 4 p.m. the first six battalions landed, without opposition, at the Bree Zand, and during the night the remainder of the troops, under the command of Sir Eyre Coote, continued to disembark, with the several brigades of artillery attached to them,—the last named being under the command of Colonel Terrot. The following detail shows the artillery attached to this part of the army:—

Captain Marsh's	Light 6-pr. Brigade,	attached to	Lieut.-Gen. Frazer.
,, Webber Smith's	,,	,,	,,	Major-Gen. Graham.
,, Massey's	,,	,,	,,	Lieut.-Gen. Lord Paget.

There was also a Heavy Brigade under Captain S. Adye.

About 3 p.m. the reserve, under Sir John Hope, proceeded to South Beveland (immediately adjoining Walcheren), accompanied by Captain Wilmot's Light 6-pounder Brigade.

On Monday, the 31st July, Ter Veer, a village at the opposite end of the island of Walcheren from Flushing, was invested, two guns of Captain Macdonald's troop and two 8-inch mortars having been landed to assist; and it surrendered the following day. Until the fall of Flush-

ARTILLERY EMBARKED for the SCHELDT EXPEDITION, under the EARL OF CHATHAM, in 1809.

Number of Troops and Companies, with Drivers attached; also Ports of Embarkation.	Field Officers.	Captains.	Subalterns.	Surgeons.	N.C. Officers.	Gunners.	Drummers.	Total.	Officers.	N.C. Officers.	Drivers.	Artificers and Trumpeters.	Total.	General Total.	Horses.
				Royal Artillery.						Royal Artillery Drivers.					
PORTSMOUTH.															
Eight companies	4	16	24	4	104	800	16	968	2	10	90	8	110	1,078	150
RIVER THAMES.															
One troop: Royal Horse Artillery (now D Batt., A Brigade)	..	2	3	1	13	81	..	100	..	..	54	8	62	162	162
Eight companies	4	16	24	4	104	800	16	968	7	41	308	37	393	1,361	515
With the battering train	..	..	..	..	..	..	..	..	7	54	500	42	603	603	1,000
Total	8	34	51	9	221	1,681	32	2,036	16	105	952	95	1,168	3,204	1,827

N.B. A few casualties occurred prior to the sailing of the Expedition. About 50 additional horses were embarked, and rather more than 100 men were left behind sick, and for other causes; but these are the numbers prepared from the official returns, both in Record Office and United Service Institution.

ing, Ter Veer was employed as a landing-place and depot for ordnance stores—the Balaclava of the Walcheren Expedition.

The army then advanced across the island, and proceeded to invest Flushing. During the siege, frequent reinforcements of the French garrison took place, their troops being transported by sea from Cadstand, and the weather being such as to render it very difficult for the English fleet to intercept them. The defence made by the French was very gallant, although the wretched inhabitants were the main sufferers during the bombardment. By Napoleon's positive order, and notwithstanding the remonstrances of the French Commandant, one of the dykes near Flushing was partly cut, and the sea poured into the English trenches to a considerable extent, increasing the discomfort and difficulties which the heavy and almost incessant rains had already produced.

The English Army was drawn up against Flushing as follows: General Graham's division on the right, General Grosvenor's next; then Lord Paget's at West Zouberg, and General Houston's at Oust Zouberg. Six batteries were formed, five of which were manned by the Royal Artillery, and one by seamen. The former were numbered and armed as follows:—

No. 1 Battery.—[1] 1200 yards from the town.

13 24-prs. . . . } This was evidently No. 5 Battery, according to the numbering of the Engineers;
2 8-in. howitzers . } vide Jones's 'Sieges.'
6 8-in. mortars .

No. 3 Battery.—2200 yards from the town.

6 10 in. mortars . { This was evidently No. 1 Battery in the Engineers' catalogue.

No. 4 Battery.—1600 yards from the town.
4 10-in. mortars.
10 24-pounders.

No. 5 Battery.—1600 yards from the town.

2 10-in. howitzers. { This was evidently No. 7 Battery in the Engineers' catalogue.

No. 6 Battery.—1700 yards from the town.
3 24-pounders.
4 10-in. howitzers.

N.B.—Two additional batteries, Nos 7 and 8, were afterwards armed: No. 7 with 2 10-inch mortars, No. 8 with 6 24-pounders.

[1] The armament and numbering of these batteries differ from those given in Sir J. T. Jones's 'Sieges;' but as they are taken from Captain Gardiner's MS. diary—written in his own hand—they must be correct. Probably they show the armament of the batteries when the bombardment *commenced*; and Sir J. Jones may give the armament when at its maximum.

These batteries were opened on the 13th August, at 1 p.m. At early morning on the 15th August Flushing surrendered. Including the ammunition expended by the sailors from No. 2 Battery, which was armed with six 24-pounders, and opened on Sunday, the 14th August, the following was the expenditure of ammunition, other than rockets, during the short siege:—

	Rounds
24-pr. guns	6582
10-in. mortars	1743
8-in. mortars	1020
10-in. howitzers	269
8-in. howitzers	380
Total	9994

N.B.—Sir R. Gardiner's MS. agrees exactly in this particular with Sir J. T. Jones's *Sieges*.

Rockets had been used before the opening of the batteries, and continued to be employed in great profusion, and with fatal effect. Great part of the city, including the Hôtel de Ville, was burnt to the ground, and hundreds of the inhabitants were killed. To this day shot may be seen in the walls of many of the houses—handing down from one generation to another the traditions of the siege.

The chief labour and hardship, however, to the English troops preceded the opening of the batteries. It was during their construction that the energies of officers and men were most severely tried. The roads between Ter Veer and the trenches became almost impassable with constant traffic and rain; the landing of the guns and stores was attended with great difficulty; it was impossible to procure cattle in sufficient quantities for purposes of draught; and many of the horses intended for the later operations had to be landed at Walcheren to draw the stores from Ter Veer. As for the trenches themselves, a few extracts from Sir R. Gardiner's diary will enable the reader to realise the conditions under which the artillerymen worked:—

August 10th. Ascertained, by the saltness of the water, that the dyke had been cut.... The water making great progress in the communication from the right to West Zouberg. The crossroads very deep and bad; great difficulty in drawing the guns from the park to the several batteries.

August 11th. A violent thunder-storm and incessant rains during the night precluded all work the greatest part of it. The water rose in the gun-battery on the left about six inches.

August 12. The roads much worse, and the water rose very high in the trenches. The water-gauge showed the rising of the water to be 4 inches. The magazine of No. 1 Battery on the right was filled with water during the night from the heavy rains, and it was feared would not be ready to receive the ammunition. *The exertions of the men, however, overcame every obstacle."*

Three companies, commanded by Captains Drummond, Campbell, and Fyers, had landed at Ter Veer on the 8th August, and proved of great service in the batteries at Oust Zouberg; but the artillery before Flushing had been weakened the previous day by the removal of the detachments of Captains Buckner's (later No. 3 Battery, 3 Brigade, R.A.) and Brome's companies, with Captains Adye and Light, under the command of Colonel Cookson, to join the force in South Beveland, in consequence of a letter received from Sir John Hope. There was considerable anxiety in South Beveland. The forts had, certainly, been occupied by the English; and Captain Wilmot had succeeded in unspiking and rendering serviceable almost all the guns which they found; but there were many reasons for disquiet.

Provisions were not so easily obtained as had been expected in such a country; the inhabitants, without exhibiting actual hostility, were decidedly cool and unfriendly; rumours were spread, which magnified every hour, announcing large reinforcements, not merely to Antwerp, but to every Dutch garrison, and describing swarms of French troops being pushed forward in waggons and boats to form a large army at Bergen-op-Zoom, or some such place, with a view to assuming the offensive; the drains made on their resources by the army in Walcheren alarmed the military chiefs; and the disagreement between the admiral and Lord Chatham as to the method of conducting future operations had already ceased to be secret.

It does not, therefore, surprise the reader to find that when, after the fall of Flushing, all the troops and horses which had been originally intended for the second operation, as the design on Antwerp was

ROYAL ARTILLERY IN ACTION

termed, were about to return to South Beveland, a decided hesitation manifested itself among the authorities, which ended in a suspense from further action. Before the end of August, the whole of the Horse Artillery, cavalry, and all the horses of the battering train had returned to England;—Captains Wilmot's, Buckner's, and Brome's companies were ordered to follow, after dismantling the forts in South Beveland;—on the 2nd September, Lord Chatham's headquarters were moved to Middleburg, in Walcheren;—on the 3rd, the embarkation of much of the ordnance, stores, &c., for England commenced;—on the 10th, Lord Chatham announced that he had received the king's commands to return home; and on the 14th, accompanied by his staff, including General Macleod, he sailed from Flushing.

The much-vaunted expedition was therefore at an end; and with the exception of the garrison of Walcheren, the army returned home by instalments. But in the successful part of the campaign—the capture of Flushing, there is more than a crumb of comfort for the artilleryman who is in search of incidents creditable to his corps. The words penned after the siege by Lord Chatham, who was observant, although incapable, are worthy of a high place in the Regimental records.

It is *impossible*, for me to do sufficient justice to the distinguished conduct of the officers and men of the Royal Artillery, under the able direction and animating example of Brigadier-General Macleod. (Lord Chatham's Despatch announcing the surrender of Flushing.)

And in a letter presently to be quoted, the reader will see that in the duller work of dismantling the works, under circumstances of great difficulty and sickness, the men of the Royal Artillery earned noble words of commendation.

Walcheren has been remembered for the sickness which scourged the English Army in 1809, when it has been forgotten as to everything else;—and the sickness certainly was fearful; although perhaps due more to exposure, injudicious diet, and inefficient hospital arrangements, than to any local influences, such as were conceived by superstition and fear. The former, it is known, *did* exist; and their results have been seen in later days, during the first winter of the war in the Crimea, much as they were in Walcheren. But the latter—the mysterious local fevers, which were believed to be indigenous to this island—seem to have marvellously disappeared, or to be innocuous, as far as the healthy, contented, and long-lived inhabitants of its beautiful

Royal Horse Artillery in action

villages are concerned.

Be that, however, as it may; the sickness among the English troops in 1809 was very great. On the 30th August there were 5000 sick; on the 3rd September the number increased to 5745; on the 5th September it rose to 8000; and on the 8th it was no less than 10,948, with fresh cases occurring every hour. The sickness in the artillery may be gathered from a return which is extant. On the 27th September there had been left in Walcheren a total strength of 1089 officers and men belonging to the Royal Artillery and Royal Artillery Driver Corps. Before the 16th October—in less than three weeks,—255 had been sent sick to England, 396 were sick at Walcheren, and 109 were in their graves. From a return of the officers who were invalided to England, we find the names of many not yet mentioned, including Captains Oliver, Monro, Parker, Wallace, Greene, and Scott; and Lieutenants J. Evans, Parker, Dalton, Pringle, Grant, Chapman, and Drawbridge. The names of others, who remained to the date of the evacuation of the island, will be mentioned presently.

After Lord Chatham's departure, it was intended at first to strengthen the island for defence in the event of a French attack. Napoleon being, however, as he said, perfectly satisfied that the English should die in Zealand without any assistance from him, and the continued sickness appalling the authorities, it was decided to dismantle the newly-armed batteries with a view to the evacuation of the place. This was done under the control and supervision of Major William Dixon, R.A., assisted by the remnants of the twelve companies, left as part of the garrison of the island. On his arrival in Woolwich, with these companies, he made a report to the deputy adjutant-general, 3 Jan. 1810, which cannot fail to be interesting.

> It would be of no use now, sir, to enter into a detailed account of the state of defence in which Walcheren was placed at the moment the order came to withdraw; but, in justice to the officers and men I had the good fortune to command, you will permit me to state that, up to the 15th November, every possible exertion was made to withstand an attack in the field, or a siege in the fortified places. All the Dutch mortars and many of the guns were exchanged for English; the extra foreign ammunition sent off to England; Flushing, Veer, and Rammekens completed; the coast strengthened by batteries mounted with heavy ordnance; the field brigades distributed to the different corps of the army;

and depots of ammunition established throughout.

These labours were effected without any assistance from the troops of the Line, and under circumstances peculiarly trying;—the companies diminished by sickness to one-third of their original strength, and even then jaded and worn by an oppression and feeling from climate, which I cannot describe, but which actually did not amount to disease. Yet, sir, notwithstanding this, I am happy to say they performed every part of their duty without a murmur, and obeyed every order with zeal and alacrity.

It will be plain to you, sir, that as we had risen to this state of defence, so in proportion were our labours increased when we came to dismantle. All that was done had to be undone; and every article of guns, ammunition, and stores throughout the island, to be embarked in the least possible time. The same diligence was continued, and within the given period not a trace remained in the works of the ordnance with which they had been defended. . . . Without meaning to take at all from the general report of the good conduct of the officers and men employed in the island of Walcheren, but as you are aware that, from various causes, there are degrees even in excellence itself, I hope I shall not be considered as acting inconsistently when I recommend the following officers as more particularly deserving your approbation. To Captains Maitland and Light I am greatly indebted for their activity and zeal in completing the defences of Walcheren.

To Captain Adye I owe everything for the assistance he gave in dismantling the works, and embarking the guns, ammunition, and stores; and to his name, which, in every respect, deservedly stands first, I beg leave to add those of Captains Rawlinson, Maitland, and Macartney, in the same undertaking. The whole of the subalterns went through every part of the duties imposed on them with zeal and goodwill, even in serving on board the *shutes* with parties of gunners to load and unload these vessels. I could place no reliance on the Dutch who navigated them, but was thus compelled to ensure their services by guarding against their escape. The navy, I presume, could not (for they certainly *would* not) grant us any assistance. Nautical skill we were not supposed to possess, but necessity, at length, helped us to find it. I shall conclude, sir, by recommending to your favour Lieutenant Anderson, the acting Adjutant, whose zeal and activity neither sickness nor fatigue could arrest, and I cannot hesitate in pronouncing him one of the finest young men I ever met in my life.

The amount of ordnance and stores captured in the islands of South Beveland and Walcheren, and either sent to England or destroyed, was very considerable. Summarised, according to date of capture, the following is a list of the guns and mortars which were taken. (From MS. return found among Sir A. Dickson's papers.)

Date.	Place.	Guns.	Howitzers.	Mortars.
Aug. 1, 1809.	Action on landing	4 6-prs. 1 3-pr.	.. ..	.. ..
Aug. 1809	Fort Haak	4 24-prs. 3 12-prs. 5 18-prs (iron) 2 „ (brass)	.. .. 3 7½-in. howitzers 1 5½-in. howitzer	3 coehorn. .. ..
Aug. 1, 1809.	Camp Veere	9 24-prs. 6 12-prs. 14 6-prs. 3 brass wall-pieces	.. .. .. 1 8½-in. howitzer	 8
Aug. 1809	Camp Veere Arsenal	2 swivel guns 1 18-pr. „ 4 8-pr. „ 4 6-pr. „ 4 18-pr. „	.. ..	 1
Aug. 4, 1809.	Fort Rammekens	6 12-pr. „ 3 6-pr. „ 3 2-pr. „	.. .. ..	.. .. ..
Aug. 1, 1809.	Coast Batteries, Walcheren	12 26-prs. „	..	7
Aug. 1809	Fort Bathz, S. Beveland	15 24-prs. „	3 8-inch 8 6 inch	4
Aug. 1809	Waarden Battery, S. Beveland	12 24-prs. „	..	..
	West Borselin Battery	12 24-prs. „	..	..
	East Borselin Battery	8 24-prs. „	..	..
	Burland Battery	12 24-prs. „	..	..
	Ounderskirk Battery	6 24-prs. „	..	..
Aug. 16, 1809	Flushing	96 brass guns 70 iron „ 122 „ carronades	22 howrs. (brass)	56 mortars (brass).

There were, in addition to the ordnance mentioned above, very large supplies of ammunition and stores of every description, of which the islands were denuded on their evacuation by the English.

The embarkation of the troops from Walcheren was conducted

under circumstances of great difficulty. The weather was unfavourable, and for many days after the men were on board, the wind was so adverse as to prevent the ships from sailing. A rear-guard had been left on shore to guard against any attack from the enemy, whose vessels had been accumulating for some weeks in the neighbourhood; and the troops on board the English ships were held in readiness for immediate disembarkation, should the expected attack take place.

Some reinforcements which reached the island from England during the embarkation, including two companies of artillery under Lieut.-Colonel Gold and Major Carncross, were not required to land, but their arrival had a moral effect in ensuring a peaceable evacuation of the place. From Colonel Gold, who landed for a few hours, a graphic description of the state of Walcheren was forwarded to General Macleod in Woolwich. Major Dixon had previously boasted of the thoroughness of his measures in destroying the fortifications.

> I am most happy, to say that not an article in point of honour or value will be found in the island when the enemy again takes possession: never was there a clearer sweep (I mean in a military point of view); and I am satisfied that he will not for years be enabled to use the Bason for the purposes of the navy. All the parapets are also thrown down, and not a vestige is to be seen of gun, ammunition, or store throughout the island. (Major Dixon to D.-A.-Gen., 4 Dec. 1809.)

This picture was confirmed and completed by Colonel Gold, who wrote to D.-A.-Gen., 10 Dec. 1809, as follows:

> I arrived just in time to witness the destruction of the Arsenal, which is completely effected; the entrance to the Bason, in which the French navy were sheltered last winter, is entirely choked up by blowing up the pieces of the flood-gates. Never was a scene of greater *public mischief*. On putting foot on shore I found Macartney in the midst of a wreck of carriages, and, at Flushing, Pilkington and Dixon surrounded by their own conflagrations; while Middleburg presented the most pacific appearance, and even at a church in Flushing, immediately opposite to the scene of destruction, divine service going on as if nothing unusual had occurred. . . . I have been across the island today, and although, from the many good descriptions I had heard, I was fully prepared, I could not have conceived any country so intolerably bad for military operations; and that you

(General Macleod) made your batteries and got your guns into them is surprising.

From these extracts, it will be seen that the first object of this much-abused Expedition was completely effected, and Walcheren rendered innocuous, as a means of menacing England. That this was mainly owing to the energy and perseverance of the troops has, it is hoped, also been made apparent. Alas! that the story of this Expedition, as of so many others from England, would be incomplete without the mention of failures in the supply departments of the army. Three months after the fall of Flushing, the troops were still suffering from want of necessary comforts. Major Dixon wrote (dated Flushing, 14 Nov. 1809:

> It will be doing us a very great favour, if you can by any means expedite the arrival of the *bedding*. It is now miserably cold, and I am convinced that much of our indisposition arises from the want of necessary accommodation and comfort. By a letter from the Honourable Board (two packets ago) I expected bedding for the whole of the Ordnance Department, but nothing of the kind has yet appeared.

From complaints like these the reader cannot fail to suspect that much of the exaggerated abuse of the climate of Walcheren was employed to shield those departments, whose members, in this as in other wars, have evinced a belief that the army exists for them, not they for the army.

It only remains to tell the singular story, whose conclusion has affected the regimental privileges of the Royal Artillery from the fall of Flushing to this day. Mention has been made several times in this work of a custom, which placed the bells of a captured city, or an equivalent, at the disposal of the commanding officer of the artillery of the besieging force. The privilege—as the reader will remember—had been exercised so recently as at the siege of Copenhagen. After the surrender of Flushing, General Macleod preferred the usual claim. The Mayor and Corporation replied through the commandant that they acknowledged with due respect a right established by custom immemorial that the bells belonged to the commanding officer of the Royal Artillery, if he thought proper to enforce his claim, but that they were persuaded he would grant consideration to their already sufficiently distressed condition, and not deprive the unfortunate town of its bells, which they would be as incapable of replacing, as they felt unable to tender any compensation for them. (Lieut.-Col. Mosheim to Lieut.-Colonel Wood, 4, Sept. 1809.)

On the following day, General Macleod replied that, in consideration of the destruction brought upon the town of Flushing by the system of defence which the French general had thought proper to adopt, he had no wish to add to the misery of the inhabitants by seizing the bells, or by demanding a strict compensation to the full amount of their value. In consenting, however, to sacrifice to a great extent his own rights and pretensions, he could not, he said, in any degree compromise those of the corps. He must, therefore, demand a modified sum in order specifically to mark the transaction, and to enable him at the same time to contribute to the comforts of the officers and men who had partaken in the artillery duties of the siege.

Valuing the bells at 2000*l.*, General Macleod expressed his readiness to accept 500*l*. This offer was communicated by the French commandant to the Mayor of Flushing, but was received with indignation, (the Dutch mayor's French petition is peculiar; but it is given as in the original):

On nous a rapporté, que Messieurs les officiers de l'Artillerie Royale persistoient dans leur demande à ce que la ville de Flussingen leur offrit un compromis en indemnité des cloches, qui—suivant une ancienne coûtume Anglaise—leur reviendroient, comme une récompense de leur service contre une place assiégée, qui s'étoit rendue par capitulation aux troupes de sa Majesté Britannique, et qu'ayant supposé les dites cloches à 2000l. sterling ils avoient fait grâce à la ville, en considération de son malheur, des trois quarts de cette somme, et se contentoient par conséquent d'un quart, montant à 500l. sterling. Vivement pénétré du sentiment de la situation malheureuse à laquelle la ville de Flussingen et ses pauvres bourgeois sont réduits, nous ne cessons cependant pas d'être nés descendans des anciens Hollandais, et tous les désastres que nous avons éprouvés ne nous ont pas tellement enlevé cet esprit franc et sincère, qui caractérise notre nation, et qui rivalise en ce point avec la nation Anglaise, que nous ne sentirions pas l'offense qui nous est faite, et que nous n'oserions l'exprimer. Oui, Monsieur! malgré tout ce qui puisse nous en arriver, nous ne pouvons que regretter l'offre qui nous est faite.... Nous avons de la peine à nous persuader que la demande qu'on nous a faite a été autorisée par le Commandant en chef. Comment, Monsieur? La ville de Flussingen, ses malheureux habitans qui excitent la compassion de tout le monde, qui sont ruinés, sans ressource, qui n'ont pas de quoi pouvoir dans leur propres besoins; cette ville de Flussingen, ces habitans, qui à plus d'un titre méritent la considération particulière du Gouvernement Anglais, et qui, nous n'en doutons pas, deviendroient les objets de sa moralité! Cette ville, et ces habitans, disons-nous, seroient-ils, après avoir passé par tous ces malheurs, réduits à cette extrémité de voir laisser enlevé ses cloches, faute de moyen de représenter la valeur supposée? Non, Monsieur, il est impossible que le Gouvernement Anglais autorise une pareille demande envers la ville de Flussingen, et nous sommes fermement résolus de lui emporter nos plaintes, en cas que Messieurs les Officiers de l'Artillerie persistent dans leur demande contraire à l'équité et à la capitulation; et nous ne doutons pas que l'âme généreuse de sa Majesté Britannique n'y fasse droit. Vous-même, Monsieur, qui connaissez la situation de Flussingen, qui savez qu'une somme de 5500f. de Hollande est au-dessus de nos forces, et qui avez déjà montré compassion à nos maux, ne manquerez pas— nous nous en flattons—d'employer vos efforts auprès de Messieurs les Officiers de l'Artillerie pour qu'ils désistent de leurs prétentions. Nous prenons la liberté de vous adresser un double de notre lettre, vous priant de l'adresser à son Excellence My Lord Chatham, *et d'appuyer auprès de son Excellence nos réclamations raisonnables.* (M. Becker to Lieut.-Colonel Mosheim, 6 Sept. 1809.)

This appeal was answered by General Macleod, (dated Middleburg, 8 Sept. 1809), to the effect that he could not, under any consideration, relinquish the rights of his corps: that he persisted in his claim, which had received the perfect approbation of Lord Chatham; but that, in consideration of the representations made by the magistrates, he again renounced the idea of deriving emolument to himself at the expense of the distresses of the inhabitants, but would persist in the right of his corps, unless the magistrates should consent to pay the still further reduced sum of one hundred guineas in establishment of the right;— "to be disposed of in charity to the soldiers' wives and widows of the Royal Artillery, as may be thought proper hereafter."

As General Macleod was on the eve of leaving Walcheren for England, he transferred the correspondence to Colonel Terrot, with the intimation that he himself would have no objection to an appeal to the English Legislature, should the magistrates of Flushing insist on it; but he wrote, (dated Middleburg, 9 Sept. 1809):

In that case, it is to be understood that the appeal is for the *whole* of the bells, or for the full amount of their value. The appeal leaves no room for generosity on either side.

The magistrates were obstinate, and the appeal was forwarded to England. On the 12th November intimation was sent to Major Dixon, in Walcheren, now in command of the artillery, that the decision was unfavourable to the claims of the corps. The following extract from the decision, (dated Doctor's Commons, 26 October, 1809) addressed by Sir Charles Robinson to the Earl of Liverpool, explains the grounds on which it was based.:

> With respect to the bells of the church, the demands of the artillery are, I conceive, altogether unsustainable. It is apparently not supported on the part of the Prize Commissioners, since they do not advert to this claim in their letter of the 4th of October. Anciently, there prevailed a law of pillage, which assigned to different corps and to different individuals a privileged claim to particular articles. Whether this was a privilege of the artillery under the ancient custom of England, as described in the Petition, I am not informed; but in the modern usage of respecting property and public edifices, and more particularly those set apart for divine worship, such a demand cannot, I conceive, be sustained. What the custom may be—whether deserving of any compensation in the division of what is properly *prize*, or from any other quarter—may be a subject of consideration according to circumstances. But I am of opinion that the demand ought not to be enforced against the town.

From subsequent correspondence which is extant, and which passed between General Macleod and Sir Anthony Farrington, it is evident that the former felt much regret that an old regimental privilege should have disappeared during operations in which he had occupied so prominent a place; but the reader will admit that no one could have conducted the cause of the corps in a more unselfish, chivalrous, and yet resolute manner.

> *N.B.*—The comments of an officer of the sister corps, on the conduct of the artillery at the siege of Flushing, were very favourable. Two extracts from Sir J. Jones's work may be given.
> The guns of the batteries on the right of the attack were more particularly directed to enfilade and take *en écharpe* the rampart of the western sea-line, in order to silence the fire of its artillery on the fleet, now preparing to force the passage of the Scheldt.

This they accomplished very effectually, by disabling or very severely wounding many of the traversing platforms and their carriages, and much injuring the guns themselves.

Again:

Discharges of carcasses and shells from the mortar batteries, with powerful flights of rockets intermixed, were kept up throughout the night on the devoted town, and frequently large portions of it burned with fury.—Jones's *Sieges*, vol. 2.

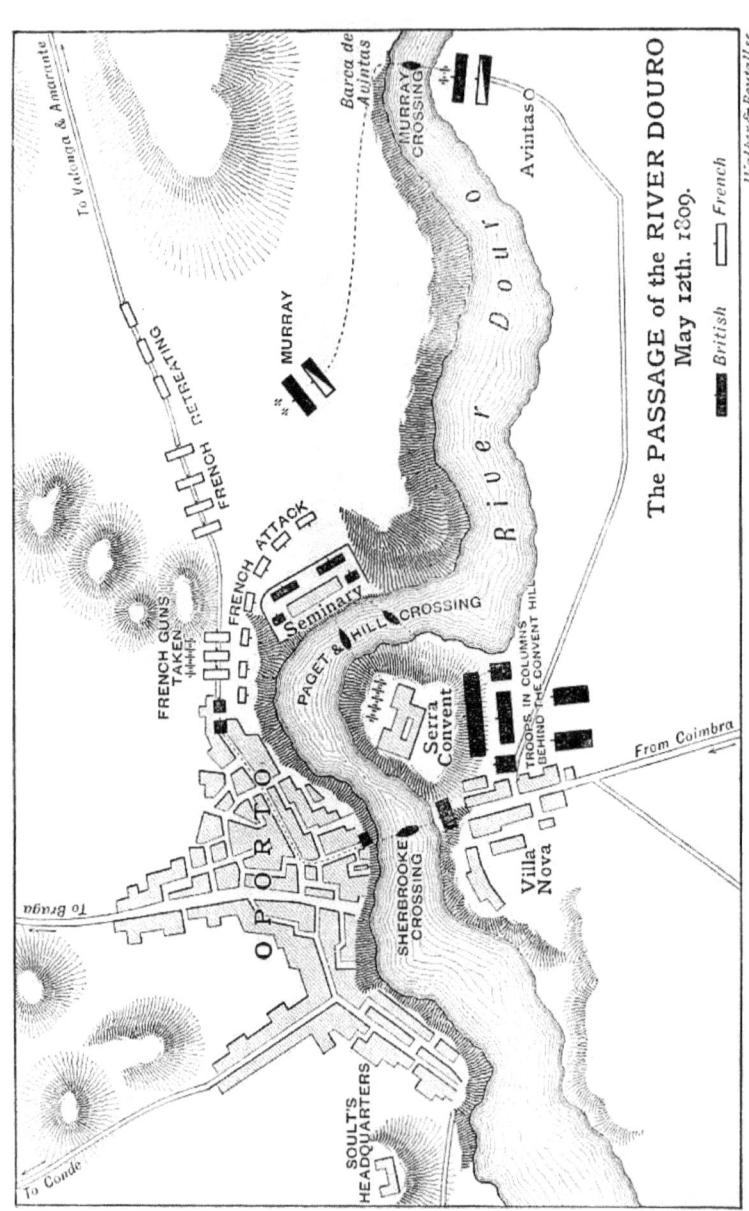

CHAPTER 4

Passage of the Douro, and Talavera

The deliverance of the Peninsula was never due to the foresight and perseverance of the English ministers, but to the firmness and skill of the British generals, and to the courage of troops whom no dangers could daunt and no hardships dishearten, while they remedied the eternal errors of the Cabinet.—Napier.

In resuming the story of the Peninsular War, it will be seen that the narrative has to go back to an earlier date than that of the expedition described in the last chapter,—Sir Arthur Wellesley having returned from England to Lisbon, to take command of the army, so early as the 22nd April, 1809. But it has been thought better to clear the ground, so to speak, of the Walcheren Expedition, and thus to enable the reader to follow uninterruptedly the story of the operations, which terminated in the victory of Talavera, and the subsequent withdrawal of the English troops from Spain to Portugal.

The British Government still resolved that the English Army in Spain should be merely an auxiliary one, and remained still undeceived as to the real state of the Spanish forces. Perhaps it was as well, therefore, that the army entrusted to Sir Arthur Wellesley was not a larger one; for the difficulty he encountered in obtaining provisions and transport from the Spaniards would have been insurmountable, had the forces under his command been more numerous. Sir Arthur wrote to Lord Castlereagh, Merida, 25 Aug. 1809:

> I do not think, that matters would have been much better if you had sent your large expedition to Spain instead of to the Scheldt. You could not have equipped it in Galicia, or anywhere in the north of Spain. If we had had 60,000 men instead of 20,000, in all probability we should not have got to Talavera to

C. Ortega
C. Penas
Santander
Corunna
Ferrol
Oviedo
Valmaseda
Lugo
Minho
Espinosa
Leon
R. Esla
Villafranca
Saldana
Astorga
Vigo
R. Sil
Carrion
Benevente
Valdaras
Villapando
Valladolid
Medina
Oporto
R. Douro
Tordessilas
Salamanca
Villacastian
Almeida
Ciudad Rodrigo
Busaco
Fuentes de Onoro
Guadarama
Coimbra
Aranjuez
Talavera
Vimieiro
Abrantes
Toledo
Tagus R.
Santarem
Torres Vedras
Badajos
LISBON
Medellin
Albuera
Guadiana R.
Sierra
Baylen
Cordova
Guadalquivir R.
Seville
PORTUGAL
SPAIN
C. St. Vincent
Malaga
Cadiz
Barrosa
C. Trafalgar
Gibraltar
40°
36°
8°
4°

fight the battle, for want of means and provisions. But if we had got to Talavera, we could not have gone farther, and the armies would probably have separated for want of means of subsistence, probably without a battle, but certainly afterwards.

The campaign of 1809, from beginning to end, was marked by obstinacy on the part of Spanish generals, and faithlessness on the part of the Spanish Government; by inadequate supplies of money from England, and by difficulties with the Portuguese troops, not the less annoying because they were often petty; as well as by hardships which tried the discipline of the English troops quite as much as the retreat to Corunna, and which drew from Sir Arthur Wellesley the bitter words to Lord Castlereagh, dated Abrantes, 17 June, 1809:

> We are an excellent army on parade, an excellent one to fight; but we are worse than an enemy in a country; and, take my word for it, that either defeat or success would dissolve us.

The success which he almost dreaded came: the 27th and 28th July witnessed as gallant an exhibition of English courage as has ever been seen; but in a few days Sir Arthur wrote to Marquis Wellesley, dated Deleytosa, 8 August, 1809:

> A starving army is actually worse than none. The soldiers lose their discipline and spirit; they plunder even in presence of their officers. The officers are discontented, and are almost as bad as the men; and, with an army which a fortnight ago beat double their numbers, I should now hesitate to meet a French corps of half their strength.

The administration which has so often marked our campaigns with passages like this, cannot be too distinctly held up to view as a perpetual warning. No troops, as Sir Arthur wrote, can serve to any good purpose unless they are regularly fed; and yet it is in this very point—the question of supply—that our military history abounds with failures.

The army which had landed in England from Corunna was speedily organised, and sent back to Portugal. Sir J. Cradock commanded the troops at Lisbon, some 14,000 in number; Marshal Beresford had been appointed to the command of the Portuguese forces, and was assisted in his task of organising them by several British officers. All arrangements were made for taking the field; and this was done immediately on the arrival of Sir Arthur Wellesley, who was appointed

Marshal-General of the united armies. Colonel Robe had remained in command of the artillery in Portugal during the interval between Corunna and Sir Arthur's arrival; but he was now superseded by Brigadier-General—afterwards Sir—E. Howorth. The number of troops and companies in the Peninsula in 1809 was only seven. There were, in addition, five at Gibraltar, five in Italy, and three in Malta.

The artillery officers first appointed for duty with Marshal Beresford were Captain—afterwards Sir —J. May and Captain Elliot, of the Royal Artillery, and also Captain Arentschild, of the King's German Artillery. Lieutenant Charles was attached to the Portuguese force raised by Sir Robert Wilson; and Captain P. Campbell and Lieutenant Wills were employed with the Spanish troops at Seville and Cadiz respectively.

General Howorth, on his arrival in Lisbon in the beginning of April, arranged, with Colonel Robe's assistance, the equipment of five brigades of guns, to take the field with the army, *viz.*, one brigade of heavy 6-pounders, three of light 6-pounders, and one of 3-pounders. These were all he could equip; and, notwithstanding the opportune arrival, from Ireland, of 170 drivers and 298 excellent horses, he yet complained of the want of mobility from which they suffered, mixed as they were with the horses of the country, mules, and oxen. However, like Colonel Harding, he took a cheerful view of matters, and pronounced the mules to be very fine animals, and "the oxen, though slow, a steady, good draught." (To D.-A.-G. Lisbon, 8 April, 1809.)

The development of the Field Artillery during the Peninsular War, from the wretched batteries employed at its commencement to those which attracted such admiration at its close, will appear in the course of this work. Suffice it, at present, to remind the artilleryman, by way of contrast, while the picture of the batteries of 1809 is yet fresh in his recollection, that before the conclusion of the Peninsular War, it was admitted by the artillerymen of the country with which England was engaged in hostilities, that "the English *matériel* might have been taken as a model by any nation in Europe," (*Le passé et l'avenir de l'Artillerie, tom v*);—that, shortly before Waterloo, Marshal Marmont remarked that the equipment of the English Field Artillery was in every respect very superior to anything he had ever seen; and that the French Committee appointed in 1818 to compare the artillery of the various countries represented in the review held that year in Paris, expressed unqualified delight with that of England.

On Sir Arthur Wellesley's arrival in Lisbon, he found that Soult was in possession of Oporto, and Victor in Estremadura. He promptly resolved to attack them in detail; and, making Lisbon the base of his operations, he requested the Spanish general, Cuesta, to watch Victor's movements, while he himself should march to the north against Soult. The moral effect of driving the French out of Portugal would, he felt, be very great—all the more so as his arrival had produced a sudden hopefulness among the Portuguese, which it was desirable not to disappoint.

Accordingly, on the 1st May, he moved his headquarters to Pombal and Coimbra, and found himself in command of an army which, after deducting the sick and absent, numbered 20,653 rank and file, with 30 guns. (Napier.) On the 9th he left Coimbra with the main body, and arrived on the Douro, opposite Oporto, on the 12th, after a march of eighty over infamous roads. General Howorth, wrote to D.-A.-G. Oporto, 14 May, 1809:

> But, neither difficulty nor danger impedes Sir Arthur: he is all fire, and establishes confidence in the troops.

On the 10th, the left column of the army, which marched from Aveiro, fell in with the enemy at Algabaria Nova. A slight affair ensued, in which the artillery and cavalry were chiefly engaged; and the enemy was repulsed with the loss of a gun. On the 11th, the right column, which marched on the Vouga, came up with the French between Algabaria Nova and Grijon, and an engagement followed which lasted two hours, ending in the retreat of the enemy. On the arrival of the English at Villa Nova, opposite Oporto, it was found that the French had destroyed the bridge across the Douro, and removed every available boat to their own side of the river. It was of the utmost importance that the English troops should cross, so as to co-operate with Marshal Beresford, who, having crossed the river higher up, was now menacing the left and the rear of Soult's army.

The crossing was effected in a gallant, and yet singular and romantic way, whose details, too long for reproduction here, render the passage of the Douro one of the most interesting episodes in the Peninsular War. Wellesley saw a building on the other side of the river—here three hundred yards wide—called the Seminary, surrounded by a walled yard, capable of containing two battalions. Close to where he himself stood was a rock, called Serra, from which artillery would well command the passage of the river, and where he therefore desired General Howorth to place eighteen guns. The guards on the other side seemed few and negligent. Soult expected no danger on the part of the river above the town, and had posted himself to the westward; if, therefore, boats could but be obtained, Wellesley resolved to cross. A small skiff was found, and Colonel Waters, a staff officer, crossed, and found three large barges, which he towed back to the Villa Nova side of the river.

The men were ordered to embark, and, in the face of an army of ten thousand men, the passage was effected. Very few, however, had crossed ere the alarm was given, and the French troops poured down upon the Seminary. The alarm acted in one respect favourably to the English; for some of the citizens hastened to unmoor some boats, and cross to Villa Nova, thus facilitating the embarkation and passage of the troops. All this time the fire of the Royal Artillery from the Serra told with great effect; and, as it completely swept one side of the Seminary, it soon limited the attack to the other. The gallantry of the infantry was unrivalled. General Sherbrooke had crossed the river a little lower down, and was now in possession of the town of Oporto, and pressing, with the Guards and 29th Regiment, on the rear of the French troops as they poured out towards the Seminary.

The Buffs and their comrades in the enclosure rained showers of bullets on the disorganised French; and in a short time, they were in full retreat, "the artillery, from the Serra, still searching the enemy's columns as they hurried along." (Napier.) General Howorth, in describing the battle, said, to D.-A.-G. 14 May, 1809, that he never saw anything like the gallantry of the English troops. Their firmness was irresistible; nor could the French make any impression; and, from the position which he occupied, he was able to form a good opinion, as he could see everything Sir Arthur, in his despatch to Lord Castlereagh, dated Oporto, 12 May, 1809, announcing the victory, after enumerating the various officers who had especially distinguished themselves, said, in describing the services of the regiments engaged:

> I had every reason to be satisfied with the artillery.

That his satisfaction was also extended to the previous operations and to the severe march of eighty miles over most difficult country, may be gathered from General Howorth's words:

> I have reason to believe that Sir Arthur is perfectly satisfied with the artillery; and, it must be owned, never was artillery put to such trial.

The French ordnance captured at the recovery of Oporto included 56 brass guns and 3 brass howitzers. A considerable supply of ammunition was also taken.

The pursuit of Soult's army was undertaken by Sir A. Wellesley with as little delay as possible, although not with sufficient promptness to satisfy the demands of certain military critics, who are ready to find fault, but slow to acknowledge difficulties in the way of armies. That it was sufficiently prompt to ensure the success of the English general's purpose, may be gathered from the fact that on the 18th May Soult and his army crossed the frontier into Spain, having been driven out of Portugal with the loss of artillery, stores, and baggage, and of no fewer than 6000 men; while of those who remained, many were without arms and accoutrements, the majority without shoes, and all utterly exhausted and miserable, (Napier); and, further, that the English Army did not delay in the pursuit may be gathered from the following letter from General Howorth to General Macleod, dated Oporto, 24 May, 1809):

> The extraordinary rapidity of events in this country, which have been accompanied by a succession of the most triumphant operations against the enemy, left me no leisure to communicate them as they occurred. However, I am at last returned here, after passing eight days in continued marches over the worst roads I ever saw, through incessant rain, a depopulated country, quartered in uninhabited houses, and with no supplies whatever, but what was scantily provided by the Commissariat Department. During the greater part of this march the luxury of a bed, or a change of clothes, which were always wet, was unknown to me. . . . . We pursued to Montalagree, where the enemy turned short to the left, over the mountains, and took the shortest way into Galicia.
>
> During the pursuit, the English overtook Soult at Salamonde, and his rear-guard being in a confined space, some guns were brought to bear on them with fearful effect.
>
> Man and horse, crushed together, went over into the gulf; and the bridge, rocks, and the defile beyond were strewed with mangled bodies. (Napier.)
>
> The furious peasantry also turned on the French troops, and rendered their retreat—which has been compared with that of the Eng-

lish on Corunna—infinitely more horrible.

As Soult sacrificed artillery and baggage in order to move more rapidly, it was but natural that he should outmarch an army which had not so disencumbered itself. (*Wellington Despatches*.) But this pursuit has an importance to the artilleryman in being a text on which much useful argument was hung by General Howorth and others, in favour of greater mobility than had yet attended the brigades of Field Artillery employed in the Peninsula. The 3-pounder brigade was the only one which was able to march with the army during its more rapid movements; and therefore, General Howorth made a demand (dated Oporto, 24 May, 1809) for additional brigades of that nature, suggesting, with the assistance of Colonel Robe, various improvements in the equipment.

Among other changes, he recommended double instead of single draught, both for guns and waggons; and that the brigades should be of four guns instead of six, the howitzers being dispensed with, and a liberal supply of spherical case being issued for the guns. Another very suggestive recommendation was made by him: "to have a small forge with each brigade of four guns; the forge to be placed on the frame of a small limber waggon; *it can then follow the brigade, which is not the case with the present one.*" The absence of a forge on the line of march must at times have sadly crippled the batteries. He also suggested that the span of the wheels should be narrowed to 4½ feet, and (to prevent liability to upset from this cause) that the gun should be lowered on its carriage by adopting *a bare iron axletree*.

His next recommendation reveals a starvation of equipment which would account for almost any shortcomings on the line of march. He urged the authorities "to have spare shafts, wheels, axles, spokes, felloes, and pintails supplied, *none having been sent with the present brigades*, and now much needed." He also made suggestions which would ensure greater mobility to the heavier brigades of 6-pounders. The artilleryman may therefore date to the campaign of the Douro some of the most valuable lessons taught in the Peninsular War, and can trace to it that change in the opinions and experience of the military authorities, which resulted in so extended a use of Horse Artillery in the Peninsula, and in so marked an improvement in the brigades of Field Artillery before the conclusion of the war.

Marshal Victor, on hearing of the disastrous termination of Soult's operations, fell back on Almaraz and Torremocha; so that Sir A. Wellesley, who had commenced his southward march through Traz-oz-

Sir Alexander Dickson

Montes, resolved to halt at Abrantes, and to commence a thorough reorganisation of his army now sadly undisciplined. The correspondence of Sir Arthur at this time reveals what one is apt to forget in reflecting on the glories of the Peninsular campaigns. (*Wellington Despatches* and *Supplementary Despatches*) The military genius of the Duke of Wellington and the courage of English soldiers are too often considered to have been the only necessary causes of success; but a study of the appeals made by him at Abrantes to officers and men,—of the strict orders, on even the smallest matters, which he found it necessary to issue,—and of the letters to ministers and friends, in which he never failed to tell the truth about the army, however unpalatable,—reveals another most necessary element in the success which attended him in all his operations.

Reference has been made to the association of English officers with the Portuguese forces. The appointment of Captain—afterwards Sir Alexander—Dickson, to the Portuguese artillery, which took place after the Douro campaign, was productive of so important results, that it deserves detailed notice. As Captain Dickson, he had acted as Brigade-Major to General Howorth during the recent operations. He had, however, come to Portugal with the intention of obtaining employment in a higher local rank with the Portuguese artillery, and had only been deterred by difficulties which had arisen as to the *status* and pay of officers so attached.

On the 4th June, he quitted Oporto with General Howorth, who had been indisposed for some time, and proceeded to Abrantes to join the army, and also to speak to Marshal Beresford on the subject of employment with the Portuguese troops. Fortunately, on his arrival, he found that Captain May, then in command of a division of Portuguese Field Artillery, was on the point of resigning, in accordance with instructions from England; and Marshal Beresford readily appointed Captain Dickson as his successor—Captain May, in exchange, assuming the duties of Major of Brigade. (Captain Dickson to D.-A.-Gen. 3 July, 1809.)

So far all was well; but Captain Dickson soon found that he had no pleasing position. The local rank of Major, which had been conferred on his junior officer, Captain Arentschild of the King's German Artillery, was refused to him by Marshal Beresford, who had been irritated by contradictory orders from the English and Portuguese Governments; so that he found himself under the orders of his junior. The Portuguese officers were also very jealous of their English comrades;

and the seniors, without incurring any risk themselves, made every difficulty in their power, when any suggestion was made which they disliked. Letters from the British to the Portuguese officers on official matters, and all applications for supplies, were left unanswered; and yet "these same men," wrote Captain Dickson indignantly, "are embracing you as often as they meet!"

He would gladly have given up his new appointment, had he not felt bound by his promise to Lord Chatham to retain it; so he set to work, in a true soldierlike spirit, to perfect the two 6-pounder Portuguese batteries which had been placed under his charge, and of which, even at the beginning, he was able to write in terms of the warmest approbation. As this narrative will show, he was rewarded for remaining at his post. The local rank was given to him ultimately; and by its means he found himself commanding many brother officers, much senior to himself regimentally, and ultimately at the head of the artillery of the armies of the Duke of Wellington, while only a captain in his own corps.

It is now necessary to follow the movements of Sir Arthur Wellesley. The English Government continued to overrate the value of the Spanish armies; and the pressure brought to bear upon the English general was such as he could not resist. He therefore proposed to the Spanish General, Cuesta, to co-operate with his army against Victor's forces, and ultimately against Madrid. Cuesta, whose treatment of Sir Arthur Wellesley was, on all occasions, of the most obstinate and boorish description, had an army of 33,000 men. Sir Arthur's army, when he quitted Abrantes, numbered 20,997 men of all arms, with 30 guns. (Napier.) The advance of the united armies against Madrid by the valley of the Tagus had been foreseen by Napoleon, and he had ordered Soult, at the head of a powerful army, to concentrate his forces in such a manner that, on the advance of Wellesley, he could pass by his left rear, and cut him off from the base of his operations,—Lisbon and its surrounding country.

The English general was far from correctly informed either of the strength or position of Soult's army; he was urged by the English representative, Mr. Frere, and by his own government, to take the offensive; the vacillation of Joseph Buonaparte tempted him to march on Madrid before further union could be effected among the French armies; he was further assured of the courage of the Spanish armies, the enthusiasm of the peasantry, and the abundance of supplies. On the 27th June, therefore, he broke up his camp at Abrantes,

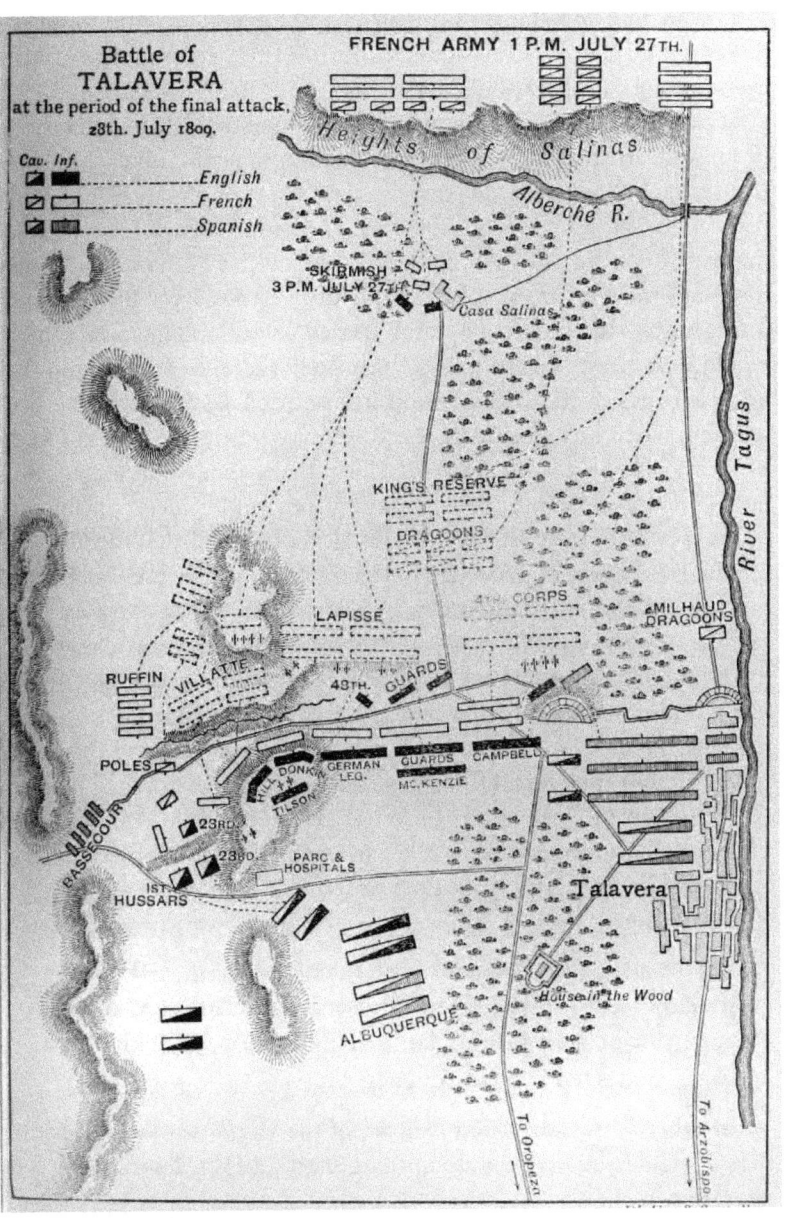

and marched towards Oropesa, to effect a junction with Cuesta. The farther he advanced, the more doubtful did he become of the sincerity of the Spaniards—a doubt which exhibited itself in the pertinacity with which he demanded from Cuesta and the *Junta* solemn promises to keep the English Army supplied, during any farther advance, with the requisite transport and supplies.

The reader does not require to be reminded how shamefully these promises were broken;—how thwarted Wellesley was, alike by the intrigues of the *Junta* and the conceited obstinacy of Cuesta;—nor how faithful he was, amid all his difficulties, to the duty which England had imposed upon him. Standing beside Cuesta like a better angel,—and receiving the treatment not unfrequently bestowed on such,—calm under insult, his judgment never heated by an indignation which would have been righteous,—he ultimately succeeded in placing the united armies in the very position in front of Talavera which he had selected, when he saw that a general action with the combined forces of Victor and Sebastiani was inevitable, if not, indeed, desirable. But not until the morning of the 27th July, nor until Cuesta's folly and rashness had courted and received, at Alcabon, a well-deserved defeat, did the English general succeed in placing the Spanish forces the position he had chosen. (Gurwood's *Despatches*: Selections.)

The quiet irony of the memorandum of Sir Arthur Wellesley on the Battle of Talavera cannot be seen without remembering the defeat just mentioned, and a panic which seized on the Spanish troops at the appearance of some French cavalry, on the afternoon of the 27th, when 10,000 infantry and all their artillery fled, terror-stricken, to the rear. Part of these were recovered before the following day; but the Spanish contingent was weaker by the greater part of its artillery, and 6000 of its infantry. With such troops as allies, no wonder that Sir Arthur wrote:

> The position of Talavera was well calculated for the troops that were to occupy it. The ground in front of the British Army was open; that in front of the Spanish Army was covered with olive-trees, intersected by roads, ditches, &c.

In other words, the offensive part of the battle was to fall on the British, while a masterly and imposing inactivity was reserved for the Spaniards.

The Battle of Talavera was fought on the 27th and 28th July. The loss of the Spanish artillery in the panic mentioned above was very serious, as the English had only 30 guns, very badly horsed and of small calibre, to oppose to 80 guns, admirably served by the enemy. Fortunately, the few guns of the Spanish artillery, which *were* brought into action, were gallantly fought; and of those of the Royal and King's German Artillery, both the officers present and all military historians speak in the highest terms.

At the defeat of the 4th French Corps by Campbell's division, the British artillery, as Napier wrote, played vehemently upon their masses:—at the critical moment, later in the day, when the English centre was almost broken on account of the injudicious advance of the Guards, and of the confusion which seized the King's German Legion, the marvellous effect which followed the arrival of the 48th Regiment, moving, amid all the confusion, with the steadiness, of a parade, was greatly heightened by the conduct of the artillery, which, as the same historian says, "battered the enemy's flanks without intermission." Sir Arthur Wellesley, in addition to an expression of his satisfaction with the corps in the general order after the battle, made use of the following expression in his despatch to Lord Castlereagh:

> The artillery, under Brigadier-General Howorth, was also, throughout these days, of the greatest service.

Compared with the loss of the other arms, that of the artillery was but small. On the 27th, only two men were wounded; on the 28th, the loss was as follows:—

> Royal Artillery.—1 officer and 7 men killed; 3 officers and 21 men wounded.
>
> King's German Artillery.—1 sergeant and 2 men killed; 3 sergeants and 27 men wounded.

The officer who was killed was Lieutenant Wyatt; those who were wounded were Lieut.-Colonel Framingham, and Captains Baines and Taylor. In reporting the severe wound of Colonel Framingham, and applying for a pension, General Howorth said to D.-A.-G. dated Badajoz, 20 Oct. 1809:

> If it were possible that any testimony or praise of mine could add to the weight of this application, or to the merit and brilliancy of Lieut.-Colonel Framingham's gallant conduct in the action of the 28th July, at Talavera, I should most freely have bestowed it; but, as he distinguished himself on that occasion by a most skilful discharge of his duty, I have only to wish him

sincerely a reward equal to his merits.

On the retreat of the army from Talavera, Captain Taylor, whose wound prevented his removal, fell into the hands of the French, and remained a prisoner to the end of the war.

There are several points connected with the Battle of Talavera which stand out prominently, and seize the attention of the student at once. The weakness of King Joseph in playing into the hands of the English general, and allowing him to fight under the terms most advantageous to himself;—the hard, honest fighting, as Napier calls it, of the English troops, who, for hours, were closely engaged with a force of double their own numbers;—the watchful tactics of Sir A. Wellesley, who never missed a point during the whole engagement, and was always ready at critical moments with the necessary remedies; and the heavy losses on both sides—over 6000 being killed and wounded on the side of the English, and more than 7000 on that of the French;—these are points which cannot escape the most superficial reader. But to the soldier there are several precious instances of steadiness and discipline among particular regiments, (*Wellington Despatches*) which shed a glow over this well-fought field,—the 45th and 5th Battalion of the 60th being conspicuous for these qualities on the 27th, and the "stubborn old 48th" on the 28th. Napier's pages glow with the enthusiasm of a soldier as he describes the movements of the last-mentioned regiment on the occasion referred to above.

> At first, it seemed as if this regiment must be carried away by the retiring crowds; but, wheeling back by companies, it let them pass through the intervals, and then, resuming its proud and beautiful line, marched against the right of the pursuing columns, and plied them with such a destructive musketry, and closed upon them with such a firm and regular pace, that their forward movement was checked.

The horrors of a battlefield, when the deadly encounter is over, were aggravated at Talavera by a fire, which caught the dry grass, and which licked the ground where the dead and wounded were lying, adding a new agony to the sufferings of the latter, and hideously scorching the bodies of those whose pain was for ever at an end.

On the 29th, Wellesley's army was strengthened by the arrival of Craufurd's brigade, consisting of the 43rd, 52nd, and 95th Regiments, with Captain Ross's, "The Chestnut," troop of Horse Artillery which, in their eagerness to reach the field of battle, and undeterred by the lies of the flying Spaniards, had marched no less than sixty-two miles in twenty-six hours, in the hottest season of the year, and in heavy marching order. (*Hew Ross of the Chestnut Troop* by Hew Dalrymple Ross is also published by Leonaur.)

✶✶✶✶✶✶

The officers of the Chestnut Troop on its arrival in the Peninsula, were Captain—afterwards Sir H. D.—Ross, 2nd Captain G. Jenkinson, Lieutenants G. J. Belson, J. Macdonald, and Smith, and Assistant-Surgeon O'Brien. The following is a copy of the Embarkation Returns. See table next page.

✶✶✶✶✶✶

But news reached the English general which determined him to fall back, and to have done with the assistance of Spanish troops, whose worthlessness he had now thoroughly tested. Hearing that Soult was pressing on by rapid marches, and with increased forces,—had already gained possession of one of his most important communications with Portugal, and was threatening the others,—he resolved to leave his wounded at Talavera, and to fall back into Portugal. He did so by means of rapid marches; but he still conducted them so as to show no appearance of flight, such as would have injured the reputation of his army in the eyes of the Spaniards—a most consideration. General Howorth, in alluding to the retreat from Talavera, emphasises this point. He wrote to D.-A.-G. dated Badajoz, 26 Oct:

> We made a retrograde movement with a dignified deliberation perfectly suitable to the gravity of Spanish deportment.

The whole of his brigades of artillery returned from Talavera complete, with the exception of one 6-pounder gun which had been damaged in the battle of the 28th, and which, the general wrote, had been *privately buried*, perhaps out of consideration for Spanish deportment also. But all the spare ammunition and stores had to be abandoned, as the carts were required to carry the sick. No less than 150 carts were so employed; for the sickness during the retreat, and even after the troops went into cantonments at Merida, was very great. The well-known sickness in the Chestnut Troop, which so nearly led to its return to England, took place at Merida after the retreat. So severely did it suffer, that, in sending in his returns of available artillery force at this time, General Howorth wrote:

> I have one troop of Horse Artillery, Bull's, (the gallant Norman Ramsay was 2nd Captain of Bull's troop) and half a one, Ross's.

Embarkation Return of a Troop of Royal Horse Artillery, commanded by Captain H. D. Ross.

Ships' Names and Masters	Captain	Second Captain	Lieutenants	Assistant Surgeon	N.-C. Officers	Trumpeters	Artificers	Gunners	Drivers	Total	Women	Children	Officers'	Troop	Total	6-pounders	5½-in. Howitzers	Ammunition Waggons	Baggage Waggons	Wheel Carriage	Forge Cart	Baggage Cart	Total
'Rodney'—G. Bowes	1	..	1	1	3	1	3	19	8	37	..	..	7	26	33	..	..	..	..	..	..	..	..
'Phoenix'—R. Oswell	..	1	2	..	3	..	2	15	9	32	2	..	7	24	31	..	..	..	..	..	..	..	..
'Amphitrite'—R. Stevenson	..	..	..	..	2	..	..	10	13	25	..	..	..	32	32	..	..	..	..	..	..	..	..
'Jane'—J. Jackson	..	..	..	..	2	..	1	15	10	28	..	..	..	30	30	..	..	..	..	..	..	..	..
'Ruby'—S. Chapman	..	..	..	..	2	..	1	13	12	28	..	..	..	34	34	..	..	..	..	..	..	..	..
'Ganges'—J. Nisbett	..	..	..	..	..	..	..	2	2	4	..	..	..	2	2	..	..	..	..	..	..	..	..
'Blessing'—R. Armstrong	..	..	..	..	1	..	..	7	..	8	1	..	..	..	..	5	1	6	3	1	1	1	18
Total	1	1	3	1	13	1	7	81	54	162	3	..	14	148	162	5	1	6	3	1	1	1	18

Ramsgate, 8th June, 1809.   (Signed)   H. D. Ross, *Captain Commanding R. H. A.*

The latter has suffered severely by sickness and death of men and horses.

The sickness was aggravated by a dearth of medical officers; and the unfortunate Chestnut Troop, which required medical assistance to an extraordinary extent, was robbed of its own surgeon in an inglorious manner. General Howorth wrote:

> Poor Doctor O'Brien, of Ross's troop, died last night, owing to his servant's getting drunk, and giving him too strong a dose of opium, which destroyed him.

Ere many weeks passed, the attempt to cope with the havoc made in the troop was almost abandoned. Two guns and their waggons were sent into store, from want of men and horses to work them; and orders were given that, on the arrival of another troop (Lefebure's) from England, the surviving men and horses of the Chestnut Troop should be handed over to it, and Captain Ross and his officers return to England to organise a new troop. Luckily for him, Captain Lefebure's troop suffered so much from a storm on its way to the Peninsula that, on its arrival, it was little more efficient than the one it was meant to relieve; so, to Captain Ross's delight, he had his vacancies completed from the new arrivals, and Captain Lefebure had, instead, the duty of rebuilding his troop. (*Memoir of Sir H. D. Ross*.)

The headquarters of the English general, on whom the title of Lord Wellington was bestowed after Talavera, were at Badajoz until the end of 1809. He devoted himself to the strengthening of his position, with the double motive of ensuring to himself the possession of Lisbon and the Tagus, and of securing the unmolested embarkation of his troops, should reverses render it necessary. The lines of Torres Vedras, which were to play so important a part in the campaign of 1810, were matured in the winter of 1809. Lord Wellington had given up all hope of succeeding by means of the Spaniards; but he by no means despaired of offering an effectual resistance to the most powerful French attacks by means of the combined English and Portuguese Army under his command. He felt confidence in his troops.

As he boasted to a correspondent, "I command an unanimous army." (Lord Wellington to Colonel Malcolm, Badajoz, 3 Dec. 1809) Supplies in Portugal were better arranged than in Spain; and, with the remembrance fresh in his mind of Talavera, which he himself pronounced "the hardest-fought battle of modern days, and the most glorious in its results to the English troops," he looked forward to the next campaign with quiet confidence, and displayed during the winter an industry in strengthening his position which, at all events, deserved success.

★★★★★★

Note.—Although the Peninsular War eclipses in point of interest any other operations in which the Royal Artillery was engaged in 1809, it would be a great omission, were no allusion made to the services of the corps, in the beginning of 1809, during the operations in the West Indies under General Beckwith and Sir George Prevost, which resulted in the capture of the French colonies of Cayenne and Martinique. Over 500 officers and men of the Royal Artillery were present under the command of Brigadier-General Stehelin, and the value of their services may be ascertained from the following extract from the general order dated 8 March 1809, issued at the termination of the campaign:—

To Brigadier-General Stehelin, commanding the Royal Artillery, for his regularity in all interior arrangements, and especially for that order and system established in this distinguished corps, which led to those eminent services rendered by them during the bombardment, and which brought the siege to an early and glorious termination . . . the Commander of the Forces is anxious to renew all those assurances of public and individual consideration, to which from their distinguished services they are fully entitled, and he requests, as an old soldier, that he may live in their remembrance and friendship.

The officers of the Royal Artillery who were present during these operations were—in addition to Brigadier-General Stehelin—Captains Blaney Walsh, Unett, Phillott, St. Clair, Cleeve, Story, Du Bourdieu, Clibborn, Butts, and Rollo; and Lieutenants Spellen, Bell, Gordon, Lewis, Mathias, Tucker, Turner, Heron, Scriven, Simmons, and F. Arabin. (B. G. Stehelin to D.-A.-Gen. 23 March, 1809.)

★★★★★★

CHAPTER 5

Busaco and Torres Vedras

It may not be uninteresting to the reader, before resuming the consideration of the Peninsular War, to study some statistics connected with the Regiment in the year 1810, the period to be treated of in this chapter. The number of troops and companies remained as before, 112—exclusive of the invalid battalion. They were distributed as follows, (Kane's list):—16 in the Peninsula, 5 in Italy and Sicily, 56 on home stations, 4 in Canada, 3 at the Cape of Good Hope, 3 in Ceylon, where they had been engaged on active service during the previous year, 6 in Gibraltar, 4 in Jamaica and 6 in the rest of the West Indies (these ten companies being actively engaged in the defence of the colonies), 1 in Madeira, 4 in Malta, 1 in Newfoundland, and 3 in Nova Scotia and Cape Breton.

The following tables show the strength of the battalions, and the proportions of the various ranks. They also show the pay of the various ranks, *less* the charges for agency, which are not deducted in the pay tables published in Kane's List. But, in addition to the strength of the Royal Artillery, the reader will find detailed statements of the other corps which swelled the total artillery force of Great Britain. It is hoped that, by publishing these tables in this form, reference will be easier, and lengthy description may be dispensed with.

It cannot be too often repeated that the services in the Peninsula of the King's German Artillery, the detail of which is given in the annexed tables, were of the most gallant description, unsurpassed by those of the corps to which they were attached. The active service of the corps, named the Royal Foreign Artillery, was chiefly in the West Indies.

From MS. Returns in Library of the Royal United Service Institution

STATEMENT OF THE ARTILLERY FORCES of GREAT BRITAIN IN THE YEAR 1810—ACCORDING TO THE ESTABLISHMENT LAID DOWN IN THE KING'S WARRANT—WITH THE VARIOUS RATES OF PAY, LESS AGENCY CHARGES.

I.—ROYAL ARTILLERY.

a. STAFF.

	Rank.		Pay per diem.		
			£.	s.	d.
1	Master-General	No pay on the			
1	Lieutenant-General	establishment.			
10	Colonels-Commandant	each	2	14	4
20	Colonels	,,	1	6	0
30	Lieutenant-Colonels	,,	0	17	11
10	Majors	,,	0	16	9
1	Deputy-Adjutant-General		1	0	0
10	Adjutants	each	0	8	6
10	Quartermasters	,,	0	7	10
1	Chaplain		0	9	11
10	Sergeant-Majors	each	0	3	7¼
10	Quartermaster-Sergeants	,,	0	3	7¼

b. COMPANY OF GENTLEMEN CADETS.

			£	s	d
1	Captain		1	4	7¼
1	Second Captain		0	13	0
2	First Lieutenants	each	0	6	10
1	Second Lieutenant		0	6	10
200	Gentlemen Cadets	each	0	2	0
1	Drum-Major		0	2	4
1	Fife-Major		0	2	4

c. TEN BATTALIONS, CONSISTING EACH OF

			£	s	d
10	Captains	each	0	11	0
10	Second Captains	,,	0	11	0
20	First Lieutenants	,,	0	6	10
10	Second Lieutenants	,,	0	5	7
40	Sergeants	,,	0	2	5¼
40	Corporals	,,	0	2	3¾
90	Bombardiers	,,	0	2	1¾
1240	Gunners	,,	0	1	5¾
30	Drummers	,,	0	1	5¾

1490 being the total for each battalion, and therefore 14,900 for the ten.

Royal Artillery, continued.

d. INVALIDS.

Rank.		Pay per diem.
		£. s. d.
1 Colonel-Commandant		2 14 4
2 Second Colonels	each	1 0 0
2 Lieutenant-Colonels	„	0 19 9
3 Second Lieutenant-Colonels	„	0 17 11
1 Major		0 16 9
1 Adjutant		0 9 0
1 Quartermaster		0 7 10
2 Staff Sergeants	each	0 3 7¼
12 Captains	„	0 11 0
12 First Lieutenants	„	0 7 10
12 Second Lieutenants	„	0 5 7
48 Sergeants	„	0 2 5½
48 Corporals	„	0 2 3¾
108 Bombardiers	„	0 2 1¾
100 First Gunners	„	0 1 9¾
620 Second Gunners	„	0 1 5¾
12 Drummers	„	0 1 5¾
48 Non-effectives	„	0 1 5¾

e. ROYAL HORSE ARTILLERY.

1 Colonel-Commandant		2 19 3
2 Colonels	each	1 12 0
3 Lieutenant-Colonels	„	1 6 9
1 Major		1 2 8
1 Adjutant		0 16 6
1 Quartermaster		0 10 9
1 Regimental Staff Sergeant		0 3 9½
1 Regimental Sergeant (for Staff)		0 2 7¼
2 Farriers and Carriage Smiths	each	0 3 5¼
1 Collar-maker		0 3 5¼
1 Trumpet-Major		0 2 3¾
12 Captains	each	0 15 11
12 Second Captains	„	0 15 11
36 First Lieutenants	„	0 9 10
24 Troop Staff Sergeants	„	0 3 9¼
36 Sergeants	„	0 2 7¼
36 Corporals	„	0 2 3¾
72 Bombardiers	„	0 2 1¾
480 Gunners mounted	„	0 1 5¾
528 Gunners dismounted	„	0 1 5¾
720 Drivers	„	0 1 5¾
12 Farriers and Shoeing Smiths	„	0 3 5¼
12 Carriage Smiths	„	0 3 5¼

Royal Horse Artillery, continued.

Rank.		Pay per diem.
		£. s. d.
24 Shoeing Smiths	each	0 2 3¾
24 Collar-makers	,,	0 2 1¼
12 Wheelwrights	,,	0 2 1¼
12 Trumpeters	,,	0 2 1¾

f. RIDING-HOUSE TROOP.

1 Captain		0 15 0
1 Lieutenant, at		0 15 0
1 ,, at		0 13 0
1 ,, at		0 11 0
1 Quartermaster		0 7 10
2 Staff Sergeants	each	0 3 2
3 Sergeants	,,	0 2 2
3 First Corporals	,,	0 2 0
3 Second Corporals	,,	0 1 10¼
1 Trumpeter		0 1 11¼
1 Farrier		0 3 2¾
1 Collar-maker		0 1 10¾
44 Riders	each	0 1 3¼

II.—FIELD TRAIN.

1 Chief Commissary.	1 Foreman.
5 Commissaries.	7 Smiths.
24 Assistant Commissaries.	6 Collar-makers.
113 Clerks of Stores.	7 Wheelers.
115 Conductors.	2 Carpenters.
13 Military Conductors.	1 Painter.

III.—ROYAL ARTILLERY DRIVERS.

1 Major		1 1 0
2 Adjutants	each	0 10 0
8 Veterinary Surgeons	,,	0 8 0
11 Captain-Commissaries	,,	0 15 0
55 First Lieutenants	,,	0 9 0
11 Second Lieutenants	,,	0 8 0
55 Staff Sergeants	,,	0 3 2
165 Sergeants	,,	0 2 2
165 First Corporals	,,	0 2 0¼
165 Second Corporals	,,	0 1 10¼

Royal Artillery Drivers, continued.

Rank.		Pay per diem.		
		£.	s.	d.
22 Rough-riders .. .. each		0	1	3¼
55 Farriers .. .. ,,		0	3	2¾
165 Shoeing Smiths .. .. ,,		0	2	1¼
110 Collar-makers.. .. .. ,,		0	1	10¾
110 Wheelers.. .. .. ,,		0	1	10¾
55 Trumpeters .. .. ,,		0	1	11¼
4950 Drivers .. .. ,,		0	1	3¼

IV.—ROYAL FOREIGN ARTILLERY.

1 Major.
4 Captains.
4 Second Captains.
12 Lieutenants.
6 Sergeants.

4 Corporals.
17 Bombardiers.
124 Gunners.
8 Drummers.

V.—ARTILLERY OF THE KING'S GERMAN LEGION.

Officers.

1 Colonel Commandant.
1 Lieutenant-Colonel.
2 Majors.
8 Captains.
8 Second Captains.
16 First Lieutenants.
16 Second Lieutenants.
1 Captain Commissary.
1 Paymaster.
1 Adjutant.
1 Quartermaster.
1 Surgeon.
3 Assistant Surgeons.
1 Veterinary Surgeon.

Sergeants and Rank and File.	Horse Artillery.	Foot Artillery.
Staff Sergeants	4	3
Sergeants	6	14
Corporals	8	18
Bombardiers	14	23
Trumpeters	8	
Farriers	2	

Artillery of the King's German Legion, continued.

Sergeants and Rank and File.	Horse Artillery.	Foot Artillery.
Smiths ..	6	
Collar-makers	4	
Wheelers	2	
Gunners	186	372
Drivers	116	Drummers .. 9

Driver Corps.

Sergeants and Rank and File.

4 Sergeants.   8 Collar-makers.
8 Corporals.   5 Wheelers.
4 Farriers.   189 Drivers.
9 Smiths.

The recruiting for the regiment during the year 1809 had been successful, no fewer than 1820 gunners and 868 drivers having been enlisted. The establishment just given was nearly maintained, and even occasionally exceeded, during 1810; and the usual decrease, caused by the discharge of men by purchase, did not occur during that year, all such discharges being forbidden. (MS 'Wear and Tear' Returns for 1809, to B. of Ordnance.) A falling off in the strength of the Regiment became apparent, however, in the winter of 1810.

The "wear and tear" among the horses of the Royal Horse Artillery and the Royal Artillery Driver Corps had been excessive during the year 1809, owing to the Peninsular Campaigns and the Scheldt Expedition. No fewer than 2786 had either died or been destroyed; and 3367 had to be purchased to compensate for these losses, and to meet the ever-increasing demand.

Very large numbers were sent to Portugal during the year 1810; and, owing to the consequent increase in the numbers of the Driver Corps attached to Lord Wellington's armies, it was decided to appoint a field officer to command them. This duty, with cavalry pay, was given to Colonel Robe. (D.-A.-Gen. to Gen. Howarth, 28 Oct. 1816.)

The numerical force of artillery, serving under General Howorth in the Peninsula, in the end of 1809, was as follows.

MS. Returns, compiled from the Monthly Returns, dated Woolwich, 17 Dec. 1809.

Royal Horse Artillery	187 of all ranks, besides a contingent of drivers attached to the Troops, numbering 106.
Foot Artillery	627 of all ranks, with 545 drivers.
King's German Artillery.	322 of all ranks, with 160 drivers.

The total being 1957, of whom 821 belonged to the Driver Corps. Of this number 357 were returned as sick; and there were in addition 39 prisoners of war.

The number of horses attached to the Artillery in the Peninsula was 951, of which 256 were returned as sick; and there were 132 mules, chiefly attached to the brigades of field and King's German Artillery.

The total being 1957, of whom 821 belonged to the Driver Corps. Of this number 357 were returned as sick; and there were in addition 39 prisoners of war.

The number of horses attached to the artillery in the Peninsula was 951, of which 256 were returned as sick; and there were 132 mules, chiefly attached to the brigades of field and King's German Artillery.

The following tables will show that before a year had elapsed a very considerable increase to this force had taken place; and are also useful, as showing the companies which were present, and the names of the senior officers. MS. Returns, Dated Woolwich, 11 Sept. 1810.

It is difficult, without a study of the correspondence of this period, to realise the energy with which General Macleod endeavoured to meet the wants of the regiment abroad. Unfortunately, there was not similar energy in the other public departments. Large reinforcements, both of men and horses, were ready early in the summer of 1810; but no ships could be found for their conveyance until the end of December. From the nature of these drafts, and from various remarks in General Macleod's letters, it was clear that the remonstrances made by the various officers concerned on the subject of the want of mobility of the field brigades had produced their effect, and the rapid increase in the force of Horse Artillery in the Peninsula which took place between 1810 and 1814 was the consequence.

Anticipating that Lord Wellington would prefer a complete troop of Horse Artillery to more of the sluggish field brigades, General Macleod suggested that the remnant of Captain Lefebure's troop, which was under orders for England, should remain in Portugal; and he despatched men and horses to complete it in that country. At the same time, he did everything in his power to improve the field brigades in the point of mobility, by sending out large numbers of horses. No fewer than 500 were embarked in the first week of January 1811.

Stations	Date of Last Returns	Colonels, Field Officers, and Captains of Companies.	Battalions and Corps.	Colonels.	Field Officers.	Captains.	Subalterns.	Surgeons and Asst.-Surgs.	N.-C. Officers.	Gunners.	Drivers.	Artificers.	Drummers & Trumpeters.	Total.	Horses.	Mules.
Portugal	1st July, 1810.	Brig.-Gen. Howorth		1				5						9		
		Lieut.-Col Framingham	H. B. 1		1	2	3	2	12	81	73	7	1	180	157	
		Lieut.-Col. Robe	3		1	2	3	1	13	45	10	5	1	80	70	
		Lieut.-Col. Fisher	10		1	2	3	1	13	81	75	8	1	184	156	
		Major Hartmann	K.G.A.		1	2	3	1	14	107			2	127		
		Captain Bull	H. B.			2	3		14	109			1	130		
		Captain Lefebure	H. B.			2	3		14	105			1	125		
		Captain Ross	H. B.			2	3		13	99			2	118		
		Captain May	1			2	3		13	117			1	137		
		Captain Ghubb	5			2	3		6	26		6	1	39	60	57
		Captain Thompson	7			2	4		14	80	53	5	2	159	7	7
		Captain Bredin	8			2	4		13	80	30	6	2	136	107	50
		Captain Lawson	8			1	4		13	80	27	25	4	144	218	72
		Detachmt. of British Art.				2	4		31		221		4	286	339	
		Captain Heise	K.G.A.			2	5	1	35		318	33		395		
		Captain Gesenius	K.G.A.													
		Captain Arentschild	K.G.A.													
		Captain Turner	R.A.D.													
		Captain Lane	R.A.D.													
		Total in Portugal		1	4	25	47	11	218	1010	817	95	24	2252	1105	186
Cadiz	1st July, 1810.	Major Duncan	6		1	1		3	7	53				4		
		Captain Campbell	2			2	3		14	98			2	64		
		Captain Owen	5			2	3		13	100			1	119		
		Captain Hughes	9			2	3		13	98			2	118		
		Captain Dickson	10			2	3		12	99			1	117		
		Captain Shenley	10			2	3		12	97		10	1	116		
		Captain Roberts	10			2	2		12		134			159	218	
		Lieutenant Wilkinson	R.A.D.													
		Total in Cadiz			1	11	20	3	84	545	134	10	8	816	218	

The numerical division of the regiment for home and foreign service in the year 1810 was as follows:—

MS. Returns, Dated Woolwich, 19 Nov. 1810.

	At Home All ranks	Abroad All ranks
Horse Brigade (incl. drivers)	1499	433
Invalid Battalions	822	39

Note:—It will be observed that, as before stated, the regiment had, before the end of 1810, fallen below the establishment shown earlier.

The force in the Mediterranean garrisons, which was considered available in event of sudden demands from the Peninsula, appears in the tables following, which also show the names of the senior officers. (MS. Returns, Dated Woolwich, 11 Sept. 1870.) With these the statistics for the year to be treated in this chapter will terminate, and the consideration of the campaign be resumed.

The campaign of 1810 in the Peninsula was, in one sense, the least active of any during the war. Napoleon certainly made a great effort to completely subdue the country, and to expel the English armies. For this purpose, Marshal Massena was placed in command of the French troops; but the duty proved to be beyond his powers. It is doubtful if in any period of the Duke of Wellington's military career he displayed more ability, more patience, more foresight, than he showed during the first nine months of the year 1810.

Not merely had he to contend with local influences, but he failed to secure the requisite support from the English Government. There was at home a fear of losing power, which led English statesmen to commit unworthy actions, and to display a nervousness in administration, which demoralized such of their agents as were not above the ordinary standard. The wisdom of publishing the private letters of a great man is certainly questionable; but once published, they become the historian's legitimate property. From the letters of the Duke of Wellington we have a graphic picture of the Government in 1810. (*Gurwood's Despatches* of the Duke of Wellington.) He wrote to Admiral Berkeley:

> What can be expected from men who are beaten in the House of Commons three times a week? A great deal might be done now, if there existed in England less party, and more public sen-

Stations	Date of Last Returns	Colonels, Field Officers, and Captains of Companies	Battalions and Corps	Colonels	Field Officers	Captains	Subalterns	Surgeons and Asst. Surgs.	N.-C. Officers	Gunners	Drivers	Artificers	Drummers & Trumpeters	Total	Horses	Mules	Remarks
Gibraltar	1st July, 1810.	Major-General Smith	3	1	..	..	..	2	..	..	..	..	..	5	..	..	N.B. At Ceuta, 1 captain, 1 subaltern, 3 N.-C. officers, and 11 gunners. At Tarifa, 1 subaltern, 6 N.-C. officers, and 61 gunners included in the general total.
		Lieut.-Colonel Ramsay	2	..	1	..	..	..	..	..	..	..	..	..	..	..	
		Lieut.-Colonel Wright	5	..	1	..	..	..	..	..	..	..	..	..	..	..	
		Captain Godby	1	..	..	1	3	..	14	87	..	..	2	107	..	..	
		Captain Dodd	2	..	..	1	2	..	17	117	..	..	4	141	..	..	
		Captain Smyth	4	..	..	2	2	..	11	83	..	..	2	100	..	..	
		Captain Morrison	8	..	..	2	2	..	13	86	..	..	2	105	..	..	
		Captain Birch	10	..	..	..	3	..	13	102	..	..	2	120	..	..	
		Captain Fead	10	..	..	2	3	..	13	101	..	..	1	120	..	..	
		Total in Gibraltar	..	1	2	8	15	2	81	576	..	..	13	698	..	..	
Malta	1st June, 1810.	Colonel Bentham	7	1	..	..	..	1	..	..	..	..	..	3	..	..	A detachment of 1 subaltern, 2 N.-C. officers, and 25 gunners belonging to these companies serving in Sicily, and not included in the general total.
		Lieut.-Colonel Harris	2	..	1	..	..	..	..	..	..	..	..	..	..	..	
		Captain Vivion	2	..	..	2	3	..	13	93	..	..	2	113	..	..	
		Captain Reynell	5	..	..	2	3	..	13	88	..	..	2	108	..	..	
		Captain Carey	8	..	..	2	2	..	10	71	..	..	1	86	..	..	
		Total in Malta	..	1	1	6	8	1	36	252	..	..	5	310	..	..	

Stations	Date of last Returns	Colonels, Field Officers, and Captains of Companies	Battalions and Corps	Colonels	Field Officers	Captains	Subalterns	Surgeons and Asst. Surgs.	N.-C. Officers	Gunners	Drivers	Artificers	Drummers & Trumpeters	Total	Horses	Mules	Remarks
Sicily	1st May, 1810	Lieut.-Colonel Lemoine	5	.	1	.	.	4	.	.	.	.	.	6	.	.	At Zante, 2 captains, 2 surgeons, 13 N.-C. officers, and 80 gunners included in the general total.
		Lieut.-Colonel Dickinson	10	.	1	1	2	.	13	99	.	.	1	116	.	.	
		Captain Gamble	6	.	.	2	3	.	14	98	.	.	2	119	.	.	
		Captain Williamson	8	.	.	2	3	.	14	98	.	.	2	119	.	.	
		Captain Fraser	8	.	.	2	2	.	13	99	.	.	1	117	.	.	
		Captain Pym	8	.	.	2	2	.	14	99	.	.	1	118	.	.	
		Captain Hickman	8	.	.	.	1	.	2	25	.	.	.	28	.	.	
		Detachment of Artillery from Malta	.	.	.	2	4	1	16	105	39	6	2	175	109	45	
		Captain Bussman	K.G.A.	.	.	2	1	.	.	.	.	.	.	40	.	.	
		Lieut. G. Smith	R.A.D.	.	.	.	.	.	5	.	32	2	.	.	.	.	
		Total in Sicily	.	.	2	11	18	5	91	623	71	8	9	838	109	45	

timent—and if there was any government.

Again, (*Gurwood's Despatches* of the Duke of Wellington.) in pleading his inability to carry out certain operations, he urged, in a letter to the Right Hon. H. Wellesley, that he would have been able to do so, "if the government possessed any strength, desire to have anything done but what is *safe* and *cheap*." The same hands that applauded the conqueror at Talavera strove, in timorous anxiety, to drag him back from any further operations. The terror of the French armies, which had obtained possession of the Portuguese Government and people, seems to have reached London. The government despatches to Lord Wellington breathed nothing but advice to guide him *when he should be expelled from Portugal.*

While *he* was ensuring in a masterly manner the safety of Lisbon, *they* were urging on him the claims of Cadiz. Their letters and the tone of the public press swelled the despondency, the presence of which in Portugal Lord Wellington lamented; and his protests, assuring the government that he had left nothing undone,—whether the event should be defeat or victory,—were treated as idle words, or as the heated expression of a mere soldier's hopes. Had Wellington been a weaker man, the lines of Torres Vedras had been got ready in vain, the Battle of Busaco had never been fought, and the unpaid arrears of the French troops would have been liquidated by the plundering of Lisbon and Oporto.

But his difficulties were not confined to the chilling advice of the government. At a time when he required the best men in the army to aid him, the exercise of home patronage inflicted on him the most incapable assistants. Not merely did he suffer from useless subordinate staff officers, but even his general officers were not always what he wished.

He wrote to Colonel Torrens:

Really, when I reflect upon the characters and attainments of some of the general officers of this army, and consider that these are the persons on whom I am to rely to lead columns against the French generals, and who are to carry my instructions into execution, I tremble; and, as Lord Chesterfield said of the generals of his day, 'I only hope that when the enemy reads the list of their names, he trembles as I do.' *(Supplementary Despatches,* vol. 6.)

And at the very time that these men were being sent out to him, he was debarred from offering reward, in the shape of promotion, to anyone under his command whose gallantry might seem to him to have earned it. No subject is more frequently alluded to in his letters than this. The government would gladly make political capital out of his successes—would greedily gather votes by making appointments to his army, but declined to strengthen him by trusting his military knowledge, or increasing his legitimate authority.

But the aggravation to which he had to submit in 1810 did not cease here. While the French were advancing into Portugal, and the English Government as little realised the strength of the lines which Wellington had prepared for his troops as Massena himself, the cry was always to embark,—to quit Lisbon,—to devote his energies to Cadiz; yet when strategical reasons and absolute necessity compelled him to leave Ciudad Rodrigo to its fate, the same voices, in querulous terror, remonstrated with him on his inaction. When he gained the victory of Busaco, the first idea with the Government was, not recognition of his merits, but political capital. And when, after a fruitless and self-destructive residence before the lines of Torres Vedras, Massena was obliged to retire from Portugal, who so loud in their cries for pursuit as the very men who had scoffed at the bare possibility of offering resistance to the French invaders?

The year 1810 was, however, not merely a year which tested the marvellous ability and patience of Wellington;—it was also the year which placed on the Portuguese troops the seal of ability to face their dreaded French enemies. At Busaco, the courage of the Portuguese, under English discipline, was nobly manifested—and the value of this discovery was beyond expression at that most critical time. As Lord Wellington said, (*Supplementary Despatches*, vol. 6) the battle had the best effect in inspiring confidence in the Portuguese troops; it removed an impression, which had been general, that the English intended to fight no more, but to retire to their ships; and it gave the Portuguese a taste for an amusement to which they were not before accustomed, and which they would not have acquired in a position less strong than that of Busaco. Had the battle been productive of no other gain than this, it ought to have found favour with a government, whose members desired that their successes might be "*cheap.*"

When the campaign commenced, the headquarters of the English Army were at Celorico; and Almeida and Ciudad Rodrigo were organised for defence. The latter city, which was defended by Spaniards, capitulated on the 10th July, after a month's siege; and Almeida, a small

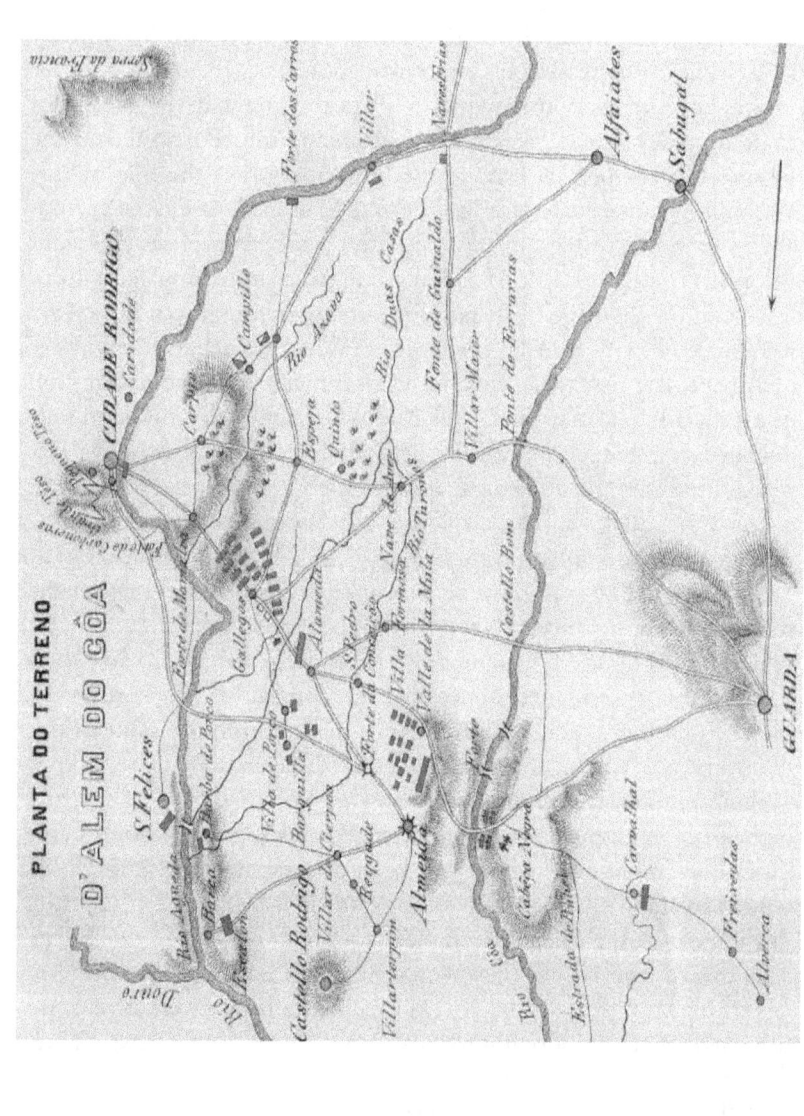

place with a Portuguese garrison, followed suit on the 28th August. During the siege of the latter place, the combat of the Coa, as it was termed, took place; and, as the Chestnut Troop took part in it, it deserves some notice. Craufurd, who commanded the Light Division, and had the outpost duties to perform, had retired before the French, after the fall of Ciudad Rodrigo, under the walls of Almeida.

The position which he took up was very dangerous. The River Coa, crossed by a single bridge, was in his rear, and an open country in front. He had been ordered to cross this river on the approach of the French, but had foolishly remained—with a small force of 5000 men and one battery of artillery, the Chestnut Troop—awaiting the arrival of Ney's force, of more than three times the number. Regardless of the fire from the guns of Almeida, Ney availed himself of Craufurd's blunder, and attacked him with vehemence.

The crossing of the bridge, now absolutely necessary, was most difficult, and could not have been effected but for the gallantry of the regiments, and the precision of the fire of the Chestnut Troop, which had been sent across the bridge early in the affair to occupy some rising ground, and to cover the retreat of the other troops. The bridge was crowded by the retiring columns of the English, so as to be almost impassable; and when, ultimately, the whole had succeeded in crossing, the pursuing columns of the French blocked the passage in a similar manner, and, under a heavy fire, were reduced into heaps of killed and wounded, level with the parapet of the bridge.

A tremendous storm of rain, which set in, flooded the pans of the French muskets, and put an end to the engagement, which, in point of losses, had been on both sides very severe. (Cust.) Of the artillery on this occasion, Napier wrote that it played on both sides across the river and ravine, the sounds repeated by numberless echoes, and the smoke, slowly rising, resolving itself into an immense arch, spanning the whole chasm and sparkling with the whirling fuses of the flying shells. Cust, in his *Annals of the Wars*, describes the Chestnut Troop, from the high ground, sending well-directed shot over the heads of the skirmishers. The gallant officer who commanded the troop wrote as follows:

> General Craufurd ordered a retreat. Lieutenant Bourchier, of the artillery, brought me the order to retire, as rapidly as in my power, across the bridge, and to get my guns into position on the opposite heights. At this time, we had five guns in action. .

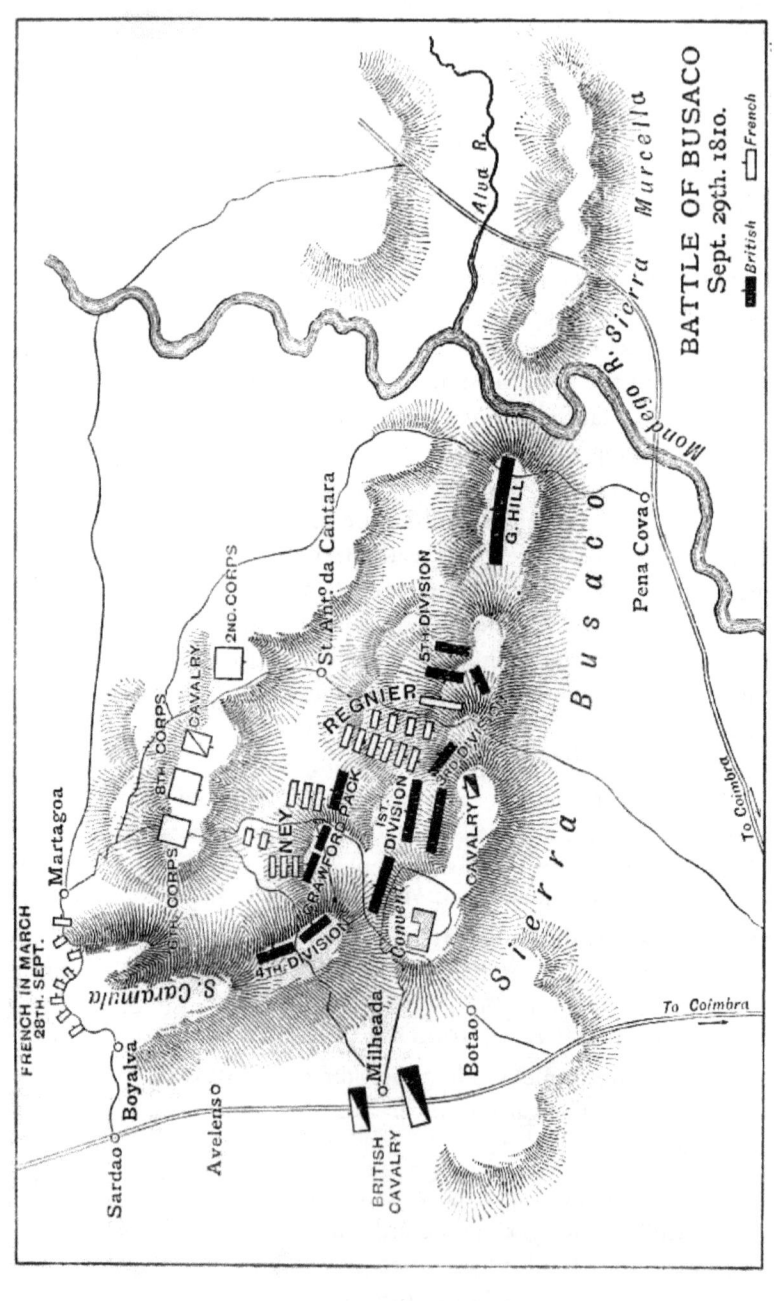

... Our fire was excellent, and broke them two or three times. (*Memoirs of Sir H. Ross.*)

Captain Ross's brother, an officer of Engineers, who was serving with the army, writes of this combat of the 24th July: "Hew's guns did their duty." The loss on the English side during this engagement was over three hundred killed and wounded; that of the French was over a thousand.

But a battle on a larger scale has now to be mentioned. Lord Wellington retreated towards Coimbra, followed by Marshal Massena on the north bank of the Mondego. The English general resolved to make a stand on the Sierra de Busaco, a high ridge which extends from the Mondego in a northerly direction about eight miles. In the battle which followed, Lord Wellington displayed an ignorance of artillery tactics, from the results of which he was happily saved by the intelligence and gallantry of the representatives of that arm. This want of knowledge, which he never overcame, was the cause of a not unfrequent irritation against artillery as an arm, and a tendency to depreciate its value.

At Busaco, instead of massing his artillery in reserve until the attack should develop itself, the guns were placed, as a rule, in the easiest parts of the position, where it was supposed the French *would* attack; and they were massed in these positions so as to form an excellent mark for the enemy's fire. (Capt. B. Strange, R.A., on Practical Artillery.) This was more especially the case with Major Arentschild's 6-pounder and 9-pounder brigades of Portuguese artillery. Fortunately, the artillery was well served, and as Sir John Burgoyne (*Life of* vol. 1) wrote, "the guns had great effect." Captain Thompson's company of the 7th Battalion—later D Battery, 11th Brigade, Royal Artillery, was of essential service, although it was broken up into divisions during the battle. Captain Lane, who was 2nd Captain of the company, thus describes the conduct of one division:

> My men did their duty. Lieutenant F. Bayley's conduct was admirable. It was the first time he had been in action, and no old soldier could have acted better. The French *Voltigeurs* (37th Regiment) came close to the guns; and one was killed only eight paces off. An immense column showing themselves in the ravine, we, with three cheers, gave them a few rounds of case and round-shot together, at about seventy paces distance, which drove them back. (MS. Letter among Cleveland's MSS.)

The same officer, who was quoted above as alluding to the services of his brother's troop at the Coa, wrote of Busaco:

> I will venture to assert that the greatest loss the enemy sustained was by our artillery; and the guns that had the most duty, and, I believe I might say, that were best placed for effect—even if nothing is said of the admirable manner in which the guns were fought—were those of Hew's troop. . . . Several officers who remained on the field the day after the retreat, among others General Craufurd himself, were convinced, more than those who only looked on it from the heights, of the immense slaughter the enemy sustained from the Shrapnel shells thrown from my brother's guns, aided for a short time by those of Captain Bull's troop. (Memoirs of Sir H. Ross.)

This opinion, which, coming from a brother, might perhaps be considered more indulgent than just, was confirmed by the great historian of the war. In the resistance offered to the attack of Loison's division, Napier says that Ross's guns were worked with incredible quickness, and their shot swept through the advancing columns. The attack having failed, Craufurd's artillery, with which was the gallant Chestnut Troop, was equally useful against the attack of Marchaud's division, which followed. Napier writes:

> It heavily smote the flank of Marchaud's people in the pine-wood; and Ney, who was there in person, after sustaining this murderous cannonade for an hour, relinquished that attack also.

Well might Lord Wellington say,:

> I am particularly indebted to . . . Brigadier-General Howorth and the artillery. (To Lord Liverpool, dated Coimbra, 30 Sept. 1810.)

The force under Lord Wellington's command on this occasion did not exceed 50,000, and extended over a distance of eight to ten miles. The French are estimated by Napier to have been 65,000 in number; but Wellington considered they exceeded that number by 5000 men. (To Lord Liverpool, dated Pero Negro, 3 Nov. 1810.) The French loss amounted to 4500 killed and wounded, while that of the Allies was under 1300, the English having lost 631, and the Portuguese 622. The absence of artillery on the side of the French, who overrated the difficulties of the ground, and the great activity shown in the use and

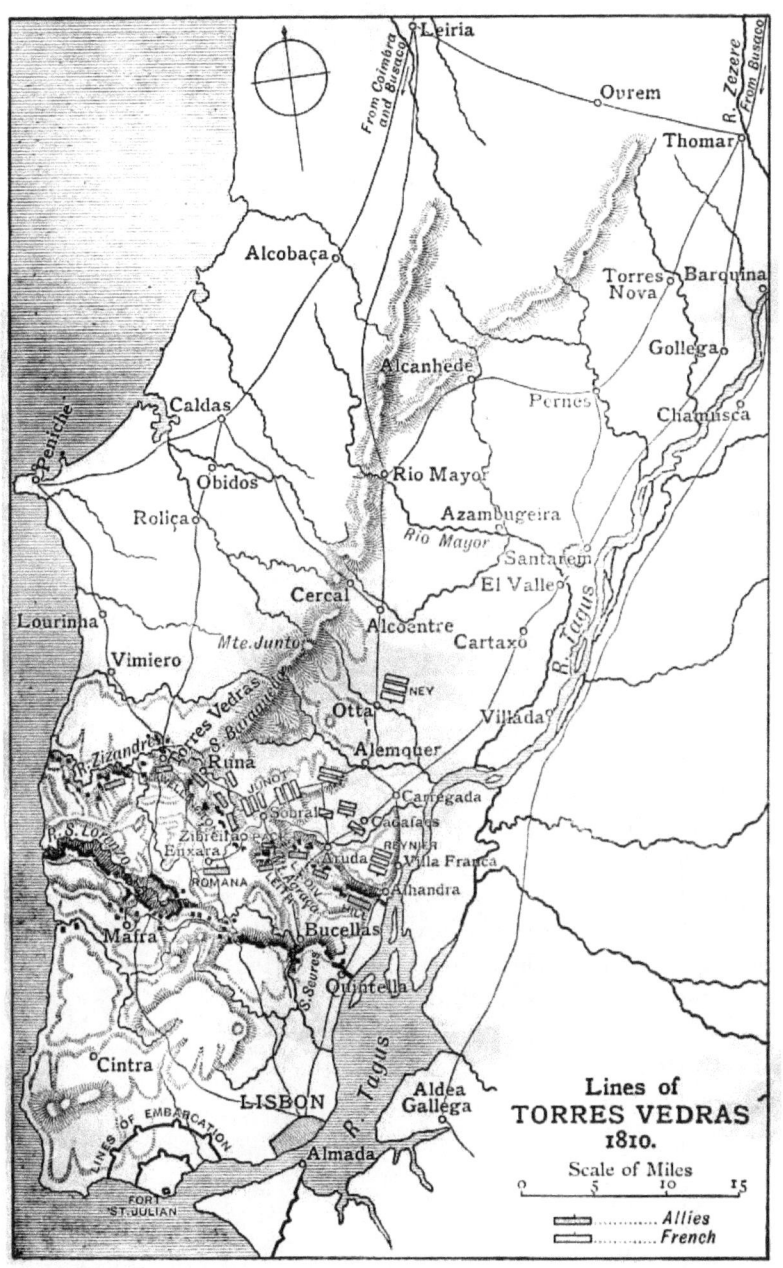

service of the guns of the Allies, accounted for the great difference in the number of casualties. Much of the efficacy of the fire of the Royal Artillery was due to the use of Shrapnel's spherical case-shot—a projectile which was daily increasing in favour—with no one more than with Lord Wellington himself. Major May wrote to Colonel Shrapnel, (dated Sabugal, 23 Feb. 1812):

> At the Battle of Busaco, your shells were of the utmost use, and their destruction plainly perceived from the heights.

Marshal Massena, finding it impossible to cross the Sierra de Busaco by either of the two direct roads, while such an enemy lined the heights, but being resolved to press on to Coimbra, turned the position by its left flank,—Wellington continuing the retreat which he had varied by so noble an episode. Massena reached Coimbra just as the English rear-guard quitted it; and his troops were there guilty of the grossest licence. The English Army continued slowly to retire to the lines which its prudent commander had prepared for it; and when Massena came up, he found it in a position which was almost impregnable, while his own communications were interrupted, and his flanks and rear annoyed by levies of Portuguese Militia. The lines of Torres Vedras were an emblem of military sagacity and of engineering skill.

Seated behind them the Allied Army received a training which proved fruitful in the campaign of the following year; the Portuguese contingent was made more efficient; and the folly of the Portuguese Government received repeated rebukes from the mouth of a general whose prudence and determination were never more clearly shown than in the history of Torres Vedras and Busaco. Croakers, as he wrote, might include the latter among useless battles; but an encounter, which made each Portuguese soldier feel himself a match for a Frenchman, was the best assistance which fortune could throw in Lord Wellington's way. Having realised the value of this beforehand, his next task was to ensure it *independently* of fortune.

CHAPTER 6

Barossa, Badajoz, and Albuera

Leaving Massena in front of Torres Vedras, the reader is requested to turn towards Cadiz. Here Spanish pride had long resisted offers of English assistance, hoping without foreign aid to raise the siege of the city; but here the English Government thought it very desirable that some demonstration should be made. In 1810 the presence of a British contingent was at length tolerated; and the artillery element has been detailed in the preceding chapter. Major Duncan and the companies under his command had originally embarked for Gibraltar; but the opening in Cadiz led to their proceeding to that city instead. Their arrival having been reported, steps were immediately taken by General Macleod to equip them for service in the field; and with this view, three batteries of six guns each, with the necessary equipment, were despatched from England, and a small supply of horses, seventy-four in number,—to form a nucleus of a larger establishment. (General Macleod to Major Duncan, dated 23 April, 1810, and 8 May.)

It had been intended that Colonel Framingham should be the officer to command the artillery at Cadiz, as soon as the Spaniards should deign to admit any. Fortunately for Major Duncan, it was found impossible to spare that officer from the headquarters of the army; and at the urgent request of General Graham, who commanded the English troops at Cadiz, the command of the artillery with his force was left in Major Duncan's hands, and remained so until 1812, when he was accidentally killed by the explosion of a powder-mill at Seville. (D.-A.-Gen. to Major Duncan, 13 May, 1810.)

In the records already given of the services of the companies of the 10th Battalion, reference has been made to the duties of the Royal Artillery at Cadiz. In this chapter it is proposed to describe a battle which was fought by General Graham's force, and in which—it has been said, the artillery covered themselves with glory. The gallant general stated, (to Lord Liverpool, 6 March, 1811), that artillery had never been better served; but it may be added that it had never been better handled than by him. His contingent was but small—ten guns—but it was never idle, and always in the right place.

The circumstances which led to the Battle of Barossa may be summarised as follows:—An attempt had been resolved upon by the Anglo-Spanish leaders in Cadiz to raise the French siege, the opportunity being favourable, as the besieging force did not at the time exceed 12,000 men. The English had 4200, and the Spaniards nearly 10,000. To facilitate matters, General Graham consented to serve under the Spanish general, La Pena, although the event proved that there never was a man less fitted to hold a command. The plan of action was to transport the allied force to Tarifa, disembark there, and effect a junction with another Spanish force; and then counter-march the whole on the rear of the besieging force at Chichlana. Inclement weather prevented the first part of the scheme from being carried out; and the landing was effected, not at Tarifa, but at Algesiras.

The whole army, however, effected a junction at the former place on the 28th February, 1811, and, driving the French before them, reached a place known as the Vigia de la Barrosa, or Barossa, at noon on the 5th March. (Cust's *Annals*.) Here they were encountered by the French Marshal, Victor, who had been warned of the expedition, and who promptly availed himself of the numerous openings which the blunders and incompetency of the Spanish general offered. The tale of these is too long to reproduce in a merely regimental history; suffice it to say that, owing to them, General Graham found himself in an extraordinary and embarrassing position.

Having been ordered to march from the height of Barossa, which was the key of the whole position, and to proceed to Bermeja through a difficult pine-wood, he obeyed, but with regret. Assuming that the important point he had just quitted would be occupied by the Spaniards, he left his baggage with a small guard. To his amazement, he soon learned that no such precaution had been taken; that the French Marshal, detecting the omission, was already ascending the height; and that his own baggage-guard was in extreme and imminent danger. Retracing his steps as rapidly as the nature of the wood would admit of, he arrived in time to see the enemy in complete possession of the height—himself face to face with the French, and utterly unsupported by the Spaniards. By what has been called by Napier an inspiration—

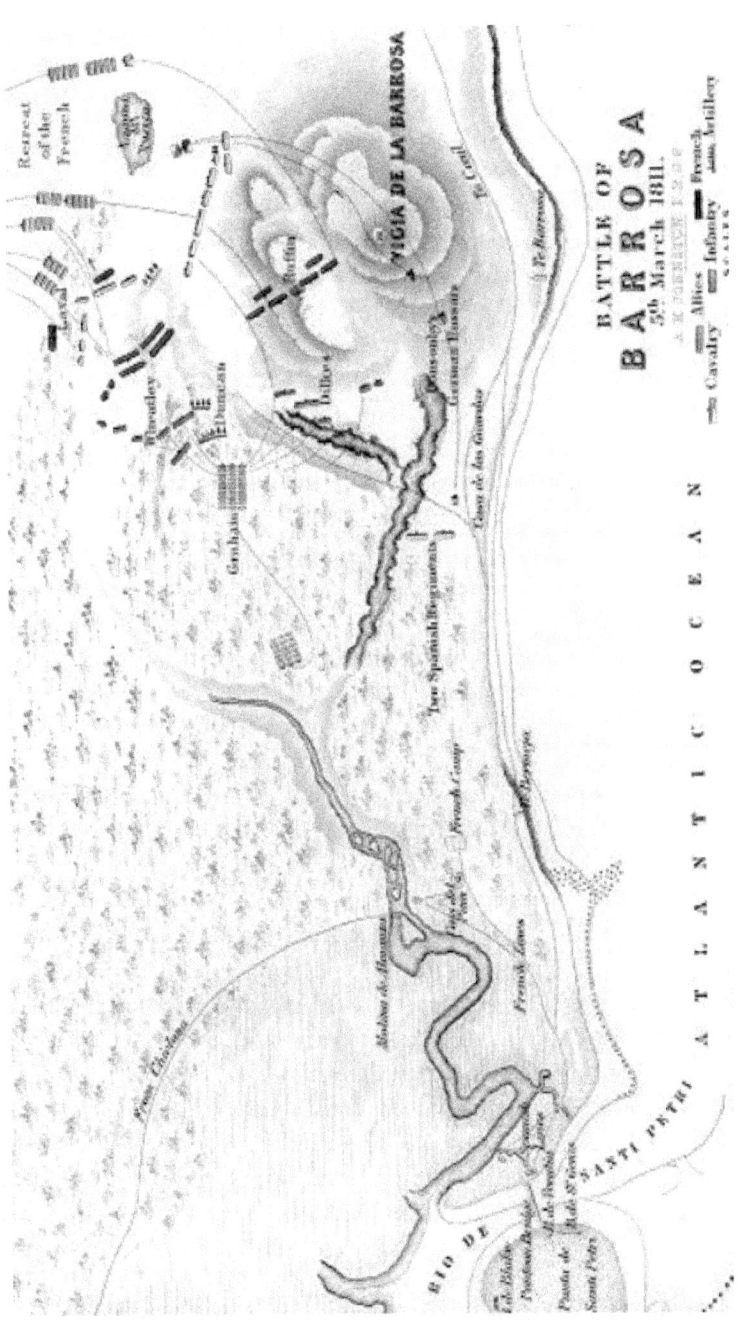

but such an inspiration as never comes to the short-sighted or ignorant—he realised that retreat would be folly, and that his only hope of success lay in immediately assuming the offensive.

Massing his artillery, he desired Major Duncan to keep up a powerful fire, while he organised his force into divisions for the attack. Of this fire Napier writes that it ravaged the French ranks. As soon as the infantry had formed, General Graham advanced his artillery to a more favourable position, whence, as he afterwards wrote, it kept up a most destructive fire on the French columns now advancing. The right division of the English, under General Dilkes, and the left, under Colonel Wheatley, encountered respectively the French divisions under Generals Ruffin and Laval. The infantry regiments engaged were the Guards, 28th, 7th, 67th, and 87th—the flank companies of the 1st Battalion 9th Foot, 2nd Battalion 47th, and 2nd Battalion 82nd, besides part of the 20th Portuguese Regiment.

Where all behaved with gallantry, it may seem invidious to select any particular regiment for notice; but, at a most critical moment, the defeat of General Laval's division was completed by a magnificent advance of the 87th Regiment. Both the French divisions were borne backwards from the hill; and, uniting, attempted to reform and make another attack. But their attempt was frustrated by the fire of the artillery, which from being terrific, as Napier (vol.3) termed it, became now "close, rapid, and murderous, and rendered the attempt vain." Marshal Victor, therefore, withdrew his troops from the field, and the English, having been twenty-four hours under arms and without food, were too exhausted to pursue.

In this battle, which only lasted one hour and a half, over 1200 were killed and wounded on the side of the English, and more than 2000 on the side of the French. Six guns and 400 prisoners also fell into the hands of the conquerors. Of the conduct of his troops generally, General Graham wrote to Lord Liverpool that nothing less than the almost unparalleled exertions of every officer, the invincible bravery of every soldier, and the most determined devotion to the honour of His Majesty's arms in all, could have achieved this brilliant success, against such a formidable enemy so posted.

Sir Richard Keats, the admiral on the station, who had superintended the transport of the troops to Algesiras, wrote, (to Admiral Sir C. Cotton, dated Cadiz, 7 March, 1811), that the British troops, led by their gallant and able commander,—forgetting, on the sight of the enemy, their own fatigue and privations, and regardless of advantage in the numbers and situation of the enemy,—gained by their determined valour a victory uneclipsed by any of the brave achievements of the British Army.

The special expressions used by General Graham in his despatch with reference to the services of the Royal Artillery on this occasion are well worthy of a place in the records of the corps:

> I owe too much to Major Duncan and the officers and corps of the Royal Artillery, not to mention them in terms of the highest approbation: *never was artillery better served.*

He recommended Major Duncan for promotion, and the brevet rank of Lieutenant-Colonel was accordingly conferred upon him.

The losses of the artillery at Barossa were as follows:—

Died of his wounds, Lieutenant Woolcombe.

Wounded: Captains Hughes and Cator,—Lieutenants Mitchell, Brereton, Manners, Maitland, and Pester.

Three rank and file killed, and 32 wounded: besides of the Royal Artillery Drivers, 1 sergeant, 2 rank and file, and 18 horses killed: 1 sergeant, 7 rank and file, and 22 horses wounded.

The ordnance captured from the French was as follows:—

Two 7-inch howitzers, 3 heavy 8-pounders, 1 4-pounder,—with their ammunition waggons, and a proportion of horses. (Major Duncan to General Graham.)

The fruits of the Battle of Barossa might have been very considerable, had the Spanish general been capable of understanding even the rudiments of his profession. As he was at once ignorant and proud, General Graham found it necessary to return with his force to Cadiz; the object of the expedition had failed, for the siege was not raised,—but Marshal Victor had received a check which alarmed him considerably, and which led to eager demands for reinforcements. In his conduct, both in the action of the 5th March, and in his withdrawal to Isla de Leon on the following day, when he separated from the Spaniards, General Graham received the warmest support from Lord Wellington, to whose movements the reader is now invited to return.

After an inactivity of five months before the lines of Torres Vedras, Massena commenced to evacuate Portugal. He had no siege artillery with which to attack the fortifications behind which his enemy was securely sheltered; and his supplies were becoming every day more difficult to obtain; he therefore had no other alternative. As he retired, he was closely followed by the English Army, and many smart affairs

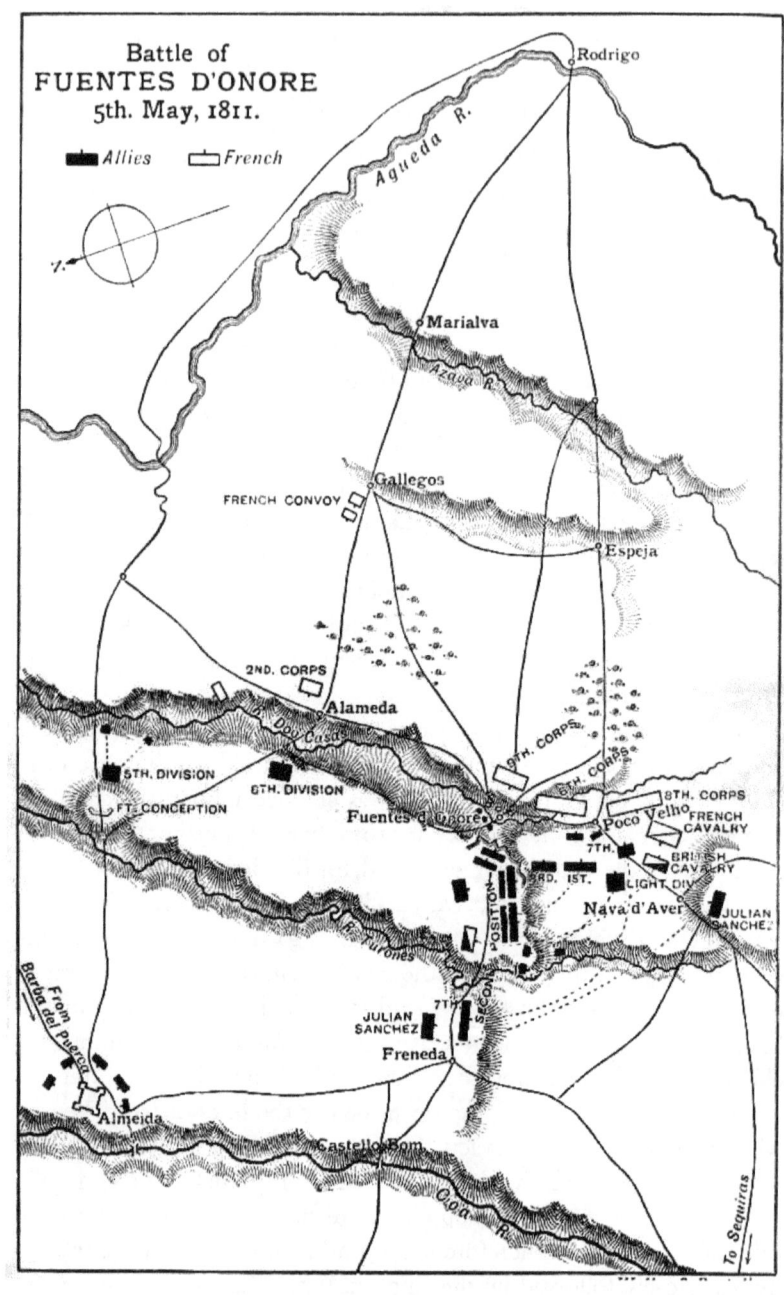

took place between the advanced guards of the latter and the rearguard of the French Army, in which the Royal Horse Artillery did good service. The limits of the largest work and the patience of the most enduring reader would be exhausted were these minor actions given in detail. Suffice it to say, that the artillery engaged on these occasions included the troops commanded by Captain Ross and Captain Bull, and that the way in which they performed their duty may be gathered, in the first place, from Lord Wellington's despatches, and, in the second, from the exhaustive narrative of Napier.

In writing of the actions of the 11th, 12th, and 13th March, 1811, at Pombal, Redinha, and Cazal Nova, Lord Wellington said (to Lord Liverpool, dated 14 March, 1811), that the troops of Horse Artillery under Captains Ross and Bull particularly distinguished themselves. At the affair of Foz d'Arouce, on the 15th March, he also wrote, (*ibid*, dated 16 March, 1811), that the Horse Artillery, under Ross and Bull, distinguished themselves. Later, in the affair which took place on the 7th April, during a reconnaissance, in which the English, under Sir W. Erskine, drove a division of the French Army before them across the Turones and Dos Casas, Lord Wellington wrote, (*ibid*, dated 9 April, 1811), that "Captain's Bull's troop of Horse Artillery did great execution on this occasion."

At the celebrated engagement of Fuentes d'Onor, the dashing affair mentioned in an early part of this work, took place, in which Captain Norman Ramsay, of Bull's troop, so greatly distinguished himself.

★★★★★★

The artillery of the Allies at Fuentes d'Onor was as follows:—

Royal Horse Artillery	12 guns
Royal Artillery	12 "
Portuguese Artillery	18 "
	42

Sir A. Dickson's MSS.

★★★★★★

On this occasion the losses of the artillery were as follows:—

Royal Horse Artillery—1 rank and file and 3 horses killed: 1 rank and file, and 3 horses wounded.

Royal Foot Artillery—1 sergeant, 4 rank and file, and 9 horses killed; 1 captain, 2 subalterns, 18 rank and file, and 21 horses wounded.

The officers wounded were Captain Thompson—whose brigade did as good service as it had done at Busaco, and the practice made by which attracted universal admiration—Lieutenant Martin, and a subaltern of the same name as the officer who fell at Barossa, Lieutenant Woolcombe. The total casualties on the side of the Allies amounted to 1786: those of the French to 2665. The battle resulted in the evacuation of Portugal by Massena, and the capture of Almeida by the English, although, unfortunately, not until the garrison had made its escape.

During these continued successes, Lord Wellington was afflicted by a want of adequate supplies and money—and by discouraging letters from England. With a temerity such as few commanders would have displayed, he did not hesitate to point out to the Government how weak and mistaken their vacillating, timorous policy was. Still undeceived as to the worthlessness of Spanish promises, the English rulers urged upon Wellington to make Spain the theatre of his operations, and yet declined to make him independent of the Spanish authorities. His protestations, also, in favour of Portugal as a base of operations fell on doubting and unwilling ears. English statesmen seemed to live in a fools' paradise: and from their dreams it seemed impossible to wake them.

On the 23rd March, 1811, Lord Wellington had actually to write, beseeching the Government to forego an intention which appeared to have been formed of withdrawing the troops from Portugal on account of the expense of the war. (To Lord Liverpool, dated Santa Marinha, 23 March, 1811.) He had already urged on them the folly of starving an expedition in the hope of securing popularity for their party; and he now boldly asserted that if they carried out their intention, and freed the French from the pressure of military operations in the Continent, they must prepare to meet a French Army in England. He wrote:

> Then, would commence an expensive contest;—then would His Majesty's subjects discover what are the miseries of war, of which, by the blessing of God, they have hitherto had no knowledge.

It was a difficult task which Lord Wellington had to perform—not merely to fight his country's battles under difficulties and discouragement—not merely to be exasperated by advice, the folly of which was glaring—but also in his few moments of leisure to have to take up his pen, and teach her senators wisdom. The superiority of England's greatest general cannot be realised without a careful study, not merely

Battle of Fuentes d'Onor

of his campaigns, but also of his correspondence.

It is necessary now to turn to Marshal Beresford's force, with which was Major Dickson, now serving in command of the Portuguese artillery. It had been hoped that this army would reach Badajoz in sufficient time to raise the French siege of that city; but a slight delay in Beresford's movements, combined with undoubted treachery on the part of the garrison, frustrated this hope, and rendered it necessary to prepare for a siege of the city with its now French garrison. From this time, the reader will enjoy an advantage which cannot be overrated, and which appears now for the first time in any narrative of the Peninsular War.

Sir Alexander Dickson was not merely a great artilleryman, but also a most methodical and industrious collector and registrar of details which came under his notice. During the various sieges in the Peninsula which were conducted by him, he kept diaries mentioning even the most trifling facts: and on his return to England he procured from General Macleod the whole of the long series of letters which he had written to him between 1811 and 1814.

The mass of information which he thus possessed was arranged, and at his death the whole passed into the hands of his son, Sir Collingwood Dickson. In the hope that the papers of the most prominent artilleryman of the Duke of Wellington's armies would be useful in framing a history of the corps in which he spent his life, Sir Collingwood kindly placed them at the disposal of the author of this history. Priceless under any circumstances, they are even more so from the fact that several of the letter-books of the deputy-adjutant-general's department during the Peninsular War have been mislaid;—and these refer chiefly to the periods covered by the manuscripts of Sir Alexander Dickson. On the latter, therefore, the narrative of the period between 1811 and 1814 will be chiefly based: and it is hoped that the reproduction of the opinions and statements of one, so able to express the former with confidence and the latter with authority, will be a welcome addition to the literature of England's wars in the Peninsula.

★★★★★★

In his notes on the various sieges in the Peninsula, Sir A. Dickson frequently differs from Sir J. Jones's well-known work. But as the latter had more to do with engineering details, and as Sir A. Dickson's MSS. contain occasional marginal notes of later date, saying that his statement is correct, and Sir J. Jones's wrong, it has been decided to accept his account, when differing from the latter work.

✶✶✶✶✶✶

On the 9th April, 1811, Marshal Beresford advanced from the Guadiana and invested Olivença. When he reconnoitred the place, Major Dickson pointed out an enclosed lunette in front of the gate of San Francisco, from which he knew, by a former visit to Olivença, that the curtain could be battered in breach. Approving of the suggestion, Marshal Beresford despatched Major Dickson to Elvas that night to bring up the siege artillery. This consisted of six heavy brass 24-pounders, each provided with all necessary stores, and with ammunition at the rate of 300 rounds per gun. To move this battery and equipment from Elvas to Olivença 104 pairs of bullocks were required, and a company of Portuguese artillery attended as escort.

On the 13th April the guns arrived at the camp before Olivença, and immediately proceeded to the neighbourhood of the point of attack. The breaching battery for four 24-pounders had been got in complete readiness, and an attempt was accordingly made at once to put the guns in battery. It was found, however, impossible to effect this on that day, on account of the dreadful state of the roads, and the circuit which the guns were obliged to take. By the night of the 14th, the communications had been made practicable, and four guns were placed in the battery, with ammunition and stores, in readiness to open fire at dawn. Two field batteries of the King's German Artillery were also placed so as to keep the enemy's fire in check. The field-pieces employed by these were five 6-pounders and one 5½-inch howitzer.

The breaching battery did not open fire until 8 a.m., on the 15th, the point aimed at being the curtain to the left of the San Francisco gate, and the distance being about 340 yards. At 11 a.m. the enemy showed a flag of truce, which occasioned a cessation of fire; but nothing definite resulting, it was resumed, and after a few more rounds the enemy surrendered at discretion. Major Dickson was much pleased with the practice made by the young Portuguese artillerymen under his command. Only 320 rounds had been fired in the four hours, and yet the breach was almost practicable. A brisk fire from five or six guns had been kept up by the enemy against the breaching battery, and had inflicted some slight loss; but the field guns of the German artillery did much to moderate it, firing about sixty rounds a gun.

On taking Olivença the following ordnance was secured:—*Mounted.* Brass, one 8-pounder and two 4-pounders; iron, five 12-pounders, two 8-pounders, and two 6-pounders. *Dismounted.* Brass, one

8-pounder; iron, two 12-pounders. (Sir A. Dickson's MS.)

On the 17th April, Major Dickson waited on Marshal Beresford at Zafra, and received orders to proceed to Elvas to make preparations for the siege of Badajoz. On the 20th Lord Wellington arrived at Elvas, and issued instructions for the carrying on of the siege to Marshal Beresford, Colonel Fletcher of the Engineers, and Major Dickson, the last-named officer being appointed to direct the artillery department of the operation. From the 21st April to the 10th May, the greatest exertions were made, both at Elvas and around Badajoz, to prepare the necessary ordnance and stores for the siege, transport them, and make and arm the batteries. The following shows, the nature and distribution of the ordnance employed:—

Prepared from various returns among Sir A. Dickson's MSS.

TABLE A.[1]

FIRST SIEGE OF BADAJOZ.

April 23, 1811.—Ordnance selected for the Siege :—

Sixteen brass 24-pounder guns.
Eight „ 16-pounder „
Two 10-inch brass howitzers.
Six 8-inch „ „

The ammunition to be at the rate of 800 rounds per gun, and 400 rounds per howitzer.

The following distribution of ordnance was determined on for the first operations of the siege, on the 8th May, 1811 :—

1. For the attack of St. Cristoval :

    24-pounders .. .. 3 } 5
    8-inch howitzers 2

2. For the false attack on Pardaleras :

    24-pounders .. .. 3 } 4
    8-inch howitzer 1

3. For the false attack on Picurina :

    24-pounders .. .. 3 } 4
    8-inch howitzer 1

On the 9th May, the following additional ordnance was sent from Elvas for the St. Cristoval attack, viz.:

24-pounders .. .. 2 ⎱ 3
8-inch howitzer .. .. 1 ⎰

Four brass 12-pounders were at the same time ordered from Elvas to enfilade the bridge of Badajoz. Four guns for the attack of St. Cristoval were replaced on the 11th May—having been damaged—by three heavy 12-pounders and a field howitzer.

On the 12th May, four 24-pounders were sent from the great park to the Cristoval attack.

On the 13th May the siege was ordered to be raised, as will hereafter be shown.

Badajoz was invested on the right bank on the 8th May, and on the morning of the 11th the breaching battery against San Cristoval opened. Being, however, totally unsupported, and having to resist a very heavy fire from that fort and the castle, the young Portuguese artillerymen proved unequal to the contest. Their practice, after a few rounds, became very uncertain; and in the course of the morning the battery was silenced, all the pieces being disabled except one howitzer.

On the night of the 11th, the battery intended to enfilade the bridge was armed, and the disabled ordnance in the breaching battery exchanged. Captain Hawker, commanding a 9-pounder field brigade of the Royal Artillery, lately arrived from Lisbon, was directed to place himself under the orders of Major Dickson, although regimentally senior to that officer, and was placed in charge of the artillery operations against San Cristoval.

The commencement of the siege was very disheartening. On the day before the solitary battery opened fire, the Allies had met with a severe loss during a sally made by the garrison; and now, in a few hours their one battery was silenced. Beresford was also disquieted by rumours which reached him that Soult was on his way to raise the siege, and that he would certainly arrive before the city could be taken. He therefore sent for Major Dickson late on the night of the 11th, and desired him not to bring forward any more ammunition or stores from Elvas, and to be in readiness to remove at the shortest notice what had already arrived. Colonel Fletcher also was ordered not to break ground that night against the castle. In event, however, of the operations proceeding, it was arranged that four 24-pounders should be moved from the south attacks to that of San Cristoval, and that they should be replaced by six additional guns of the same calibre from Elvas.

On the morning of the 12th intelligence reached Beresford which led him to doubt the accuracy of the reports which had reached him on the previous day, and he ordered active operations to recommence at once. Additional guns were therefore sent forward from the park at Elvas, and at night ground was broken for the batteries against the castle. The new activity, however, was but short-lived; for positive information was received at midnight as to the enemy's movements. On the morning of the 13th the siege was ordered to be raised, and Major Dickson directed to send the heavy ordnance, ammunition and stores back to Elvas. This duty was admirably performed.

As many pieces of ordnance were at once despatched, as the means of conveyance would permit; and in the first instance it was thought sufficient to take the pieces across the flying bridge, and to park them in a situation not visible from Badajoz. On the Cristoval side the guns were removed from the battery on the night of the 13th; and at the same time the battery in the false attack against Picurina was dismantled. The 14th May was spent in carrying away the ordnance and stores in such a way as to conceal from the enemy the fact that the siege was being raised; and by noon on the 15th the whole of the besieging artillery and ammunition from the great park had been sent across the river, and the flying bridge removed, while the park of the Cristoval attack had been taken back to the vicinity of Elvas.

The investing troops on the south bank were then withdrawn; but a corps remained on the north bank to cover the removal of the heavy artillery to Elvas. Of the duty performed by Major Dickson on this occasion, under Marshal Beresford's orders, Napier writes that "the arrangements for carrying off the stores were admirably executed; ... and that the transactions were so well masked by the 4th Division, which, in concert with the Spaniards, continued to maintain the investment, that it was only by a sally on the rear-guard, in which the Portuguese piquets of the 4th Division were very roughly treated, that the French knew the siege was raised."

The same author visits the failure of this siege, and the heavy losses attending all the subsequent sieges carried on by the British in Spain, on the absence of any properly-equipped corps of sappers and miners to assist the officers of engineers. The want of such a corps, with the necessary implements, rendered, according to Napier, the British sieges a mere succession of butcheries. But Sir Alexander Dickson was ready to accept part of the responsibility of this failure for his own department. In his diary of the first siege of Badajoz he wrote:

Every praise was due to the Portuguese artillery for the activity, zeal, and willingness they displayed in this service. Indeed, nothing could exceed their personal exertions; but, from their professional inexperience, Major Dickson has great doubts whether a satisfactory result would have been obtained without the assistance of a of better-trained artillerymen. (Sir A. Dickson's MS.)

At the same time, however, he distinctly stated, in a letter to General Macleod, (dated Elvas, 22 May, 1811), that his wish was not to begin the fire from any one battery until the whole attack should be more advanced, and that the Cristoval attack should be supported from other points. He added that the battery against the Picurina, although well placed as an auxiliary for general attack, afforded no support to that against San Cristoval. In these points, he wrote, "my opinions coincide entirely with those of Colonel Fletcher (R.E.), with whom it is a pleasure to serve."

Marshal Beresford was brave, but was better as an administrator in peace than as a general in war. No praise can exceed his deserts in reference to the organisation and training of the Portuguese Army, or his fidelity to Wellington; but his abilities as a commander in the field were feeble, and the success of his troops in the battle which followed the raising of the siege of Badajoz was won in spite of, rather than by him. Albuera was one of the fiercest battles of the Peninsula; with it the name of Beresford will always be associated; but its chronicler will always have to register with the stories of its gallantry that of his incapacity. The policy of fighting the battle at all—a question which lies with a general alone—was more than doubtful; but, even admitting that it was wise, his tactics were extremely faulty, and the errors were expiated only by the courage and losses of his men.

With a general like Soult against him, the arrangement of his army on the morning of the 16th May revealed a childlike innocence, which, in a general charged with the lives of men, was criminal. Part of his army was still at Badajoz, and could not possibly reach his position in time for the battle;—part had barely succeeded in doing so on the eventful morning;—he had, on the previous day, allowed the French to occupy a wood on the other side of the Albuera River, where they could conceal their intentions;—and, with marvellous blindness, he had allowed them to secure a hill in the immediate front of his own right, behind which they organised the famous attack, which so nearly proved fatal.

On the afternoon of the 15th, Major Dickson, having completed his duties at Badajoz, proceeded to Albuera, where the army had taken up its position, and resumed the command of his two brigades of Portuguese Field Artillery. About the same hour on the morning of the 16th as that on which General Cole's division happily succeeded in joining Beresford's army, the enemy showed himself in force. The first appearance was the advance of seven or eight squadrons of cavalry, some light infantry, and a troop of horse artillery, from the wood towards the bridge of Albuera by the Seville road.

This was a feint, but not immediately recognised as such by Marshal Beresford. They drove in the English piquets, and formed in the plain, where they opened an artillery fire towards the village of Albuera, a small place, which, with the exception of its church, was almost in ruins, and which was without inhabitants. This fire was answered by some of Major Dickson's and of the German artillery, which directed their practice against the cavalry. At first Major Dickson thought it was merely a reconnaissance; but it was soon seen that the real attack was intended against the right, which was composed of Blake's Spanish troops. Beresford sent orders to Blake to throw back the right at right angles to the line; but the command was not obeyed until he went in person to enforce it, by which time the French were upon them, harassing them, as they wheeled, with a murderous fire.

From the position occupied by Major Dickson near the bridge, which was opposite the centre of the line, he first saw a column of infantry advancing to the bridge by the same road as had been taken by the cavalry, on which a brigade of General Stewart's division was at once sent to the village to support Baron Alten, who commanded there. Very soon afterwards, however, he saw another column moving through the wood in the direction of the Allied right, and as, at the same time, the column approaching the bridge first halted, and then commenced to retire, it was evident that the real French effort would be made against the right. Stewart's British brigade, therefore, at once marched from the village to the right, followed by the rest of the division, and Cole's division formed up in support.

By this time a heavy shower of rain had commenced, which greatly favoured the approach of the French columns against the Spaniards on the right, and during which they passed the river, and advanced upon and came round the height which the latter occupied, and on which they were then, in great confusion, wheeling into a new position. In describing the conduct of the Spanish troops at Albuera, Major Dickson, referring to this particular episode in the battle, wrote to General Macleod as follows:

> The fact is, the Spaniards, once in line, could not be moved—I mean, could not manoeuvre—and the marshal was obliged to use the British, that knew how to move, or else our flank must have been completely turned. (To D.-A.-G. dated 22 May, 1811.)

This quite corroborates Napier's account of the battle. It was on the hill occupied by the Spanish that the contest was decided; it was there that the gallantry of the French cavalry and the heroism of the English Infantry were manifested; there a murderous artillery fire of grape at close range was maintained incessantly on both sides; and it was there that the grand final episode took place which was described with poetic fervour by the great historian.

> The fusilier battalions of Cole's division advanced in gallant line, but, struck by the iron tempest, reeled and staggered like sinking ships. But suddenly and sternly recovering, they closed on their terrible enemies; and then was seen with what a strength and majesty the British soldier fights. . . . Nothing could stop that astonishing infantry. No sudden burst of undisciplined valour, no nervous enthusiasm, weakened the stability of their order; their flashing eyes were bent on the dark columns in their front, their measured tread shook the ground, their dreadful volleys swept away the head of every formation, their deafening shouts overpowered the dissonant cries that broke from all parts of the tumultuous crowd, as, slowly and with a horrid carnage, it was pushed by the incessant vigour of the attack to the farthest edge of the height. . . . At last the mighty mass gave way, and, like a loosened cliff, went headlong down the steep. The rain flowed after in streams discoloured with blood; and eighteen hundred unwounded men, the remnant of six thousand unconquerable British soldiers, stood triumphant on the fatal hill!

Before this final charge took place, Beresford thought the battle was lost, and commenced arrangements for a retreat. He ordered the withdrawal of Alten's Germans and Major Dickson's guns from Albuera bridge. This was strongly asserted by Napier, although denied by one of his critics; and it is confirmed by a passage in one of Major

Dickson's letters:

> The marshal himself, for a moment, thought he was defeated, as I received an order to retreat, with my artillery, towards Valverde, and Baron Alten absolutely, by order, quitted the village for a moment. All this was, however, soon countermanded and rectified. (To D.-A.-G. dated 22 May, 1811.)

To Colonel Hardinge was due the credit of ordering the final and successful advance.

The artillery force at Albuera, on the side of the Allies, comprised:—

> (Sir A. Dickson to General Napier, dated 16 Dec. 1830, and to Lord Beresford, dated 19 March, 1831, in correction of the former.)
>
> Captain Lefebure's Troop of Royal Horse Artillery, consisting of 4 6-pounders.
>
> Captain Hawker's Brigade of Royal Artillery, now No. 4 Battery, 7 Brigade, R.A., consisting of 4 9-pounders.
>
> Captain Cleeve's Brigade, King's German Artillery, consisting of 5 6-pounders and 1 5½-inch howitzer.
>
> Captain Sympher's Brigade, King's German Artillery, consisting of 5 6-pounders and 1 5½-inch howitzer.
>
> Captain Braun's Brigade, Portuguese Artillery, consisting of 6 9-pounders.
>
> Captain Arriaga's Brigade, Portuguese Artillery, consisting of 6 6-pounders.
>
> Spanish Artillery, consisting of 6 6-pounders.

No explanation is given in any of the regimental records why Captain Lefebure had only four guns; it may, however, be assumed that his troop had not yet recovered the drain on its resources which was made on its arrival in the Peninsula, when it was called upon to fill up the vacancies in the Chestnut Troop.

A detailed statement of the services of the artillery at Albuera was forwarded by Major Dickson to General Howorth, for transmission to England, but, unfortunately, was lost. The student has, therefore, merely a private letter from Major Dickson to General Macleod to rely upon, whose details are, of course, less ample than could be wished. In it he mentioned that the cannonade on both sides was tremendous during the whole battle, and that probably on few such occasions had there been more casualties from artillery fire. Major Hartmann was in command of the British and German artillery; Major Dickson of the Portuguese. These latter behaved admirably.

Captain Lefebure's troop also distinguished itself, one gun having been, for a short time, taken, but afterwards recovered. Captain Hawker's brigade, from Major Dickson's personal observation, did great execution. General Cole spoke in the highest terms of Captain Sympher's brigade; and Captain Cleeve's guns went through a number of vicissitudes. Being placed on the hill, where the great attack was made, the whole of them fell into the enemy's hands, but were afterwards recovered, with the exception of one howitzer. They were admirably served until the French were actually amongst them; and then retreat was impossible, the enemy's cavalry having swept round the hill, and taken them in rear.

Modern battles may dwarf those of the Peninsula in point of the numbers engaged; but it is questionable if the British courage displayed at Albuera, and the proportionate losses to the number engaged, have ever been surpassed.

The severe fighting lasted about four hours; and in that time nearly 7000 of the Allies, and over 8000 French, were killed or wounded. On the side of the Allies, over 4000 of the casualties were among the British troops, only 1800 of the total number engaged being untouched. Major Dickson, in describing the scene, said that everyone declared they had never seen such a field; that on the hill where the great struggle had been, in the space of from 1000 to 1200 yards, there were certainly not less than 6000 lying dead or wounded. Napier's description of the field after the battle is characteristically graphic, and leaves an indelible impression on the reader's mind.

Such was the crippled and famished state of the Allies, that, had the French attacked again on the 17th, resistance would have been impossible. Fortunately, Soult resolved to retire; and Lord Wellington, reaching Albuera on the 19th, sent Beresford to watch his movements, while he himself proceeded to reinvest Badajoz. The order issued by Marshal Beresford, after the battle, included the following paragraph:—

> To Major Hartmann and Major Dickson, and to the officers and soldiers of the British, German, and Portuguese artillery, the greatest praise is due, and the marshal returns them his best thanks.

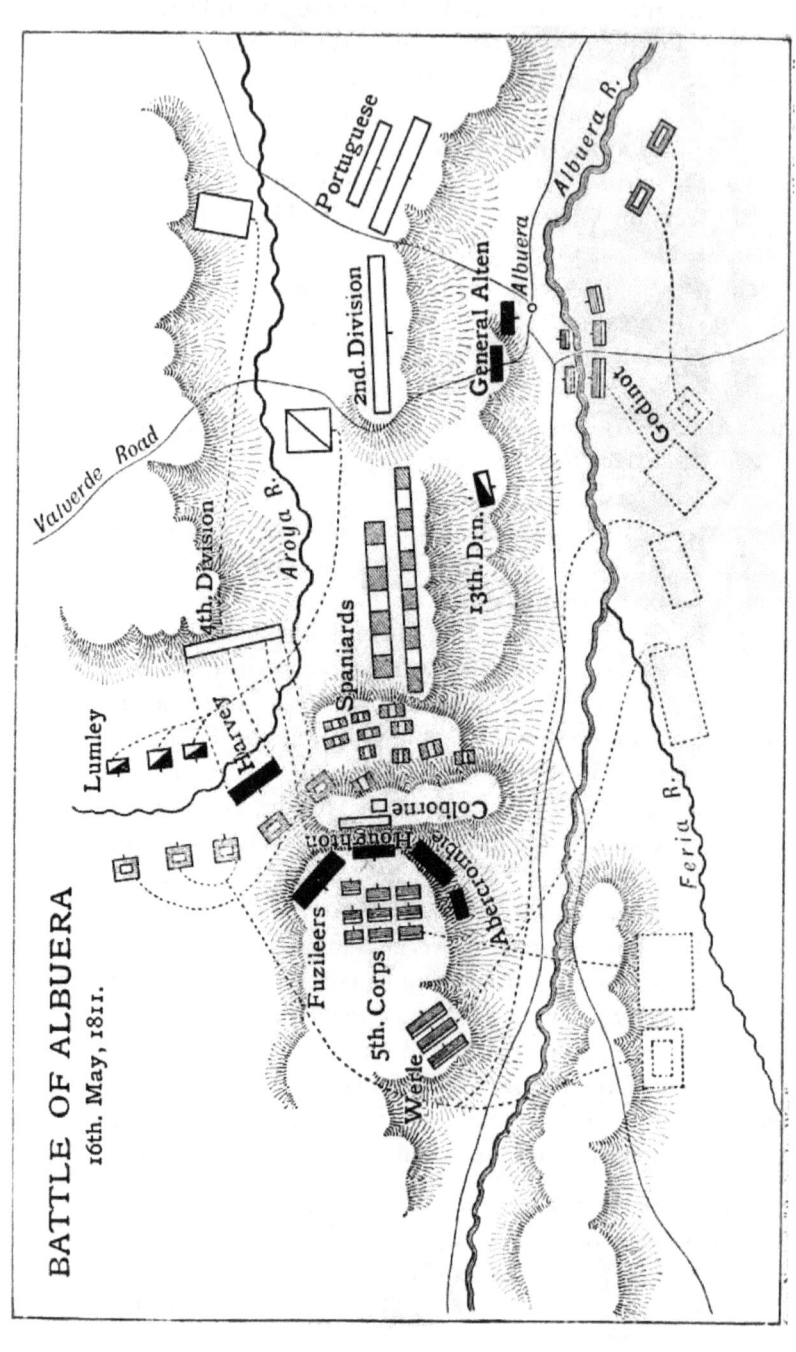

In forwarding to the Ordnance a copy of this order, Major Dickson, with soldierlike generosity, added:

> The Marshal's orders are not strong enough in favour of the Fusilier Brigade, who really saved the day. (To D.-A.-G. dated Elvas, 29 May, 1811.)

In Lord Wellington's letter to Admiral Berkeley, dated 20th May, 1811, he said that he considered the Battle of Albuera one of the most glorious and honourable *to the character of the troops* of any that had been fought during the war. In Marshal Beresford's report to Lord Wellington, dated 18th May, 1811, he said:

> I have every reason to speak favourably of the manner in which our artillery was served and fought. Captain Lefebure's troop of Horse Artillery did great execution.

On the 19th May, 1811, Lord Wellington, Colonel Fletcher, and Major Dickson arrived at Elvas, from Albuera, to make preparations for resuming the siege of Badajoz. Colonel Framingham had joined at headquarters, and assumed command of the Royal and other artillery; but Lord Wellington expressed a wish that Major Dickson should continue to direct all the arrangements for the siege, and communicate directly with himself.

This distinction caused no jealousy in Colonel Framingham's mind; on the other hand, that officer spoke of Major Dickson to Lord Wellington in the highest terms, and during the siege assisted him in every way. This was the beginning of a confidence between Lord Wellington and Major Dickson, which only increased as the war went on; and it is interesting to find, even thus early, the latter officer speak of his great chief as follows:

> I have transacted business with many generals, but never such an one as Lord Wellington, both for general knowledge, and attention to reason and suggestion. (To D.-A.-G. dated Elvas, 29 May, 1811.)

The story of the second unsuccessful siege of Badajoz, as of the first, may be prefaced by showing in a tabular form some of the more important artillery statistics connected with it. These have been extracted from the voluminous diary and almost daily correspondence of Major Dickson, on which the summary, given afterwards in the form of narrative, is also based.

TABLE B.

SECOND SIEGE OF BADAJOZ.

May 22, 1811.—The following was the appropriation of ordnance determined upon for the siege:—

CRISTOVAL ATTACK.		SOUTH, OR CASTLE ATTACK.	
24-pounders (brass)	12	24-pounders (brass)	14
16-pounders	4	10-inch howitzers	2
10-inch howitzers	2	8-inch howitzers	4
8-inch howitzers	4		—
	—		20
	22		

In reserve: 24-pounders (brass) 4

Detail of men for siege artillery:—

1st Regt. Portuguese Artillery: officers and men						100
2nd	,,	,,	,,	,,		100
3rd	,,	,,	,,	,,		300
Royal Artillery	,,	,,	,,	,,		110
						610

Many of these guns were replaced during the siege, as may be gathered from the following table:—

	24-pounders.	10-in. howitzers.	8-in. howitzers.	
Disabled by the fire of the enemy	3	..	3	
Disabled by the effects of their own fire	15	2	1	
Total	18	2	4	= 24.

The expenditure of ammunition during the siege was as follows:—

No. of rounds.	24-pr. round shot.	24-pr. grape shot.	16-pr. round shot.	Shell 10-in.	8-in.
North, or San Cristoval Attack	5950	200	1134	62	989
South, or Castle Attack	8419	441	..	640	1090
Total	14369	641	1134	702	2079

N.B.—The totals given above, and in the first table (Table A), agree with those given by Sir J. Jones; but the details here are more minute. It was but natural that Sir J. Jones, being an Engineer officer, should devote more space and detail to the labours of his own corps; but his artillery details in most sieges in the Peninsula were obtained from Sir A. Dickson and Sir J. May, and generally agree with the MSS. of the former.

On the 10th June Lord Wellington determined on raising the siege. On the night of the 30th May the trenches were opened on both attacks, and great progress was made. The whole of the guns for the batteries were also set in movement, with ammunition at the rate of 300 rounds per gun.

Captain Rainsford's company (now No. 7 Battery, 17th Brigade) having arrived from Lisbon, the artillerymen were divided as follows:—

ATTACK AGAINST THE CASTLE.

Major Dickson commanding.

			Officers' Names.
Royal Artillery	.. .. ..	55 officers and men.	Captain Rainsford.
1st Reg. Portuguese Artillery	100	,,	Captain Latham.
2nd ,,	,, 100	,,	Lieut. Saunders.
3rd ,,	,, 50	,,	Lieut. Willis.
	Total .. 305		

ATTACK AGAINST SAN CRISTOVAL.

Captain Cleeves, (K.G.A.), commanding under Major Dickson.

			Officers' Names.
Royal Artillery	.. .. ..	55 officers and men.	Lieut. Hawker.
3rd Reg. Portuguese Artillery	250	,,	Lieut. Connel.
	Total .. 305		

This gave but a very small relief; and Lord Wellington remarked, after the raising of the siege, that some of the Royal Artillery were indefatigable, and had never quitted their batteries. (Lord Wellington to the Earl of Liverpool, dated 13 June, 1811.)

Captain Latham was the 2nd Captain of Captain Hawker's Field Brigade, and was lent for the service of the siege train. Of him Major Dickson afterwards said, (to D.-A.-G. dated 13 June, 1811):

I assure you the assistance I derived from his professional knowledge and activity can never be forgotten by me.

Instances like this, and others hereafter to be mentioned, when even Horse Artillerymen served in the trenches, are arguments against the necessity of any *complete* divorce between the Field and Garrison branches of the artillery service. Of Captain Rainsford's company—now 7 Battery, 17th Brigade—Major Dickson wrote (*ibid*):

It was of wonderful assistance; it is an uncommon fine one.

On the 1st June the batteries on both sides were in a very forward state, and two on the north side received their armament. (To D.-A.-G. dated 20 June, 1811.) On the south side several guns were brought into the parallel, ready for mounting on the following night, when the batteries should be prepared for them. By half-past 8 o'clock on the morning of the 3rd everything was ready; and on the south side a fire was commenced with fourteen guns against the point which it was intended to breach. The fire was most vigorous, and, although well replied to, gave considerable hopes of success. Two of the guns became disabled from the effects of their own fire—a casualty whose recurrence during the siege was most monotonous.

On the north side No. 1 Battery was partly employed to breach San Cristoval, and partly to enfilade the castle front; No. 2 to breach San Cristoval; No. 3 against the defences of the same fort; and No. 4 to keep in check the *tête de pont* and enfilade the bridge. The breach in San Cristoval was begun in the shoulder to the right of the work, where it formed a dead angle; and in firing at this from a battery on the north side, a gun, on the very first night, became disabled by muzzle-drooping. These incidents will prepare the reader for the verdict of condemnation which was unanimously passed on the armament of the Allied siege trains in the earlier Peninsular sieges.

The howitzers were used as mortars, by taking the wheels off the carriages and inventing means of elevating them. Major Dickson had carefully tested what was the extreme elevation at which they could be used with safety, and found the *maximum* was an angle of 30°. Righteous, therefore, was his indignation when he learnt that, in spite of his own and Captain Cleeves' positive orders, an officer on duty on the north side, whom he tersely stigmatised as "a brute of a Portuguese Captain," had thought proper to elevate them to 40° or 42°, with a charge of 2½ lbs. to 3 lbs., the result being that both carriages were rendered entirely unserviceable, without any means of replacing them.

On the 4th June, the fire from the south side continued, but with less effect, the shot entering the wall without bringing down any part of it worthy of mention. On this day another gun was disabled at the vent by the effect of its own fire; and one was rendered unserviceable by that of the enemy. On the 4th very considerable progress was made in the breach at San Cristoval. During the night a new battery was opened in the south attack, and the guns from No. 1 Battery removed to it.

The 5th of June was a very disheartening day. The progress in the breach of the south attack was little more hopeful than on the 4th; and before afternoon the batteries were reduced—principally by their own fire—to nine serviceable guns. Major Dickson, therefore, proceeded to Lord Wellington, and obtained his permission to bring six *iron* 24-pounders from Elvas to the south attack. The breach in San Cristoval made by the north attack made apparent progress, but was not yet deemed practicable. Here, also, one or two of the guns showed symptoms of giving way.

On the 6th June, Lieutenant Hawker of the Royal Artillery was killed in the north attack:—a gallant young officer, of whom Major Dickson wrote, "He has never been out of No. 1 Battery from the commencement of the fire." In the south attack, a steady fire was kept up from the nine serviceable guns during this day, and more progress was made in breaching the wall, than had been effected during the two preceding days. Before night, the breach was practicable for a single person. In the evening, the breach at San Cristoval was also considered practicable for an assault, which accordingly was ordered, but repulsed. The enemy had previously cleared the breach, leaving a certain portion of the wall standing perpendicular: and their fire was so warm that the troops could not face it at the breach for any time. Attempts were made to escalade at one or two other points, but the ladders were too short; so, the party had to retire with a loss of 130 men.

On the 7th June, another battery of the south attack, No. 3, was completed; and the iron guns, having arrived from Elvas, were mounted during the night. The breach on this side was a little improved, but the resistance of the wall was far in excess of Major Dickson's expectations.

On the 8th June, under a fire from 16 24-pounders in the south attack, the breach on that side seemed large enough to admit several persons abreast. On the north side, the fire continued, but the breach was not yet deemed again practicable. During the night of the 8th, grape-shot was fired from the south side, but the Portuguese grape was extremely bad, and the enemy was successful in clearing away all the rubbish from the breach, in spite of the fire, leaving to view a considerable height of wall yet uninjured. A quantity of 3-pounder shot was therefore brought up from Elvas, which, when tied up in bags containing eight or ten each, formed a better description of grape. Various guns in both attacks showed symptoms of distress during this day.

On the 9th June, there were only twelve or thirteen guns left serviceable on the south side after the day's firing, but the breach was decidedly larger, and grape was fired all night to prevent the enemy working at it. On the north side, there were only eight or nine guns left undisabled in in the evening, but the breach at San Cristoval was pronounced practicable; and another attempt was made, at 9 o'clock, to carry it by assault. It was, however, again repulsed; for it was found that, notwithstanding the appearance of the breach, there was a perpendicular wall about 6 or 7 feet high still standing, which had been concealed from view by the counterscarp: and the enemy had taken every precaution to keep it clear of the *debris* of the breach. The gallantry of the assailants was as great, as the defence of the French was resolute. The ladders were thrown down—grenades thrown among the stormers in great abundance, and masses of stone hurled down upon them. (Major Dickson to D.-A.-G. 26 June, 1811) With the loss of 150 men, the assailants were obliged to retire.

On the following morning it was found that the grape-shot from the south attack had been successful in preventing the enemy from working at the breach, and preparations for resuming the battering had been ordered, when Major Dickson received a summons from Lord Wellington. He met him with Colonel Fletcher on the north side: and they were informed that he had decided on raising the siege. (Dickson's MSS.) He mentioned his reasons; but he particularly pointed out the impossibility of getting possession of San Cristoval without advancing to the crest of the *glacis*;—the still difficult situation of the main breach on the south side;—the imprudence of attempting it, even when practicable, without first having Cristoval;—the strong entrenchments which the enemy had had time to construct within the breach;—and finally the approach of the enemy in such force that prudence would not allow him to be caught by them in the midst of a siege.

Soult was at this time in force at Llerena, and Drouet's corps was reported as having joined him; while the Northern French Army under Marmont was also in motion. (Major Dickson to D.-A.-G. Elvas, 13 June, 1811)

Major Dickson immediately set to work, and by the evening of the 12th the whole of the guns, stores, and ammunition were either in Elvas again, or at such a distance as to be in perfect safety in all circumstances.

Major Dickson wrote to General Macleod:

> Thus, ended this siege, in which everything that artillery could do was done, considering our miserable means; and this Lord

Wellington was good enough to express, both to Colonel Framingham and myself. The brass guns could not stand the necessary fire, and their destruction, I am of opinion, was considerably occasioned by the lowness of the shot, which generally had so much windage that you could put your fingers in between the shot and the bore.... On the whole I have to observe that our batteries were too far off....The whole principle of the attack was founded on the supposed weakness of the castle wall, which it was thought could be beat down at a distance. On discovering the difficulty of this, the batteries were thrown forward as far as they could, at the same time avoiding the fire of the modern fronts, nor could they be advanced farther until Cristoval was in our hands. Indeed, if that had been carried, I think we should have got the place.... Lord Wellington was good enough to say that everything that could be done on our parts, had been done.

The casualties among the artillery during the siege were as follows:—

		Killed.	Wounded.
Officers, Royal Artillery	Lieut. E. Hawker, killed.		
	Lieut. W. Saunders, wounded.		
Officers, Portuguese Artillery	Captain Barreiros, wounded.		
	Lieut. Lopez, wounded dangerously.		
N.-C. officers and men, Royal Artillery		0	4
" " Portuguese Artillery		6	28
	Total	6	32

The total loss of the Allies amounted to 118 killed, and 367 wounded and taken prisoners.

In his despatch to Lord Liverpool, announcing the raising of the siege, in addition to expressing his great satisfaction with the corps, Lord Wellington said that the British service had derived great advantage in the different operations against Badajoz from Major Dickson's zeal, activity, and intelligence.

The subsequent sieges of Ciudad Rodrigo and of Badajoz, which took place in 1812, were in marked contrast to those described in this chapter; and the rapidity with which the breaches were then made was mainly due to the employment of iron ordnance from England, instead of the miserable brass Portuguese guns which were employed in the sieges of 1811.

★★★★★★

In answer to an inquiry from General Macleod about these guns, Major Dickson, writing from Oporto, on 27 Aug. 1811, said: "They were brass Portuguese guns of the time of John IV. and his son Alfonso, bearing dates 1646, 1652, and 1653, &c.; also, some Spanish guns of Philips III. and IV.—dates 1620, 1636, &c."

★★★★★★

Of these guns, Lord Wellington truly said (to Lord Liverpool, 13 June, 1811), that they were very ancient and incomplete, and that their fire was very uncertain. It had at first been intended to fire at the rate of 120 rounds a gun *per diem*: but that was soon found to be impossible with the wretched brass pieces at the disposal of Major Dickson. It was therefore reduced to 80 rounds; but even with this limited expenditure the guns were repeatedly disabled by the effect of their own fire.

The Peninsular sieges cannot be thoroughly understood without two points being borne in mind. First, the besieged cities belonged to, and were inhabited by, the allies of England, and the war was only with the garrison. The artillery fire, therefore, was confined to breaching, and dismounting the ordnance in battery—not used for bombardment. Secondly, the sieges were mere episodes in Wellington's general operations, not goals to which these operations tended. Hence, in 1811, the raising of sieges, without hesitation, after but a brief continuance; and hence, also, in 1812, the rapidity and loss of life with which he stormed cities, rather than complicate his plans by indulging in siege operations of a longer and, perhaps, more regular description.

CHAPTER 7

Ciudad Rodrigo and Badajoz

The enemy approaching in force, after the raising of the second siege of Badajoz, the Allies crossed the river on the 17th June, 1811, and on the 19th encamped between Elvas and Campo Maior. Elvas had been put in a state of siege, and a position had been marked out behind Campo Maior, in case the French should show any inclination to attack. The bold front which Lord Wellington here showed deceived the two French marshals, Marmont and Soult, who had now united their armies, and entered Badajoz in triumph congratulating its gallant governor, Philippon. They concluded that he must have received great reinforcements; and although they crossed the Guadiana with a great body of cavalry supported with infantry, and one or two small affairs with the outposts took place—they declined a general engagement. (Major Dickson to D.-A.-Gen. dated 26 June, 1811), want of *entente cordiale* between Marmont and Soult led soon to a separation—the latter moving towards Seville, whither Wellington despatched Blake's Spanish troops—and the former marching away by the valley of the Tagus towards Almaraz. Thus, relieved of their presence, Lord Wellington took up his quarters at Pontalegre, and allowed his army to have some repose after its recent exertions. (Cust.)

This seems a favourable moment for placing before the reader a tabular return which shows the gradual increase in the artillery element of Lord Wellington's army in the Peninsula. Prepared from the monthly returns, it shows the numbers at different periods, distinguishing between the Royal and Foreign Artilleries. The point which will doubtless strike the reader most is the steady increase in the force of Horse Artillery and artillery drivers, which took place; marking the growing recognition of that which had hitherto been overlooked to a great extent—the value of mobility in Field Artillery.

Return of the Royal, British and German Artillery attached to the Army under the Command of the Duke of Wellington in the Peninsula and France at the undermentioned periods.

(Extracted from the Monthly Returns.)

	1811.		1812.			1813.			1814.	
	March.	May.	January.	April.	May.	July.	December.	January.	April.
1. General, Field, and Staff Officers, not included on Company Rolls	8	8	9	10	11	11	9	10	8
2. Royal Horse Artillery	495	499	699	728	926	988	1,016	1,007	1,012
3. Royal Foot Artillery	884	1,111	996	1,327	1,876	1,862	1,950	1,985	1,966
4. Royal Artillery Drivers	777	858	1,040	1,159	2,154	2,150	2,683	2,719	2,734
5. Ordnance Medical Staff	9	10	13	18	27	26	29	29	29
6. Field Train or Commissariat Department of the Ordnance	84	86	129	121	130	128	153	154	148
General Total of Royal British Artillery	2,257	2,572	2,891	3,363	5,124	5,165	5,840	5,904	5,897
King's German Artillery	421	412	449	434	450	446	439	439	412

N.B.—The Field Train Department attached to the Engineers is not included, as it did not appear in the Monthly Returns of the Artillery.

General Howorth vacated the command of the artillery in the Peninsula in July 1811, being obliged to return to England on account of ill-health—and was shortly afterwards succeeded by General Borthwick. This officer was wounded at Ciudad Rodrigo, and returned to England—a coolness having sprung up between him and Lord Wellington, which recurred with one of his successors, and continued until the command of the artillery devolved upon his favourite, then Colonel Dickson, a few months after the siege of Burgos.

On the 19th July, 1811, Lord Wellington sent for Colonel Fletcher, Colonel Framingham, and Major Dickson, and informed them that it was his intention to attempt the siege of Ciudad Rodrigo; and after a little conversation as to the means of transport, &c., he desired Major Dickson to proceed to Oporto, to superintend the conveyance of the English battering train up the Douro to Lamego, and thence by land to Francoso, whence it would also be conveyed by land to its final destination. (Major Dickson to D.-A.-G. dated Castel Branco, 23 Jul. 1811)

This battering train had arrived in Lisbon in the first instance, and had been carried secretly to Oporto, with a view to the proposed siege of Ciudad Rodrigo, its ostensible destination being Cadiz. (This battering train consisted of 78 pieces, according to Sir J. T. Jones, but, as will be seen presently, only 64 pieces went up the country with Major Dickson from Oporto.) Two new companies of artillery which had arrived in Lisbon were now ordered to Oporto to assist Major Dickson. In all these arrangements Lord Wellington underrated the strength of the French Army in the north of the Peninsula.

Major Dickson reached Almeida, on his way to Oporto, on the 28th July, and arrived at the latter place on the 3rd August, where he found Captain Bredin's and Captain Glubb's companies—later H Battery, 1st Brigade, and 5 Battery 5th Brigade—waiting his orders. (To D.-A.-Gen. dated 27 Aug. 1811.) Before the 13th the whole of the train had been embarked in boats, about 160 in number, and despatched to Lamego; but the work and the climate proved too much for Major Dickson, and before he could follow the train he was struck down with a violent fever, accompanied by delirium.

When first attacked, he requested Lord Wellington to send someone to take up his duties, and, accordingly, his friend Captain May was sent, and superintended the movement of the train until the 5th September, when the gallant Dickson, only half recovered, and travelling in a litter, arrived at Lamego. Here he found that all the guns and stores had marched for Villa da Ponte, and that Captain May was on the point of following them.

On the 8th Major Dickson left Lamego, and reached Villa da Ponte on the 10th, where he fell an immediate victim to a relapse of fever, which lasted acutely several days. (Major Dickson to D.-A.-G. dated Villa da Ponte, 13 Sept. 1811.) Captain Bredin's company had, in the meantime, been recalled to the headquarters of the army, to take over the brigade of guns from Captain Thompson's, which was almost *hors de combat* from sickness. (Captain Thompson's company was later employed in the operations on the east of Spain.) The troops left with the battering train were therefore reduced to Captain Glubb's company of Royal Artillery, about 250 Portuguese artillery, and from 1200 to 1400 Portuguese Militia, intended to assist on the march. Captain Holcombe's company of Royal Artillery was hourly expected. That company was later No. 4 Battery 2nd Brigade.

On the march, the battering train had been arranged by Captain May as follows. It was divided, as far as the ordnance was concerned, into five divisions; each gun marched with 350 rounds, and each howitzer and mortar with 160 rounds. (Major Dickson to D.-A.-G. dated Villa da Ponte, 20 Sept. 1811.) An officer was placed in charge of each division, and each division marched separately. The remaining stores and ammunition requisite to furnish a total of 800 rounds per gun, and 400 for each howitzer and mortar, were under the charge of the Commissary and other officers, and marched in rear.

While at Villa da Ponte, awaiting orders from Lord Wellington for a further advance, Major Dickson's correspondence was of a nature which reveals to the reader more of the personal element than his letters, as a rule, allow to become visible. The alternate hoping and despairing as to orders for advance,—the *ennui* produced by enforced idleness,—the impetuous way in which he would fling himself into professional discussions with General Macleod, merely to occupy his leisure—the spasmodic fits of zeal in improving the arrangement of the immense train,—all unite to present to the reader a very vivid picture of him whose hand, so long still, penned these faded letters. His recurring attacks of fever—followed by apologies like the following:

> The fact is, when I am well, I forget all, take violent exercise at all times and seasons, and knock myself up; but I am determined to be more careful in future.

Followed by an inevitable relapse, in proof of the failure of his good resolutions—combine to bring before the reader a very lovable picture of a very earnest man. It is by such study alone that the artilleryman can realise the characters of the great among his predecessors in the corps, and by such links that he can bind them to himself with that almost family tie, of which the Regimental union is but an expansion.

The extent of the battering train under Major Dickson's command was as follows:—34 24-pounders, 4 18-pounders, 16 iron 5½-inch howitzers, 2 8-inch howitzers, and 8 10-inch mortars; and much of his leisure at Villa da Ponte was devoted to improving and renewing the somewhat shattered carriages of this ordnance. (To D.-A.-G. dated 27 Sept. 1811.)

On the 16th November he received an order from Lord Wellington to commence moving the battering train to Almeida; and by the 21st the last division, spare carriages, &c., had left. (To D.-A.-G. dated 22 Nov. 1811.)

The march was most successful. No fewer than 1100 bullocks were employed for the divisions alone, apart from the reserve of stores; and in no case did the march occupy more than six days, although the country was very mountainous; nor did a single accident occur. (To D.-A.-G. dated 4 Dec. 1811.) The bringing up the reserve of ammunition and stores was delayed by want of means of conveyance; and pending its arrival, Lord Wellington requested Major Dickson to superintend the unspiking of the ordnance in Almeida, and the placing the batteries in a state of defence. In this occupation the reader is requested to leave him while he returns to the movements of Lord Wellington, which were now assuming an active form.

The English general had moved northward, with the view of besieging Ciudad Rodrigo; and a summary of his movements may be given from some admirable MS. letters, written by Captain May on his return to the headquarters of the army. On the 23rd September the enemy's advanced guard was near Ciudad Rodrigo. The French Army was under Marmont and Dorsenne, and numbered 60,000 men, including 6000 cavalry. On the 24th, the whole of this cavalry had crossed the Agueda, about 10,000 infantry remaining on the other side. On the 25th the enemy advanced, and Wellington disputed the ground, retiring gradually to the position at Fuente de Guinaldo. In this advance the enemy's cavalry and artillery were principally engaged; and on the side of the Allies, the cavalry, Portuguese artillery, and Cole's and Picton's divisions of infantry.

During this forward movement the enemy, by a charge of cavalry, gained possession of five Portuguese guns, which, however, were

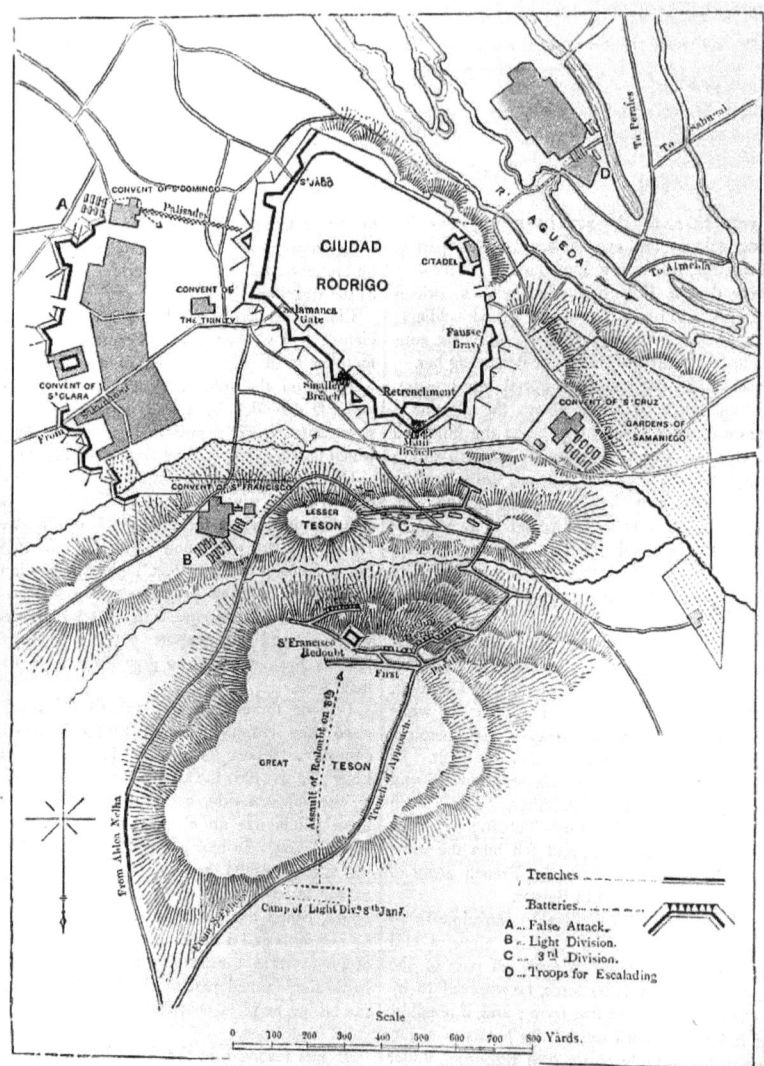

PLAN OF THE ASSAULT ON CIUDAD RODRIGO.

speedily recaptured by the 5th Regiment of Foot, in a most gallant and intrepid manner. On the 26th, the Allies remained all day in the position of Guinaldo, which extended from the right and front of the town for four miles towards Ituero, the woods being occupied by two Infantry brigades from the right down to the Agueda. Thus posted, they witnessed the arrival of the whole French Army, the last of which did not arrive until sunset. On satisfying himself as to their numbers, and bearing in mind the great extent of country to be watched, Lord Wellington determined to retire in the evening to a more favourable position for concentration and battle.

The army, therefore, began its march to the rear at 10 p.m., and next day, the 27th, everything was in the neighbourhood of the new position, which occupied a length of about six miles. The left was near Reudon, on the Coa, and the right in the rear of Çouta, resting on the mountains. When daylight revealed to the enemy the masterly retreat which had taken place, some cavalry and infantry were pressed forward, and the Allied piquets were driven in; but Wellington, suddenly assuming the offensive, drove them back from Alfaites to Aldea da Ponte, his troops occupying the latter village. After sunset, however, the enemy advanced in such force, in front and also on the flanks of the village, that the officer commanding there wisely withdrew his troops to Alfaites. This final advance of the French was made to cover a retreat which had now been determined on.

On the morning of the 28th nothing could be seen of them; and on the 29th it was learnt that they were moving back on Ciudad Rodrigo. After they had thrown provisions into that city, they continued to retire, and went into cantonments in the neighbourhood of Salamanca. The British Army did the same between the Coa and the Agueda, Lord Wellington, with his headquarters at Freneda, keeping watch on the city which he had determined to take.

The only brilliant affair which took place between this time and the successful sieges, which will now have to be mentioned, was the surprise of Girard's division by General Hill, at Arroyo de Molinos. As, however, the artillery with Hill's force was Portuguese—Major Hawker's 9-pounder brigade of Royal Artillery having been unable to get up on account of the state of the roads—its further notice in this work will be unnecessary.

Taking advantage of the French troops being scattered in their cantonments, and having ascertained that large reinforcements from Marmont's army had been detached to Valencia, Lord Wellington re-

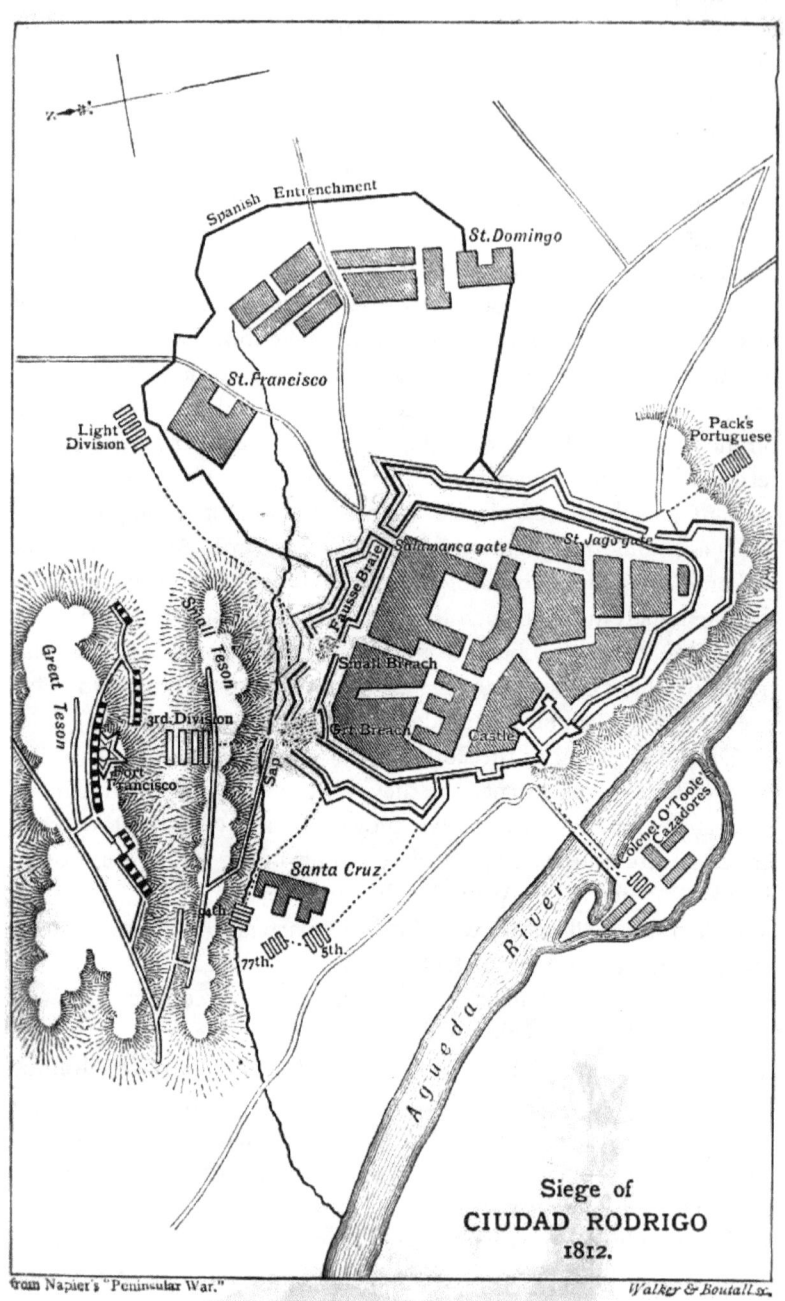

solved on a short, sharp siege of Ciudad Rodrigo. In the end of December, he sent for Major Dickson, and directed him to move forward the battering train and stores from Almeida, Galegos being made the intermediate depot. (Major Dickson to D.-A.-G. 1 Jan. 1812.) To the latter place the army headquarters were moved on the 7th July.314

The main interest to the military reader in the sieges of Ciudad Rodrigo and Badajoz, in 1812, attaches to the gallantry of the Infantry. The monotonous, albeit short-lived, work in the batteries is drowned in the recollection of the scenes of valour at the final assault. In these pages, therefore, the artillery share in the sieges will assume, of necessity, the form of a few dry statistics.

The artillery present at the siege included 185 of the Royal Artillery and 370 of the Portuguese. The names of the officers of the Royal Artillery who were present were General Borthwick, Major Dickson, Captains Holcombe, Thompson, Power, Dundas, and Dyneley; Lieutenants Bourchier, Love, Johnstone, Ingilby, Smith, and Grimes; and Captain May, Brigade-Major.

The batteries opened in the afternoon of the 14th January, 1812, the guns having narrowly escaped being spiked in the morning of that day. On the night of the 19th, the breaches were pronounced practicable, and Wellington announced in orders, "Ciudad Rodrigo *must* be stormed this evening." Except on the 16th and part of the 17th, the weather was clear and admirably suited for artillery practice, and the batteries were in action daily for an average of eight and a half hours.

The guns employed were as follows:—On January 14th, 20 24-pounders and 2 18-pounders; on January 15th, 23 24-pounders and 2 18-pounders; on January 16th and 17th, the same; on January 18th, 30 24-pounders and 2 18-pounders; and on January 19, 30 24-pounders. (According to Sir J. Jones, the guns in action on the 19th were 29 24-prs. and 1 18-pr.; but Sir A. Dickson, who was in charge of the artillery, says as above. The difference is, however, infinitesimal.)

The expenditure of ammunition during this short siege was as follows—the total number of guns in battery having been 34 24-pounders, and 4 18-pounders:—

24-pr. guns: Round shot, 8950. Rounds expended per gun, 263.
18-pr. guns: Round shot, 565. Rounds expended per gun, 141.

The absence of mortars and howitzers from this siege was explained by the increased amount of transport required for shell, compared with shot, and by the fact that Lord Wellington had resolved on an assault the moment a breach was practicable, without any other siege operations. Shot were, therefore, all that was necessary, except for keeping the enemy from working at the breach.

The following extract from a letter written by Major Dickson to the D.-A.-G. dated 29 Jan. 1812, after the siege, is interesting:—

> Lord Wellington has certainly made a most brilliant *coup*, and, I am convinced, astonished the enemy by the rapidity of his operations. They intended to relieve the place and raise the siege about this day (29th January). We were certainly favoured by the most delightful weather—excessively cold, but perfectly dry. It was not even necessary to put the powder under the laboratory tents, which I was enabled to spare to keep the poor fellows from the pinching frost; for we were nearly without cover. . . . I am hard pressed for time, but I must say a word in favour of our fine fellows of the corps. They were (Portuguese and all) at relief and relief, off and on; but nothing could exceed their zeal and activity, and their work speaks for itself. *Never was better practice made.* I had only 430 artillerymen of both nations—about 130 British, and the rest Portuguese. We had somewhere more than 50 artillerymen killed and wounded, but no officer materially hurt. The latter days, to make it up, I had some help from our own field artillery:—part of Lawson's company was one day in the trenches, and part of Sympher's German company another.

The actual number of killed and wounded between the 14th and 19th January (MS. Return dated 26 Jan. 1812)—while the siege lasted,—was as follows, excluding Portuguese artillery, (N.B. Sir J. Jones's statement *includes* the Portuguese artillery):—

> Captains Dyneley and Power, wounded.
>
> Captain Glubb's company, now 5 Battery, 5th Brigade; 2 gunners died of their wounds; 2 gunners wounded slightly.
>
> Captain Holcombe's company, now 4 Battery, 2nd Brigade; 1 gunner killed; 17 non-commissioned officers and men wounded.
>
> Captain Lawson's company, now H Battery, 8th Brigade; 1 gunner died of his wounds; 2 gunners wounded.
>
> Captain Sympher's company (K.G.A.); 1 gunner killed; 3 gunners wounded.
>
> The ammunition expended was:—

8950 rounds from 24-pounders, and 565 from 18-pounders.

In Lord Wellington's despatch to Lord Liverpool, dated 20 Jan. 1812, announcing the successful termination of the siege, he—after extolling Major Dickson's conduct of the artillery operations—proceeded to say:

> The rapid execution produced by the well-directed fire kept up from our batteries affords the best proof of the merits of the officers and men of the Royal Artillery, and of the Portuguese artillery, employed on this occasion; but I must particularly mention Brigade-Major May, and Captains Holcombe, Power, Dyneley, and Dundas, of the Royal Artillery.

General Borthwick's name is not mentioned, either in the despatch or among the wounded; but he appears in Kane's list—generally most accurate in its details—as having been in command of the artillery, and also as having been wounded, during the siege.

Ciudad Rodrigo had hardly fallen, before Lord Wellington resolved to attempt a third siege of Badajoz—now that he had suitable ordnance. He ordered Major Dickson to proceed on the 30th January to Setubal, calling at Elvas to make some necessary arrangements. From Setubal he was directed to send 16 24-pounders of a new battering train, which had arrived, to Elvas—as well as 20 guns of the same calibre, which were to be furnished from the navy.

The whole of these guns were to travel on block carriages. The difficulty of sending the heavy guns of the train at Almeida to Elvas led to this arrangement: but it was decided to send the 24-pounder howitzers, as being much lighter, and also a number of 24-pounder carriages, which were stored at Almeida. By this means it was hoped to have speedily equipped at Elvas a new battering train of 36 iron 24-pounder guns, and 16 24-pounder howitzers—an armament very different from the brass Portuguese guns which had assailed the stronghold of Philippon twice before.

So incessant was the work which now devolved on Major Dickson that he had no time for correspondence, and there is a great blank, where the student had hoped to find much that was interesting. From other sources, therefore, the artillery details of a siege, which can never be forgotten, must be procured. As at Ciudad Rodrigo, the Infantry share in the operations dwarfs all other;—but it dwarfs it to even a greater extent. The story of the storming of Badajoz is one which will thrill the heart of every Briton for all time; which will bind together

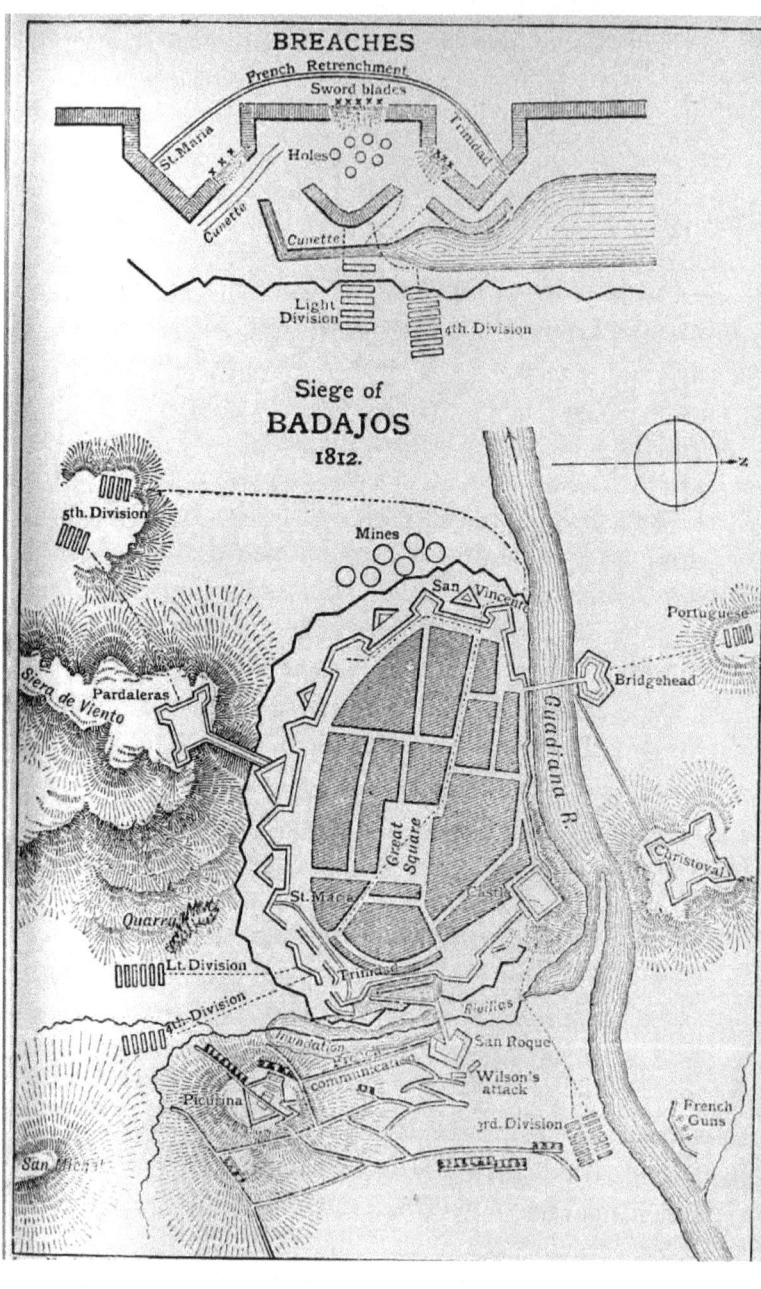

by sacred memories the regiments which were so nobly represented on that day; and which will impress on all, who study it, the truth of Napier's words, that "a British Army bears with it an awful power."

The scene on the night of the 6th April, 1812, was one before which the energy, zeal, and proficiency of the artillery on the preceding days pale away into nothingness; and the chronicling of their humble statistics seems almost an impertinence. For, the night of the 6th was, indeed, one in which "many died, and there was much glory;" (Napier), it was one in which death took many and hideous forms,—"the slain dying not all suddenly, nor by one manner of death; some perishing by steel, some by shot, some by water, some crushed and mangled by heavy weights, some trampled upon, some dashed to atoms by fiery explosions;" and yet it was a night in which the most cruel death was fair to look on,—because hallowed by marvellous courage and rare devotion.

The breaches, which were rendered famous by this combat "so fiercely fought, so terribly won," were virtually made between the 30th March and the 6th April. (Tables published by an officer of the artillery in 1819.) On the 30th March 8 18-pounders were in action for purely breaching purposes; on the following day, this number was increased, by 12 24-pounders, and 6 18-pounders, to 26 guns; and these remained in action, for 13 hours a day, until the storming of the place. Of round shot, alone, no fewer than 18,832 24-pr., and 13,029 18-pr., were expended during the short siege; besides 1163 24-pounder grape shot, and 496 of the same from the 18-pounders. Of the round shot, 23,896 were employed in forming the three breaches. Besides the breaching guns, there were 10 24-pounder and 18-pounder guns, and 16 5½-inch howitzers, employed for enfilading and other fire. From the last mentioned, 507 common shell and 1319 spherical case were fired during the siege.

The three breaches were rendered practicable from a distance of between 600 and 700 yards; and the curtain breach was made in one day, the day of the assault. To the rapidity of the making of this breach was much of the success in the final storming due; because, had several days been required, measures would have been adopted by the defenders during the intervening nights to render it wholly impracticable. In making this curtain breach, 14 guns were employed, with an expenditure of 3514 rounds. (Tables published by an officer of the artillery in 1819.)

Colonel Framingham commanded the Allied artillery during the siege, but Major Dickson virtually directed the operations. From a rough MS. diary in the Record Office, in the handwriting of the latter officer, it would appear that the strength of the artillery was as follows:—

	N.-C. officers and men.
Captain Holcombe's company	110
Captain Gardiner's ditto[1]	110
Captain Glubb's (commanded by Captain Power) company	78
Captain Rettberg's (King's German Artillery) ditto	30

[1] Now No. 7 Battery, 17th Brigade R.A., Captain Gardiner having been posted *vice* Raynsford.

There were also 377 of the 3rd Regiment, and 249 of the 2nd Regiment, of Portuguese Artillery.

In his despatch to Lord Liverpool, 7 April, 1812, after the storming of the city, Lord Wellington said:

> Major Dickson conducted the details of the artillery service during this siege, as well as upon former occasions, under the general superintendence of Lieut.-Colonel Framingham, who, since the absence of Major-General Borthwick, has commanded the artillery with this army. I cannot sufficiently applaud the officers and soldiers of the British and Portuguese artillery during this siege, particularly Lieut.-Colonel Robe, who opened the breaching batteries, Majors May and Holcombe, Captain Gardiner and Lieutenant Bourchier, of the Royal Artillery; Captain de Rettberg, of the King's German Artillery; and Major Tulloh, of the Portuguese. Adverting to the extent of the details of the Ordnance Department during this siege, to the difficulty of weather, &c., with which Major Dickson had to contend, I must mention him most particularly to your Lordship.

Besides the officers named in the despatch, there were present in the batteries Captains Power, Latham, Dundas, and Dansey; and Lieutenants Weston, Connel, Grimes, and Love.

The loss of the Royal Artillery during the siege was as follows:—

Killed: Captain Latham, Lieutenant Connel, and 23 non-commissioned officers and men.

Wounded: Captain Dundas, Lieutenants Grimes and Love, and 48 non-commissioned officers and men.

N.B These numbers, which differ from those given by Napier, are taken from the official MS. Regimental Returns prepared immediately after the siege, which include all, even *slightly* wounded. Doubtless many such were not included in the Army returns.

Major Tulloh, an officer of the Royal Artillery attached to the Portuguese, was also wounded.

The troops of Horse Artillery commanded by Majors Bull and Ross were present at the investment and siege of Badajoz; and although not included in the detail out by Major Dickson for duty in the trenches, it is evident that they must have taken part in the operations, for Major Ross was severely wounded by a grape-shot. But his name does not appear in Lord Wellington's lists. (Major Ross to Sir H. Dalrymple, 8 April, 1812.)

The losses in the other arms of the service employed in the siege were very great. No fewer than 5000 officers and men fell during the siege, and of that number 3500 fell on the night of the 6th April. Sixty officers and upwards of seven hundred men were slain on the spot.

No wonder that:

> When the extent of the night's havoc was made known to Lord Wellington, the firmness of his nature gave way for a moment, and the pride of conquest yielded to a passionate burst of grief for the loss of his gallant soldiers. (Napier.)

The recollections of such a night are among the greatest treasures which an army can cherish. Even the reaction after success, the irregularities and licence displayed by the troops in the captured city, while certainly dimming, could not permanently injure the glory of the marvellous assault. Such traditions are a weapon for discipline, which only a soldier can estimate. Inspired by them, men will feed the lamp of their present lives with the oil of past glory, and strain every nerve to make the flame burn pure and clear.

Perhaps one of the highest motives, which can influence a soldier, is the desire to be worthy of his predecessors, and true to the reputation which they have earned for their corps. It carries him at once out of himself, and introduces an unselfish element even into his own ambition and aims. Only those who have served long in a regiment which they love can understand the fond jealousy for its honour, which will inspire its members. Its history never dies; the deeds of the years that are gone are the living possession of all; the valour which may have been exhibited in former days lives again in the breasts of those, who hunger for an opportunity of similar display; and the men who, by their courage and skill, may have earned honour for their corps, still haunt in no shadowy form the dreams of the young aspirant, and the memories of the old.

Note.—In alluding to the services of the two scientific corps at this siege of Badajoz, Sir J. Jones wrote that "as an engineer and artillery operation, it succeeded to the utmost letter."

CHAPTER 8

Salamanca and Burgos

After the fall of Badajoz, Lord Wellington decided on marching northward, and carrying the war into Spain. In the meantime, however, he directed General Hill to storm the forts at Almaraz, a great French depot—and so weaken the chance of union between the armies of the North and South. Colonel Dickson was detailed as commanding officer of the artillery for this service, which consisted of a brigade of 24-pounder howitzers, horsed by the mules of one of the Portuguese Field Brigades, and manned by Captain Glubb's company of the Royal Artillery, and a Portuguese company. (The rank of lieut.-colonel had at first been conferred on Colonel Dickson by the Portuguese government. He received the same—by brevet—from the English Government on 27th April, 1812.)

The ammunition, which was carried in Spanish mule carts, comprised 600 24-pounder round shot, 300 5½-inch common shells, 240 5½-inch spherical, and 5½-inch common—case shot. (To D.-A.-G. dated, Elvas, 6 May, 1812.)

Six pontoons accompanied the guns on this expedition, which was perfectly successful; and in which General Hill was pleased to say that he found the exertions of Colonel Dickson, and his officers and men, to be unwearied. (General Sir R. Hill to Lord Wellington, dated 21 May, 1812.)

Before turning to Lord Wellington's movements in the north, which culminated in the Battle of Salamanca, and the temporary occupation of Madrid, a statement of the strength of the artillery force of England during this eventful year may possibly be found interesting. Two dates have been chosen, and it will be seen that the numbers—already large in the beginning of the year—continued to increase; more especially in the item of drivers for the brigades in the Peninsula.

These tables give one an idea of the strain on the resources of England which was caused by the Peninsular War. No fewer than 1811 recruits joined the artillery alone, and over 1200 became non-effective from various causes during the same period. (MS. 'Wear and Tear Return' of the regiment for 1811.)

RETURN of the ARTILLERY FORCES OF ENGLAND on the 25th June, 1812, distinguishing the ROYAL ARTILLERY from the ROYAL HORSE ARTILLERY, and specifying the Numbers serving at home and abroad.

	At Home.		Abroad.		Total.	
	Officers.	N.-C. Officers and Men.	Officers.	N.-C. Officers and Men.	Officers.	N.-Com. Officers and Men.
Royal Horse Artillery . .	49	1,417	21	696	70	2,113
Royal Artillery	391	8,812	331	6,599	722	15,411
R. A. Drivers	63	3,521	24	1,950	87	5,471
King's German Artillery .	21	430	28	587	49	1,017
Royal Foreign Artillery .	6	158	15	327	21	485
General Total . .	..	..	..	..	949	24,497

RETURN of the ARTILLERY FORCES of ENGLAND on 25th Dec. 1812, &c.

Royal Horse Artillery . .	51	1,452	19	733	70	2,185
Royal Artillery	405	8,723	333	6,817	738	15,540
R. A. Drivers	70	3,554	25	2,305	95	5,859
King's German Artillery .	21	392	27	638	48	1,030
Royal Foreign Artillery .	7	123	15	348	22	471
General Total . .	..	..	..	..	973	25,085

The year 1812 was the most eventful in the Peninsular War. Already marked by the successful sieges described in the last chapter, it was to be distinguished by events, both in Spain and elsewhere, which were to have a great effect on subsequent hostilities. The English general—who opened the year with an unexpected attack on Ciudad Rodrigo—was destined, ere it should be much more than half over, to defeat his enemy in a pitched battle, drive him ignominiously before him, and enter the capital of Spain in triumph. These successes were to be further heightened by Soult raising the long-continued siege of Cadiz, in alarm at the intelligence of the French disasters in the north. Scarcely, however, were these advantages to be realised, ere the whole picture should change.

The conqueror at Ciudad Rodrigo and Badajoz should find himself fretting hopelessly before the castle of Burgos; and the general, who entered Madrid in triumph at the head of a victorious army, should lead that same army—in disorder and semi-mutiny—from Salamanca to Portugal, in retreat. The light and shade in the military operations of the Peninsula were also to be intensified by news from without, which should mightily affect the powers whose armies had faced one another for so many years. In the colds of Russia, the greatest army that even Napoleon had ever commanded, should dissolve, as utterly as the snows amid which they died should melt before the strengthening sun.

It was, indeed, a year of great events: but of these the two with which this history has most interest were the Battle of Salamanca and the siege of Burgos.

Colonel Dickson, with the brigade of howitzers which he had commanded at Almaraz, left Elvas on the 5th June to join Lord Wellington's army in the north. Passing the Tagus at Alcantara, he joined the army at Salamanca by way of Zarza, Fuente Guinalda, and Ciudad Rodrigo. (Colonel Dickson to D.-A.-Gen. dated Orbada, 30 June, 1812.) Wellington was engaged at this time, with very limited means, in endeavouring to reduce the French Fort St. Vincent at Salamanca, a strongly entrenched work, having a large convent as its stronghold, and mounted with 36 pieces of ordnance. The Allied siege artillery—previous to Colonel Dickson's arrival—consisted of only 4 18-pounder guns, and a battery of long 6-pounders, under Lieut.-Colonel May. (Appointed Brevet Lieut.-Colonel on 27th April, 1812.)

That officer had performed his duty, with inadequate means, in a manner which called forth universal admiration; and Colonel Dickson when he arrived with his howitzers to assist him, expressed the great satisfaction it afforded him to be able now to repay, in a small degree, the many acts of kindness and co-operation, which he had enjoyed at Colonel May's hands. Several points of the defence were breached by the fire of the Allied artillery, but the whole work was so strong, and the defences so connected, that no assault could be attempted on the body of the work.

An assault made on two outworks failed at first, but the gorge of one of them having been subsequently breached, they were carried with little or no loss a few hours before the surrender of the chief fort. The means at their disposal being very small, Colonels May and Dickson employed hot shot from the howitzers against the convent, and succeeded, after firing 260 rounds, in setting fire to it, and destroying the whole of the enemy's provisions. The surrender followed almost immediately. These operations had been mainly conducted by General Clinton, under the supervision of Lord Wellington; and, in his despatch, dated Fuenta la Pena, 30 June, 1812), Lord Wellington reported that that officer had mentioned in strong terms Lieut.-Colonel May, who commanded the Royal Artillery under the direction of Colonel Framingham, and the officers and men under his command. The capture of the forts was delayed until the 27th June, it having been necessary to send to the rear for more ammunition, a step which caused a delay of six days. As soon as they fell, the French Army commenced to retire, pursued by the Allies.

The loss of the Royal Artillery at the siege of these forts was as follows:—

Killed: Captain Eligé, and 9 rank and file.

Wounded: 1 lieutenant (Love), and 25 rank and file.325

In the various movements of both armies between the 27th June and the 22nd July, 1812, on which day the great engagement known as the Battle of Salamanca was fought, no use appears to have been made of the artillery, with the exception of the Horse Artillery attached to the cavalry division. In one affair, on the 18th July, at Castrejou, when the troops under Sir Stapleton Cotton were attacked, Lieutenant Belson, an officer in the Chestnut Troop, was wounded. For honest, conscientious hard work, and staunch performance of his duty, this officer was unsurpassed by any in the Regiment. On reference to his record of service, it appears that between the 3rd August, 1809, and 14th April, 1814, Lieutenant Belson was present in no fewer than thirty-three engagements. Beside such services, which received but little official recognition, those of men in more recent campaigns, who have received lavish, although merited, rewards, sink into insignificance.

It is impossible, without exceeding the limits of this work, to describe in detail the services of the Horse Artillery in the Peninsula— the branch of the regiment to which young Belson belonged. The tables at the end of the preceding volume give some idea of what these services were, but are totally inadequate. The history of some of the

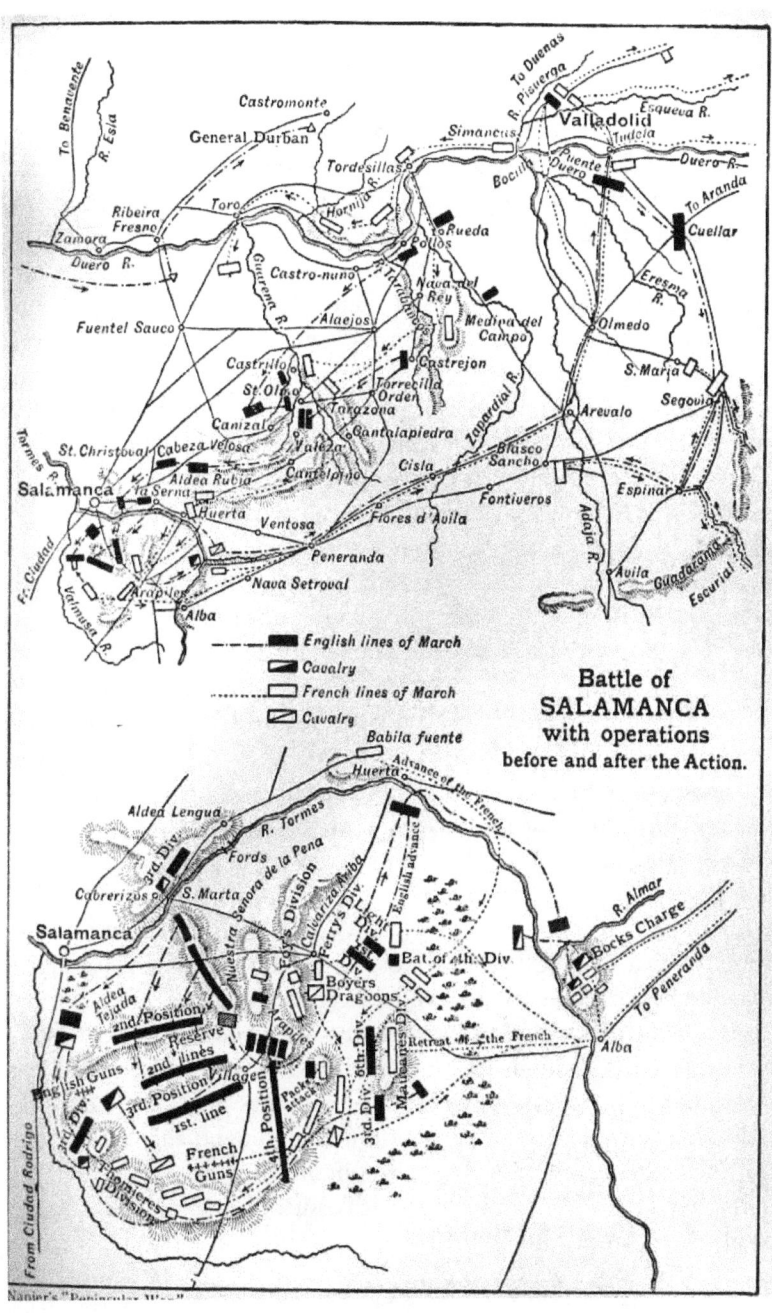

individual troops would alone fill a volume; and the writing of such a history will doubtless be undertaken by some officer, who may find himself in the proud position of commanding one. Their active duties were incessant; even during the sieges, when they ostensibly formed part of the armies of investment or observation, they were ready to volunteer at all times to do additional duty in the trenches.

At San Sebastian, as will be seen shortly, their services in the sieges, as siege artillerymen, were invaluable. The details of their services in the great battle now to be described are, unfortunately, not given in any of the documents in the Record Office. The fact of the presence of three troops, Ross's, Bull's, and Macdonald's, is known, but little more. They were included in the general mention of the corps, by Lord Wellington, after the battle, when he said that "The Royal and German artillery under Lieutenant-Colonel Framingham distinguished themselves by the accuracy of their fire;" (despatch dated Flores de Avila, 24 July, 1812), but no further details are given. From another pen (Browne) we learn that the whole of the troops and batteries were more or less engaged during the eventful day; but this general statement is neither satisfying, nor quite exact. In a letter from Colonel Dickson, written three days after the battle, he mentions that one of his heavy brigades was not ordered up, but was kept in the rear, ready to move in case of retreat.

Possibly this brigade may have been manned by Portuguese, and the howitzer brigade, which he commanded during the battle, may have been manned by Captain Glubb's company, which was under his orders;—in which case the author referred to would be right; but it is extremely rare in Colonel Dickson's correspondence to find him alluding to any action, in which he commanded men of his own corps, without particularizing some by name. On the other hand, it must be admitted that Napier describes Colonel Dickson's howitzers as being manned by British and Portuguese brigaded together.

Lord Wellington's letters show that he was by no means anxious for a general action at this time, if it could have been avoided; and this fact was apparent to those around him. When it was inevitable, he found that the enemy had a better position than himself; and but for the unexpected opening given by Marmont, in the over extension of his left, it would have been a very doubtful issue. Colonel Dickson wrote to D.-A.-G. dated 25 July, 1812:

I really believe that Lord Wellington fought against his inclination, and that if Marmont by his manoeuvres had not pushed him so hard, he would quietly have fallen back, and relinquished Salamanca to the French. The audacity of the enemy was such, however, that British honour required it should be checked; and most severely Marshal Marmont has been punished for playing tricks with such a leader as Lord Wellington. When at last his Lordship determined to attack the attacker, his dispositions were splendid, and his operations rapid and overpowering. I can compare the close-fighting part of the battle more to one of those battles between the French and Spaniards, of which there have been so many, with always the same result, than to a contest between armies equally powerful. It was a rapid succession of overthrows, with some failures, but none that for a moment impeded the grand result.

There were two hills on the left of the Allied line, called Dos Arapiles or Los Hermanitos, situated within easy artillery range of one another. The French had obtained possession of the loftier of these, and by this means had acquired an undoubted advantage. But this advantage was modified by the artillery fire on the left of Lord Wellington's line, which was very effective. It was here that Colonel Dickson's howitzer brigade was in action, taking part in an artillery duel, which is mentioned in the correspondence of several artillery officers who took part in it. Major Macdonald, who commanded a troop of Horse Artillery on the occasion, said that the French artillerymen were driven from their guns on the hill opposite, and prevented from returning, by the destructive fire of Shrapnel shell from the English guns. (To Colonel Shrapnel, dated 9 May, 1813)

In another letter, from an officer who was also present, the same statement is endorsed; and the reader learns that the brigades of artillery chiefly engaged were Ross's, Bull's, and Macdonald's troops, Colonel Dickson's and Captain Douglas's brigades, and Major Sympher's of the King's German Artillery. (Lieut. Sinclair to Colonel Shrapnel, dated 22 Oct. 1814.)

From the same sources it is ascertained that in the staunch final advance of the enemy against the village of the Arapiles, the fire of Shrapnel shell from the howitzers of the English artillery produced great effect; and that, on another important occasion during the battle, a battery of the enemy's guns was disabled by the same means. It will be in the recollection of the military student that Marmont's extension and weakening of his left sprang from a desire to cut off the retreat of the Allies on Ciudad Rodrigo, while he should yet retain the strong position on his right, afforded by the possession of the hill already mentioned. The division Thomières was selected for the flank movement, and against it Pakenham's division was despatched by Lord Wellington, accompanied by 12 guns.

The service performed by these guns was most valuable. Being placed in a commanding position, they suddenly took the French troops in flank, and aided materially in ensuring a victory, which Lord Wellington's quick judgment and military skill had placed in the way of his troops. Then followed the stern battle all along the line, which resulted in the "beating of forty thousand men in forty minutes;" the French seeing general after general fall, and fighting at times in bewilderment, for want of orders;—the English fighting with all the courage of their race, and all the confidence which a general like Wellington inspired,—who seemed to be always at the right place at the right time:—then the French falling back from their first position only to make a new effort; and then the utter rout and confusion, redeemed but by the coolness and skill of the brave Foy, who with his rear-guard strove to cover the headlong flight of the others.

The strength of the Allied Army at Salamanca was 46,000, that of the French 42,000; but the superiority in point of numbers on the side of the Allies was caused by the presence of some utterly useless Spanish troops. The French had 74 guns on the field, the Allies only 60. These, according to Napier, were as follows:—

Royal Horse Artillery. Three troops	18 guns.
Royal Foot Artillery. Two 9-pounder brigades	12 ,,
Royal Foot Artillery. Two 12-pounder ,,	12 ,,
King's German Artillery. One 9-pounder ,,	6 ,,
Portuguese and British brigaded together	6 24-pr. howitzers.
One Spanish battery	6 guns.
Total	60 pieces.

There would certainly appear to be an error in this statement. In none of Colonel Dickson's manuscripts can it be traced that there were more than five 24-pounder howitzers with his brigades; it would therefore seem that the strength of the Allied artillery at Salamanca was even more disproportionate than that given, and that Lord Wellington had only 59 guns against Marmont's 74.

The losses on both sides at Salamanca were very heavy. The Allies lost 1 general, 24 officers, and 686 men killed; and 5 generals, 182 officers, and 4270 men wounded. The loss of the French has never been exactly stated. They lost 7000 prisoners alone, besides 11 guns and other trophies. An approximation to their real loss has been obtained by taking General Clausel's statement of the army on the 18th of the following month. (Cust's *Annals of the Wars*.) He had succeeded Marshal Marmont in the command, on the latter being wounded; and on the 18th August he reported that the army, which had been 42,000 strong on the 22nd July, had fallen to 21,800, with 50 instead of 74 guns. Much of the loss may have occurred during the pursuit after the battle, but the whole was virtually attributable to the contest of the 22nd.

Important as the results of the victory were, they would have been more so, had not the retreat of the French across the Tormes been facilitated by a blunder of the Spanish general, Espana, who left the bridge of Alba open to them. This enabled Clausel to get as far as Peneranda with far less punishment than an army so beaten as his was should have received from his pursuers.

******

A few days after the Battle of Salamanca, the troop of Horse Artillery, under Captains Lefebure and Whinyates (which was on the Tagus with Hill's force), distinguished itself in a brilliant affair, resulting in the total defeat of the French cavalry at Ribera. Major-General Long, who commanded, spoke in the highest terms of all the troops under his command, particularly the Horse Artillery, who displayed great activity in their movements, and rapidity in their fire.—Browne.

******

Wellington followed him to Valladolid, but failed to overtake him; so, while Clausel continued his flight to Burgos, Wellington, after a pause of some days, turned towards Madrid, to free the capital from the presence of Joseph Buonaparte and his army.

******

On the 10th August an engagement took place with a body of the enemy's cavalry which had been sent forward to watch the movements of the Allies. This force was driven in by General D'Urban, but made another attack. General D'Urban ordered the Portuguese cavalry, with which was Captain Macdonald's troop of Horse Artillery, to charge. Before reaching the enemy they were seized with panic and fled, leaving Macdonald's guns, which had been moved forward in support, utterly unprotected. The exertions of the troop got the guns moved off, but owing to the state of the ground, three got damaged and fell with Captain Dynely and their detachments into the enemy's hands.—Browne.

******

He entered it in state on the 12th August, Joseph having quitted it without waiting for the Allies; and he remained there until the 1st September, receiving from the Spaniards a perpetual ovation, and learning from England how valuable his services were deemed, by their further recognition in the form of a Marquisate.

Affairs in the Peninsula forbade longer repose, nor was Wellington the man to risk his army finding a Capua in Madrid. Soult, alarmed at the news from the north, raised the siege of Cadiz, and let Seville fall into the hands of the Allies, while he moved northward himself. An expedition from Sicily landed in the east of Spain, to co-operate with Lord Wellington, of which it must suffice here to say that the Royal Artillery accompanying it was commanded by Captain—then Brevet Lieut.-Colonel—Holcombe, the same officer whose company had been at the sieges of Ciudad Rodrigo and Badajoz. And, lastly, the French general, Clausel, had reorganised his army, and was taking the offensive against the Allied troops left in the north. Of the operations of Wellington to check this general, and to defeat him again before Soult's army could join him from the south, it is proposed to select one, as being a specially artillery subject—the siege of the castle of Burgos.

After the fall of the forts at Salamanca, the heavy artillery employed there continued to be attached to the reserve artillery under Colonel Dickson, and followed the movements of the army during the campaign. (Dickson's MSS.) It consisted of three 18-pounder guns on travelling carriages, and five 24-pounder howitzers, to which were attached Captain Glubb's company of the Royal Artillery, commanded by Captain Power, and a company of Portuguese artillery, commanded by Major Arriaga, with some additional detachments of the artillery of both nations. After the Battle of Salamanca, the whole eight pieces were brought forward to the neighbourhood of Madrid, preparatory to the attack of Fort la Chine, which was still occupied by the French, but which ultimately surrendered without a contest. On the 1st September, Lord Wellington quitted Madrid, to proceed to Arevalo, where the 1st, 5th, 6th, and 7th Divisions were ordered to assemble preparatory to a movement to the northward; and Colonel Dickson, with his 18-pounders and howitzers, was ordered to accompany this corps.

Previous to this movement, measures had been taken to bring forward from Ciudad Rodrigo the following proportion of ammunition, viz.—

24-pr round shot   600
18-pr   800
With powder, and all necessary small stores

On the 9th September, this small siege-train arrived at Valladolid, and on the following day continued its march towards Burgos. On the 19th, the castle of Burgos was invested, the artillery park being formed near Villa Toro.

That Lord Wellington undertook this siege with wholly inadequate means has been well known; but how inadequate these means were will appear from the following statement. First, as regards *personnel*: how many artillerymen had he to carry on the duties in the batteries against a place which held a commanding situation, and was powerfully armed? He had merely

	No. of men
Capt. Glubb's company, under Capt. Power	45
Lieut.-Col. May's company under Lieut. Elgee	45
Major Arriaga's company of Portuguese artillery	57
Total	147

As mentioned above, he had only eight guns; and the following was the total ammunition of all sorts, including the additional supply from Ciudad Rodrigo.

24-pr. round shot	900
24-pr. common shell	208
24-pr. spherical case	236
18-pr. round shot	1306
18-pr. spherical case	100

To swell this amount, Colonel Dickson offered a reward for bringing in any shot fired by the enemy. He found that the enemy's 16-pounder shot fitted his own 18-pounder guns, and that his

8-pounder shot would fit the 9-pounders of the English field brigades. Before the end of September, about 1400 shot were brought in, in this way. Colonel Dickson also obtained detachments from the Horse and Field Brigades occasionally, to give his siege artillerymen relief; but the duties of the Field Artillery were so active at this time round Burgos that men could with difficulty be spared.

The names of the officers of the Royal Artillery engaged in the siege were as follows:—

Lieutenant-Colonel Robe, commanding.

Lieutenant-Colonel Dickson, in immediate charge of the operation.

Captain Power		Captain Greene	Belonging to
Lieutenant Robe	Present during	Captain Dansey	Field Bri-
Lieutenant Pascoe	the whole	Captain Gardiner	gades, but
Lieutenant Elgee	operation.	Lieutenant Monro	occasionally
Lieutenant Hough		Lieut. Johnstone	employed.

Captain Blachley, joined 1st October.

Of the Royal Artillery, small in numbers, the casualties were very great in proportion. Fifteen men were killed, and forty wounded, during the siege, and in the operations immediately attending or succeeding it. The officers who were wounded were Colonel Robe, Captains Dansey and Power, Lieutenants Elgee and Johnstone.

After severe loss, a hornwork in front of the castle had been carried by assault on the night of the 19th September, and on the following night a battery for five guns was commenced. This battery was armed on the night of the 22nd with two 18-pounders and three 24-pounder howitzers, in readiness to open on the inner lines, in the event of an assault, which had been determined on for that evening on the outer line, proving successful. At the same time, a second battery for six guns was commenced to fire against the keep of the castle. The assault, which was premature, failed; and its leader was killed.

On the night of the 24th, the two 18-pounders were taken out of No. 1 Battery, and drawn along a trench, part of the way towards No. 2, being replaced in the former by howitzers. On the 25th, the five howitzers in No. 1 Battery opened a fire to destroy some palisades, which were used to flank the works of the castle. The fire was not successful; the howitzers were found to be very deficient in precision when firing round shot; and the result was inadequate to the expenditure of ammunition,—141 rounds,—a consideration of some importance under the existing circumstances.

******

The total expenditure of ammunition during the siege was as follows:—

920 24-pr. round shot	288 French 4-pr. round shot.
1854 18-pr. ,,	203 24-pr. common shell.
333 French 8-pr. round shot.	182 ,, spherical case.
90 ,, 6-pr. ,,	192 French 6-pr. shot."

—Jones's 'Peninsular Sieges.'

******

Lord Wellington, conscious of the deficiency of his guns, worked now by means of mining; and on the night of the 29th September, a mine was sprung which threw down part of the outer wall. An assault was immediately ordered; but from the darkness of the night the detachment missed its way, and those who were leading—having gained the top of the breach—were driven down again for want of support. The whole, therefore, returned to the trenches.

On the 30th September, the howitzers in No. 1 Battery were of essential service. About 10 a.m. they opened fire, with the addition of a French 6-pounder gun, taken in the hornwork, to demolish a stockade upon the top of a tower in the outer line a little to the enemy's right of the breach, from which the French with musketry annoyed the English in the sap,—the fire being so close that every man, who exposed himself in the slightest degree, was sure to be hit. The stockade was strengthened by sand-bags, &c., but, after three hours' firing, it was utterly destroyed. The ammunition expended for this purpose was 136 rounds;—90 24-pounder shot, 40 6-pounder French shot, and 6 5½-inch common shell. It was on this day that Captain Dansey, who had volunteered for service in the trenches, was wounded.

The next episode in the artillery portion of the siege was the moving the three 18-pounders into a breaching battery so close to the outer wall, that the guns of the upper work could not bear on them. The French commander, Dubreton, lost no time, however, in bringing down a howitzer and a light gun from the upper work, followed by others as quickly as he could; and as the breaching battery was very slight, the result was serious.

The defences of the battery were quite demolished, two of the gun-carriages were disabled, a trunnion was knocked off one of the 18-pounders, and the muzzle of another was split. (Napier and *Memoir of Sir Hew Ross*.)

A second, stronger, breaching battery was then formed, but the plunging fire from the castle was too severe; the guns which were yet serviceable were therefore removed back to No. 1 Battery, on the hill of San Michael. From this position, on the morning of the 4th October, they opened again on the old breach; and a mine having been exploded with great effect in the same evening, another assault took place—the fourth during the siege. This was more successful, and a lodgement was effected; but on the following evening, a large body of the enemy charged down upon the guards and workmen, and got possession of the old breach, besides killing and wounding 150 men, and destroying their works. (Napier.)

On the 7th, the besiegers, who had continued their advance, and were now close to the wall, were again charged with fatal effect by the garrison; and the guns from San Michael, although effecting a great breach in the second line, suffered severely from the artillery fire of the enemy,—another 18-pounder losing a trunnion.

Guns were, however, too few and too valuable to be considered unserviceable, even after so serious an injury as this; and the ingenuity of Colonel Dickson produced a species of carriage, from which the damaged ordnance could fire with reduced charges. Between the 7th and the 10th October, the San Michael guns continued to make breaches in the works; on the 10th, some ammunition arrived from Santander; on the 18th, another breach was pronounced practicable, and Wellington ordered a fifth assault. This also was unsuccessful; the Allies lost 200 men killed and wounded; and the siege was at length raised—on the 20th—by Lord Wellington, who had received alarming intelligence of the approach of a French Army to relieve Burgos, and of the movements of Soult.

The siege of Burgos is a blot on the military reputation of the Duke of Wellington; and revealed an ignorance of what artillery could and could not do, which every now and then manifested itself in his military operations. If Sir Hew Ross was correctly informed, the error made by Lord Wellington was almost criminal, as there was no necessity for attempting such a siege with so inadequate a siege-train. (Sir Hew Ross to Sir Hew Dalrymple, dated Madrid, 18 Oct. 1812.) Major Ross wrote from Madrid:

> Why he should have undertaken the siege of such a place, with means so very inadequate appears very extraordinary, *especially as there was little or no difficulty in augmenting it to any extent*, either from the guns and ammunition found here, or the ships at St. Andero.

SAVING THE GUNS

That Sir Hew wrote with reason seems all the more probable from the fact that, while the last assault was actually taking place, two 24-pounders sent from Santander by Sir Home Popham had passed Reynosa on their way to Burgos. But it may be urged that the responsibility of undertaking a siege with insufficient artillery lay not with the general, but with the artillery commander. (Napier.) Those who are familiar with the character of the Duke of Wellington, as shown in the various narratives of the Peninsular War, will not make use of this argument. It was not his wont to allow his plans to be altered by the representations of his subordinates, nor was he addicted to the habit of consulting them. Besides, in this particular instance, he officially relieved the artillery and engineer officers of the responsibility. He wrote to Lord Bathurst, dated Cabeçon, 26 Oct. 1812:

> The officers at the head of the Artillery and Engineer departments, Lieut.-Colonel Robe and Lieut.-Colonel Burgoyne, and Lieut.-Colonel Dickson, who commands the reserve artillery, rendered me every assistance; and the failure of success is not to be attributed to them.

The Duke of Wellington believed in the bayonet beyond any other weapon; and if a legitimate belief became occasionally credulity, it is hardly to be wondered at, when one reflects on the gallantry of the Infantry which it was the duke's good fortune to command. What seemed to be impossibilities, when ordered by him, were proved possible in the result; and the consequently increased belief in the power of the bayonet seems but natural. But his creed was supported at a terrible cost. When we find Napier himself—Wellington's idolater—pronouncing his sieges a succession of butcheries, the criticism of a more temperate student may be excused. Doubtless, the want of adequate ordnance was often severely felt by the Duke of Wellington, and compelled him to an exaggerated use of the other arms; but this fact was hardly an excuse for neglecting its employment, when available in sufficient quantities, and obtainable with moderate exertions.

Nor was the fact that he—as he justly complained—*never* had a proper amount of artillery with his armies any excuse for his making occasionally but an indifferent use of that which he had. Fortunately, the Duke of Wellington had merely to encounter Napoleon's Marshals in Spain: had he had to meet their master, it is probable that the creed which he believed and practised might have received some rude assaults. If one could free oneself of all but purely professional consid-

ROYAL HORSE ARTILLERY

ROYAL ARTILLERY

erations, one would wish, for the sake of the student in the art of war, that Napoleon, instead of Marmont and Clausel, had faced Wellington in the campaign of 1812. The result would, doubtless, have been the same; but the ways and means would have been very different.

As it happened, Wellington's sole encounter with Napoleon took place on ground chosen by himself, and under circumstances which yet further assisted his military creed, by testing yet again that which he had so often extravagantly proved, the marvellous endurance, discipline, and courage of the British Infantry.

The results of the mistaken siege of Burgos are curtly described by Sir J. T. Jones, in his *Journal of the Sieges in the Peninsula*.

> By its means, a beaten enemy gained time to recruit his forces, concentrate his scattered armies, and regain the ascendancy.

The same author writes, with regard to the service of the Royal Artillery during the siege:

> It is a pleasing act of justice to the artillery officers, employed in this attack, to state that they vied with each other in their exertions and expedients to meet the hourly difficulties they encountered, and that no set of men could possibly have drawn more service than they did from the limited means at their command.

Chapter 9

Vittoria and San Sebastian

The threatening appearance of the various French armies in Spain, which compelled Lord Wellington to raise the siege of Burgos, compelled him ultimately to withdraw into Portugal for winter quarters. In leaving Burgos he found the activity of the commanding officers of artillery very beneficial. (Despatch to Lord Bathurst, dated 26 Oct. 1812.) It enabled him to carry off all his serviceable guns and stores in a single night; but the absence of cattle prevented his removing the few French guns which he had captured in the storming of the hornwork. During the retreat, the services of the Horse Artillery, under Major Downman, were of a high order, and called forth the commendation of Lord Wellington.

The troop which most distinguished itself was Major Bull's, commanded by Captain Norman Ramsay, Major Bull having been twice wounded—on one occasion so severely—when in advance with the cavalry at Torquemada on the night of the 12th September, 1812—that he was obliged to be invalided. He does not reappear in the story of his gallant troop until the Battle of Waterloo.

The retreat terminated on the 24th November, and the troops went into cantonments, the headquarters being stationed at Frenada, and the artillery at Malhada Sourda, three miles distant.

An old friend reappears, in the winter of 1812-13, to the burrower among artillery records. Captain—now Brevet-Major—Frazer, who last was mentioned in this work in the account of the operations at Monte Video and Buenos Ayres, arrived to take command of Major Bull's troop during that officer's absence. His own troop being on home service, he more easily obtained permission to assume this duty. He had not been many weeks in the Peninsula before he received a more important command—that which had hitherto been held with such distinction by Major Downman—the command of the Royal Horse Artillery with Lord Wellington's armies. (Sir A. Frazer's *Letters*.) Although a reserved man in public, and fond of solitude, he was almost diffuse in his correspondence.

Happily, for those who have succeeded him in the corps, his letters from the Peninsula have been collected and published by one who served in his troop for seven years—General Sir Edward Sabine. These letters, and the unpublished letters of Sir A. Dickson, give together a most graphic picture of the operations of 1813, 1814, and 1815, which cannot but lose by the necessary condensation of the historian.

In the beginning of 1813, Lord Wellington proceeded to Lisbon to make the necessary arrangements for the coming campaign. The intelligence of the French disasters in Russia had reached him; rumours also came that Soult and many of the best troops in the French Peninsular armies had gone to France; and, from his preparations at Lisbon, it is evident that he had already resolved on offensive operations, which should, if possible, have the effect of driving the French out of the Peninsula. That he succeeded is well known to the reader; it remains to single out, in this and the following chapter, some of the more salient points in the campaign.

Colonel Dickson had been ordered to Lisbon, to consult as to some means of making the Portuguese artillery more available for service than it had as yet been, (Colonel Dickson to D.-A.-G. Lisbon, 16 Jan. 1813); and while there, he was sent for by Lord Wellington, who had also arrived, and was directed to superintend the equipment of a pontoon train of thirty-four large pontoons, which was to be sent by river to Abrantes, and there handed over to the master-pontonier, for use in the coming operations of the army. (*Ibid* to D.-A.-G. Lisbon, 30 Jan. 1813.) This train was destined to be a sore grievance to the artillery. It had always to be horsed *first*, even at the expense of the artillery brigades; and its possible wants in that respect haunted, like a nightmare, the commanding officer of the corps.

At this interview Lord Wellington also expressed considerable anxiety about the brigade of 18-pounder guns, which, he said, he was determined to have early in the field, as the French were understood to be fortifying positions everywhere. Some new 18-pounders were expected daily from England; and, on their arrival, he desired that they should be sent up the Tagus to Abrantes. This was safely effected; and bullocks were ordered to bring them thence to headquarters, at Malhada Sourda. (Colonel Dickson to D.-A.-G. dated, 24 Feb. 1813)

They were ultimately manned by Captain Morrison's and Captain Glubb's companies of the Royal Artillery; and the number of carriages in the brigade was no less than 57, (Colonel Dickson to D.-A.-G. 18 April 1813), *viz.*:—

6 18-pr. guns on travelling carriages
2 spare carriages
6 platform waggons
2 forges
18 ammunition (limber) waggons
3 store waggons
20 bullock carts

N.B.—Ammunition was carried at the rate of 150 rounds per gun.

The guns, and nine of the ammunition waggons, had horses in addition to their bullocks; the remaining carriages were drawn by bullocks only.

About the same time as the 18-pounders arrived from England, another troop of Horse Artillery, under the command of Captain Webber Smith, also reached Lisbon. (Colonel Dickson to D.-A.-G. dated, 24 Feb. 1813.) A change in the armament of the troop, from 6-pounders to 9-pounders, was immediately ordered by Lord Wellington,—a change which, on more than one occasion, and in more than one campaign, has been ordered in the armament of the Royal Horse Artillery. At this time, also, a recognition was made by the Portuguese Government of the services of the artillery—Colonels Robe and Dickson being made knights of the Tower and Sword.

The old difficulty as to horses reappeared in the beginning of 1813. The sickness among these animals during the winter had been excessive; and the difficulty of purchasing any in the country seemed daily to increase. (Colonel Dickson to D.-A.-G. dated, 24 Feb. 1813.) This led to many changes. Among others, Lord Wellington reduced the whole of the Portuguese artillery for service in the field to three brigades—one 9-pounder and one 6-pounder brigade to be with Sir Rowland Hill's force, and one 9-pounder brigade to be attached to the general artillery reserve of the army. These three were made very efficient by this means, and the purchase of a considerable number of horses avoided.

The campaign of 1813 was distinguished by a feature of considerable importance. Lord Wellington was now Commander-in-Chief of all the Spanish Armies, and all necessary correspondence came direct to him, instead of through Cadiz. The assistance of the *Spanish* regular troops was never of much value, even under the new system, except at the combat of San Marcial and the Bidassoa; but the part taken by the Partidas, or irregular forces, during the campaign was not unimportant, and increased the difficulties of the French troops.

The French commenced to fall back from Salamanca towards Burgos, and in the beginning of April had not above a thousand men in the former place. At the same time, supplies were arriving from England weekly, and were disembarked in the northern ports of the Peninsula, with a view to the advance of the English Army. (Colonel Dickson to D.-A.-G. dated Corilhaa, 4 April 1813.) An organisation of the Allied troops was taking place, superior to anything which had yet been witnessed; and the corps, whose history is treated in these pages, improved with the other arms in this respect. It seems a suitable time to touch on the improvement in the Field Brigades which had already taken place; and, at the risk of wearying the reader, to place before him a specimen of these in the spring of 1813.

The brigade, *i.e.* battery, which it is proposed to describe belonged to the 10th Battalion, and was commanded by the 2nd Captain, R. M. Cairnes, a gallant officer, who afterwards fell at Waterloo. It was pronounced by various inspecting officers to be the best field brigade with the army; but Captain Cairnes in his correspondence declined to accept this honour, as he considered others equally efficient. It may, therefore, be accepted as a fair type. From a letter written by Captain Cairnes himself, dated Penamacor, 4 April, 1813, to Captain Bedingfield, the following particulars are obtained; and they exhibit a startling contrast to the oxen-draught brigades of the commencement of the Peninsular War. His system was based on that of the Horse Artillery, now universal in field batteries, in which each officer was wholly and solely responsible to the captain for his division, whether in matters of men or *matériel*.

He declined to allow the officer of the Driver Corps, who commanded the drivers attached to the brigade, to have any control over his men, except as far as their pay and subsistence were concerned; and by thus giving his own officers complete responsibility, he received the reward which such conduct generally ensures, and was able to say:

> My subalterns, Raynes, Bridges, James, and Talbot, are all most excellent, full of zeal, activity, and intelligence; they run be-

fore me in everything I can desire concerning their respective charges, and are never more happy than when in stables.

The chief difficulty in field brigades had always been in the divided allegiance of the men of the Driver Corps. The solution of this difficulty, which was adopted by Captain Cairnes, gradually obtained favour, and ended in a most natural manner—the abolition of the Driver Corps and the absorption of the drivers into the regiment. It took, however, some years to educate the authorities up to this point; and not until 1822 was the corps actually abolished. (Kane's List.)

Another point in Captain Cairnes's system to which he attached great importance, and which he said had been generally adopted in the other brigades, was that of having promotion among the non-commissioned officers to go, not by *battalion*, but by *company* seniority; and of waiving even the question of seniority in the presence of undoubted superiority. There were faces in Woolwich which grew very long, and fossil old gentlemen whose remaining hairs stood on end, at such a perversion of the old order of things; but Lord Wellington supported the captains of companies in a measure which on service gave them a powerful engine for discipline. So, time after time, does the reader find the real artillery unit asserting itself.

The artificers with a brigade were 2 wheelers, 2 collar-makers, 1 farrier, 1 jobbing smith, and 4 shoeing smiths. The non-commissioned officers of the Driver Corps attached to a 9-pounder brigade were, 1 staff-sergeant, 2 sergeants, and 6 corporals, one of whom acted as forage sergeant, under the acting storekeeper of the brigade (a *company*, not *driver* non-commissioned officer), who, again, was under an assistant commissary-general attached to the brigade (under the immediate orders of the captain commanding). This officer was responsible for the rations and the supply of corn, for which purpose he had a number of forage mules, at the rate of one mule to two horses.

Sixteen round tents and two horsemen's tents were carried; and, for the convenience of the artificers, two store waggons accompanied the brigade. The other extra carriages were the forge waggon, spare wheel carriage, and the captain's cart. The brigade itself consisted of 6 guns and howitzers, 6 ammunition waggons, and 2 reserve ammunition waggons. The proportion of ammunition carried was as follows:—

For each 9-pr. gun: 70 round shot, 34 spherical case, and 12 common case. Total 116 rounds.

For each 5½-in. howitzer: 44 spherical case, 8 common case,

and 32 common shell. Total 84 rounds.

In each reserve ammunition waggon there were 57 round shot, 21 spherical case, and 6 common case. Total 84 rounds.

The number of drivers with a brigade was one hundred. Five of the spare carriages were drawn by mules; those being selected which were the least likely to go under fire.

This was altogether a most desirable command for a young 2nd Captain to have on active service; and keenly did Captain Cairnes enjoy it. His dismay may therefore be imagined, on receiving, on the 5th May, 1813, a letter from Colonel Fisher, then commanding the artillery in the Peninsula, announcing that Lord Wellington had decided to take away the horses of his brigade for the service of the pontoon train, leaving him to the chance of any horses which might hereafter come from Lisbon. He was not allowed any time to brood over his troubles, but was ordered to meet the pontoons at Sabugal in three days' time, and hand over to the Engineer the whole of his stud.

Colonel Fisher's letter, which was a private communication, sent a few hours in advance of the official order, held out hopes of a speedy restoration (which fortunately took place) of the equipment of his brigade for the field. (As will be seen, on reference to the chapter on the Old Tenth Battalion, Captain Cairnes had also to give up to the pontoon train his second supply of horses in the end of this year.) Captain Cairnes' reply to this letter, dated 6 May, 1813, was so soldier-like, that it is well worthy of a place in the records of his corps:

> I return you, my dear colonel, my sincere thanks for your communication of yesterday's date, anterior to the arrival of any *order*, which would, I think, have set me perfectly *crazy*. As it is, I have read your letter over twenty times, and am yet very unwilling to understand it. Lord Wellington having fixed on this brigade, I trust we shall be entitled to every consideration, when it is recollected that a junior one in all respects is within a league of the same distance from Sabugal as this place.
>
> The pain of urging anything prejudicial to my valued friend Parker is superseded by the promise held out to us of a speedy re-equipment. . . . . I know, my dear colonel, that you cannot avert the blow from us, and that the necessity of the service has forced Lord Wellington to this measure; therefore, however sorely affected and hurt we may now feel, you will assure yourself that the whole shall be given over to the pontoons in as

complete and efficient a manner, as if they were going to be put to our own carriages. I am full of dread and alarm that our new equipment of horses and harness will not come up in time to march with the army; and that (without being so extravagantly sanguine or conceited as to *build on* future successes and good fortune) we shall be too late for the golden opportunity that a few days will probably offer to other brigades.

This allusion of Captain Cairnes to the other artillery brigades with Lord Wellington's army suggests the propriety of placing before the reader their distribution at the opening of the campaign of 1813. This would appear to have been as follows:—

With 1st Infantry division :	Captain Dubourdieu's Brigade, R.A.		
,, 2nd ,, ,,	Captain Maxwell's	,,	,,
,, 3rd ,, ,,	Captain Douglas's	,,	,,
,, 4th ,, ,,	Major Sympher's K. G. Artillery.		
,, 5th ,, ,,	Captain Brandreth's Brigade, R.A.		
,, 6th ,, ,,	Major Lawson's	,,	,,
,, 7th ,, ,,	Major Gardiner's Troop, R.H.A.		
,, Light Division :	Major Ross's	,,	,,
1st Division of Cavalry :	Major Frazer's (Bull's) Troop, R.H.A.		
2nd ,, ,, ,,	Captain Beane's	,,	,,
Reserve	{ Captain Webber Smith's Troop, R.H.A.[1] Captain Cairnes' Brigade, R.A. Captain J. Parker's ,, ,,		

[1] It would appear from Sir A. Frazer's letters that Webber Smith's troop was for a time attached to the Hussars, but ultimately to the 7th Division, in lieu of Captain Gardiner's troop, which joined the Hussar Brigade.

In the middle of May the plan of the campaign was arranged. The army was ordered to move in two columns, the headquarters to leave Frenada on the 22nd May. One column was to cross the Douro at the mouth of the Coa, and to advance by Miranda de Douro; the other was to go by Ciudad Rodrigo. (Colonel Dickson to D.-A.-G. dated 19 May 1813.) Lord Wellington was to accompany the latter column, which consisted of Sir Rowland Hill's corps, the Light Division, cavalry, &c. The other column, composed of the rest of the army, was under Sir T. Graham; and with it went the pontoon train. It was decided to lay the pontoon bridge across the Douro, near Miranda, and thus unite the two columns; this operation to be followed by the siege of Zamora, which, when concluded, would leave the Allies masters of the Douro. Following the headquarters, the reader finds that they moved to Ciudad Rodrigo on the 22nd May, to Tamames on the 23rd, and to Matilla, about six leagues from Salamanca, on the 25th.

(Colonel Dickson to D.-A.-G. dated Matilla, 25 May, 1813.)

On the way, Lord Wellington inspected the Portuguese Division, commanded by General Silveira, and found the men better equipped than they had ever yet been. The brigades of artillery with them were commanded by Colonel Tulloh, an officer of the Royal Artillery, whose zeal and ability were repaid by the efficiency of the men under his control. The whole of the reserve artillery of Lord Wellington's army, with the exception of the brigade under Captain Cairnes, which was now re-equipped, had gone with the main body, under Sir T. Graham.

Colonel Dickson was now in command of the artillery, although junior to many in point of regimental rank; and as the way in which he obtained the command is not so generally known in the regiment as the fact, it seems desirable to state it. While he was at Corilhaa, preparing the reserve artillery for the coming campaign, Colonel Fisher, who had succeeded to the command of the artillery after Colonel Robe was disabled at Burgos, but who had not held the command as yet in the field, wrote to him, requesting his attendance at head quarters without loss of time. On his arrival, he ascertained that a misunderstanding had arisen between Lord Wellington and Colonel Fisher, which had ended in the latter's requesting permission to resign, and return to England.

Lord Wellington inquired of Colonel Dickson whether he was senior to Colonel Waller, who had arrived in Lisbon, and on learning that he was not, he said, "Colonel Dickson, then, will take the command of all the artillery in the field, both British and Portuguese; and Colonel Waller and General Roza, as commandants of the artillery of the two nations, will remain at Lisbon for the purpose of forwarding supplies." He then desired Colonel Fisher to give such explanations of the state of affairs as would enable Colonel Dickson to enter on his charge.

There would seem to have been considerable hastiness and injustice on the part of Lord Wellington in this matter. Colonel Dickson himself, while naturally flattered, could not but say, to D.-A.-G. 25 May, 1813:

> I am convinced, if Lord Wellington had known Colonel Fisher's talents and abilities, he would never have allowed any such circumstance to take from him such an officer; and I hope you will forgive my thus presuming to discuss in so particular a

manner the merits of a superior, which I am only induced to do in order that you may better know the merits of an officer I love and esteem; and I am sure every man of sense or ability in the corps of artillery in the Peninsula will subscribe to what I now state.

The honour paid to Colonel Dickson was an embarrassing one. Although his Portuguese rank placed him over all officers under the rank of colonel, many such were senior to him regimentally. This fact demanded great tact from him in the execution of his duty. Fortunately, he met with ready, soldierlike co-operation from all; and one, who had commanded him on service before, in writing to his friends on the subject, expressed the general feeling when he said, (*Letters of Sir A. Frazer*):

> I shall get on very well with Dickson; he was second to me in the South American Expedition, and then obeyed my orders with the implicit readiness which I shall now transfer to his. He is a man of great abilities and quickness, and without fear of anyone.

And again (*ibid*):

> Colonel Fisher left us the day before yesterday, sincerely regretted by all. I hope Dickson's reign may be long for the sake of the service, but the times are slippery.

Yet once more, (*ibid*):

> Dickson showed me yesterday a very sensible, plain letter, which he had written to Colonel Waller, and was just going to send off. Dickson, too, feels himself awkwardly off, but will bear his honours well. There is an open, manly simplicity about Dickson very prepossessing. I hope and trust he will long enjoy the confidence of the Marquis; and this I should desire for the sake of the service, independently of any regard I might have (and I have a very sincere one) for Dickson.

To return, however, to the movements of the army. (Colonel Dickson to D.-A.-G. dated 6 June, 1813.) On the 26th May the headquarters moved forward in the direction of Salamanca, on approaching which place columns of the enemy's infantry were observed, halted at each side of the town, a part of their cavalry being, however, on the left bank of the river to watch the movements of the Allies. As the latter advanced, the cavalry retired across the bridge into Salamanca, but the infantry for a considerable time remained unmoved. In the meantime, Sir Rowland Hill's cavalry and Captain Beane's troop of Horse Artillery were ordered to push for the ford of Santa Martha, a little above the town. As soon as the French saw these troops approach the river, they moved off with their whole force, which included about 2500 infantry, two or three squadrons of cavalry, and three or four guns.

General Fane, who was in command of Sir R. Hill's cavalry, passed the river in a moment, and came up with the French before they had gone three miles from Salamanca. They were retiring *by squares* along the Arivalo road, which leads up the Tormes by Aldea Langua; and, on overtaking them, the Horse Artillery opened upon their squares with considerable execution. The pursuit was thus continued for five or six miles, the Horse Artillery cannonading them from every available point. The artillery fire was interfered with by the repeated interposition of the cavalry between the guns and the enemy; but was nevertheless very efficient.

According to Colonel Dickson—of 400 killed, wounded, and prisoners, lost by the enemy—100 were victims to the artillery fire alone; and the squares were so shaken by it, that, if the regiments moving on the flank had pushed on, the whole force might have been captured. Lord Wellington, however, seeing that the pursuing cavalry were somewhat exhausted, desisted from further pursuit. The headquarters halted at Salamanca on the 27th May, and orders were issued for their transfer to the other army, north of the Douro.

On the 28th, therefore, the headquarter staff proceeded to Almeida, and on the 29th to Miranda, crossing the Douro at a ferry near the latter place. Lord Wellington, himself, remained one day later at Salamanca; and on the 29th proceeded the whole distance to Miranda. On the 30th the headquarters were moved to Carvajales, and on the same evening the Esla was reconnoitred, and preparations made to cross it on the following morning.

Small parties of the enemy were seen on the opposite bank with two guns. Early on the morning of the 31st, the Hussar Brigade, Gardiner's and Webber Smith's troops of Horse Artillery, and two regiments of infantry crossed—upon which the French parties immediately retired. The infantry found the greatest difficulty in crossing—the river being both deep and rapid—and several men were drowned. A pontoon bridge was therefore made in a couple of hours, over which the rest of the army passed, with the exception of the cavalry, artillery,

The Duke of Wellington passing the R.H.A. on the march

and waggons, which forded the river. A special pontoon bridge was made for the 18-pounder brigade, over which it passed with safety. On the 1st June headquarters proceeded to Zamora, and the army completed the passage of the Esla—the French evacuating Zamora as the Allies approached.

Colonel Dickson wrote:

> Thus, we succeeded in our manoeuvre of turning the Douro, and getting possession of that river without sustaining the smallest loss. It has been a bold one; but, by his Lordship's rapidity in moving the army, and transferring himself from one point to the other, I think the French did not succeed in discovering our real intention until it was too late for them to hinder it. Otherwise, we found the Esla such an obstacle, that if they only had had ten or twelve thousand men on that river, the passage of it would have been a serious operation to us, and could not have been effected without either great loss of time or of men, and probably both.

On the 2nd June, the French abandoned Toro, and Wellington's headquarters proceeded there—remaining over the 3rd, on which day, and on the 4th, the force which had advanced by Salamanca, under Sir R. Hill, crossed the Douro. On the 4th, the army moved forward in three columns—the right, under Sir R. Hill, in the direction of Valladolid; the centre upon La Mota, and the left under Sir Thomas Graham towards Rio Seco. The headquarters proceeded to La Mota on the 4th, to Castro Monte on the 5th, and to Ampudia on the 6th; the French abandoning Valladolid, as the Allies advanced, and retiring upon Palencia and Duenas. The armies continued to keep within a day's march of one another: indeed, when the Allies reached Palencia, on the 7th June, the rear-guard of the enemy was clearly visible from the high ground.

On the 12th (the pursuit still going on steadily, and Wellington continuing this, his greatest, march in the most persevering, relentless manner) the French Army had reached Monasterio and the neighbourhood of Burgos—but indicated no sign of discontinuing its retreat. Warned by past experience, Wellington had decided to take no active measures against Burgos, but merely to blockade it with part of the Spanish Army, leaving the English troops undiminished. In the meantime, Sir Thomas Graham, with the left column of the army, inclined to his left in the direction of the upper part of the Ebro;

with the view, it was believed, of turning or crossing that river. The events of the next few days, however, modified matters very much. On reaching Villa Diego, Lord Wellington ascertained that the castle of Burgos had been blown up by the French, and was in utter ruins.

Sir Richard Fletcher, of the Engineers, accompanied by Colonels Dickson and May, and Major Frazer of the artillery, penetrated into the place, although the French rear-guard was still close at hand, and brought back the report. Joseph Buonaparte had meditated taking up a position at Burgos, but it having been pronounced unwise, he continued to retire on Vittoria. His army—which was known to be *en route* for France—was embarrassed with huge convoys of spoils—and crowds of followers, male and female, who were unwilling to be left in Spain, unprotected by the French troops. Lord Wellington now executed a very brilliant strategical manoeuvre—the crossing of the Ebro.

The route by which he abruptly moved his army was unfrequented and considered impracticable. The descent to the river by the Puente de Arenas was by a very narrow and steep pass, opening into a small but fertile valley, entirely surrounded by high mountains, with the river running through it. (Colonel Dickson to D.-A.-G. dated 19 June, 1813.) The *sortie* from the valley of Puente de Arenas was by a road running for a considerable distance close to the river, with stupendous rocks overhanging on either side. Had this movement been foreseen, a very small body of the enemy could have impeded the passage of the army. The advantages of this manoeuvre were many. French communications with the coast were cut off, and a new base was opened for the operations of the Allies. (Cust's *Annals of the Wars*.)

The English fleet entered Santander, and commissariat communication was opened with the coast. Wellington was also in a position to threaten the communications between Vittoria and the Pyrenees, and the French found the English already in rear of their right. An engagement took place between Sir Thomas Graham and the French General, Reille, who had been detached to protect the communications between the French Army and their own country; and the Light Division—with which Lord Wellington himself was—succeeded in surprising General Mancune's division on the march,—killing a good many, dispersing one brigade, and capturing an immense quantity of baggage, and 300 prisoners. (Colonel Dickson to D.-A.-G. dated 19 June, 1813.) But these were merely the preliminaries to a battle, which, in its results, was unsurpassed in the whole narrative of the Peninsular War. Writing on the evening of the 19th June, from Subijana de Morillas, three leagues south-west of Vittoria, Colonel Dickson said:

> We can see the whole French Army on their march to Vittoria;—the column is not more than six or seven miles off. Tomorrow we expect to move forward upon Vittoria, which, I think, must lead to something.

In proceeding to discuss the share of the Royal Artillery at the Battle of Vittoria, it has unfortunately to be premised that the most valuable letter on the subject has been mislaid, or lost. In writing to General Macleod after the battle, dated 23 June, 1813, Colonel Dickson said:

> I know Frazer has given you some account of it, so I will not enter into further details at present, except on our own matters.

And in two subsequent letters, he said:

> Frazer's letter will have explained everything.

Now, in the published letters of Sir Augustus Frazer, this letter is not to be found; nor is there much in his allusions to the battle in his other letters to assist the artilleryman in tracing the services of his corps. The loss of the letter is, to a certain extent, compensated by details given in subsequent letters from Colonel Dickson, but still remains irreparable.

It would be beyond the province of this work to describe the Battle of Vittoria, as a whole. In the pages of the *general* military historian such a description can be found. In these, the regimental statistics alone need be reproduced.

The general plan of the battle is, doubtless, familiar to all:—the plain in front of Vittoria, into which—as into a trap—Joseph Buonaparte poured all his troops and convoys;—the one road available for the retreat of his forces to France, which was menaced—but not with sufficient decision—by Wellington's left;—the confusion in the space between the French Army and the town of Vittoria, where mobs of terrified fugitives were mingled with heaps of vehicles and stores;—the three-handed assault of the Allies, advancing with steadfast purpose from three quarters at once;—the frequent artillery duels, in which the artillery on both sides so greatly distinguished themselves;—the grand final effort of the French artillery, when "more than eighty guns, massed together, pealed with such a horrid uproar, that the hills laboured and shook, and streamed with fire and smoke, amidst which the dark figures of the French gunners were seen, bounding with a

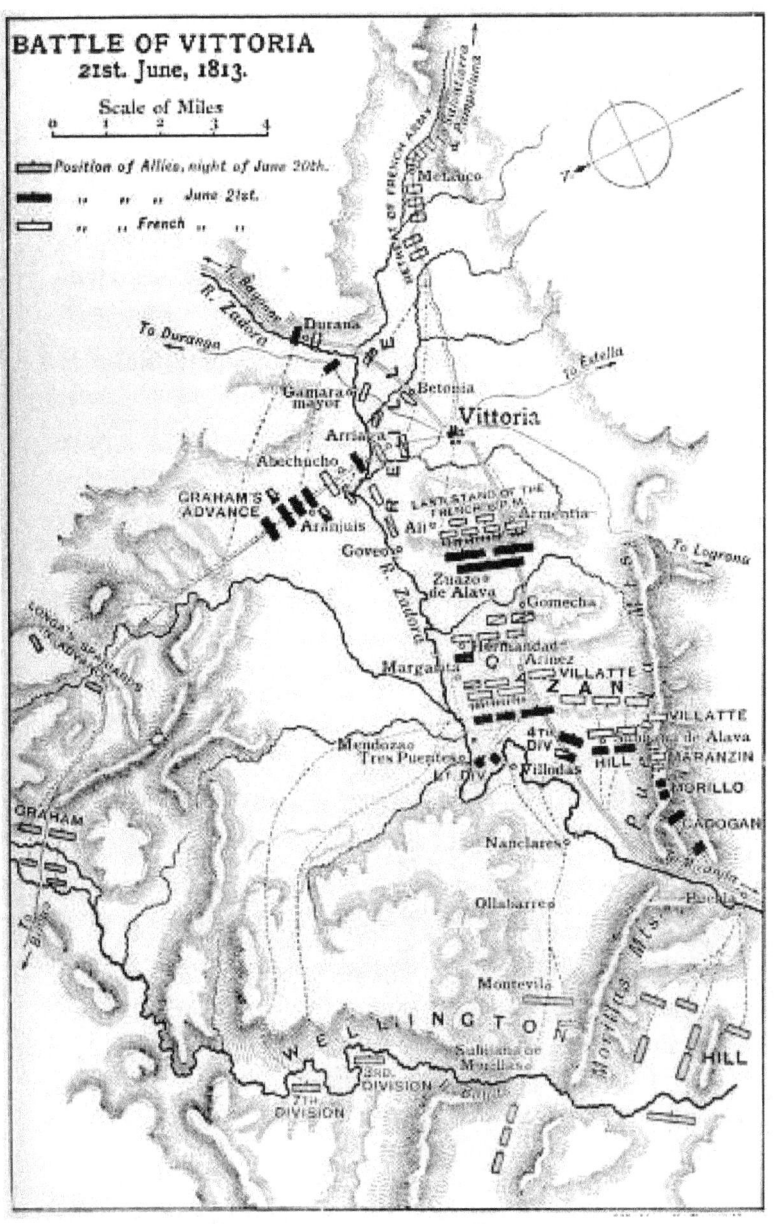

frantic energy (Napier);" and then the wild rout, the headlong flight of an army leaving its guns and everything behind it;—the shrieks of women, the terror of men, rising so vividly before his mind as he wrote, that Napier exclaimed, "It was the wreck of a nation!" But no such ambitious description is required in detail from the mere regimental historian. What is demanded from him is the narrative, from old records that have never seen the light, of the share taken by his corps on this eventful day.

Let the distribution of the various troops and brigades of artillery at Vittoria first be given. Official Report to the master-general, dated 23 June, 1813. Colonel Dickson was in command, assisted by the following field officers:—

> Lieut.-Colonel Hartmann, K.G.A., commanding the reserve artillery.
> Major Carncross, with Sir Rowland Hill's column.
> Major Buckner, with column of 3rd and 7th Divisions.
> Major Frazer, commanding the Horse Artillery.

The troops of Royal Horse Artillery were distributed as follows:—

> Captain Webber Smith's, with the Reserve.
> Major Ross's, with Light Division.
> Captain Beane's, with General Fane's Cavalry.
> Major Gardiner's, with the Hussars.
> Captain Ramsay's, with the Cavalry Division.

The Field Brigades were distributed as follows:—

> Major Lawson's, with 5th Division.
> Captain Douglas's, with 3rd Division.
> Captain Maxwell's, with 2nd Division.
> Captain Dubourdieu's, with 1st Division.
> Major Sympher's (K.G.A.), with 4th Division.
> Captain Cairnes', with 7th Division.
> Captain Parker's, with the Reserve.
> Lieut.-Colonel Tulloh, R.A., commanded two Portuguese brigades with Sir R. Hill's corps, and Major Arriaga commanded the Portuguese Reserve Brigade.
> Lieut.-Colonel May acted as Assistant Adjutant-General, and Lieut. Woodyear acted as Brigade-Major. Lieutenants Ord, Harding, and Pascoe, were employed as staff officers by Colonel Dickson.

The number of guns, exclusive of the Spanish, which were brought into action by the Allies at Vittoria was ninety; but the French had considerably more. There happened in this battle, on the 21st June, 1813, what rarely happens;—*every* brigade of artillery was brought into action. In his official report, Colonel Dickson said that he had reason to be satisfied with the conduct of the officers and men of the Royal Artillery on this occasion; that their skill and bravery were highly conspicuous, as were their exertions in bringing forward the artillery through a difficult and intersected country, both during the attack and the pursuit. "In short," he added:

> I can safely assert that artillery could not be better served; and, to the credit of the officers, I have to add that from the beginning of the day to the last moment of the pursuit, it was always to be found where it was wanted. (Dated 23 June, 1813.)

In his private letter to General Macleod, Colonel Dickson particularised some of the officers who had especially distinguished themselves; and the following extract deserves publication:

> I cannot close this letter without mentioning the valuable assistance my friend Frazer afforded during the whole business. I may truly say he flew from one troop to another—accompanying them into action and attending to their supply, or looking out for roads for them to move. You, who know Frazer so well, can easily anticipate what he would be on such an occasion.

The massing of the English artillery was effected at Vittoria to an unprecedented extent, and with most happy results. It might at first be assumed that the admirable use made of this arm on that occasion is a sufficient reply to any insinuations against Lord Wellington's knowledge of artillery tactics. Unfortunately for him, a letter has survived which proves, on the best authority, that to accident alone was this artillery display due. Colonel Dickson wrote:

> The nature of the country, and want of roads, was the means of throwing a large proportion of our artillery together, away from their divisions, which I availed myself of, and by employing them in masses it had a famous effect. This was adjoining to the great road to Vittoria; and the French brought all the artillery they could to oppose our advance, so that the cannonade on one spot was very vigorous. In none of our Peninsular battles have we ever brought so much cannon into play; and it was so

well directed that the French were generally obliged to retire ere the Infantry could get at them. There were few or no instances of the bayonet being used during the day.

Considering the duration of the battle, the casualties among the artillery were singularly few. They were as follows (MS. Official Return to D. A. Gen.):—

Staff.—*Wounded*: Colonel May, and Brigade-Major Woodyear (died of wounds).

	Killed	Wounded	Missing
Royal Horse Artillery	4	36	2
Royal Artillery	8	19	—
Horses of R. H. A.	28	23	8
Horses of R. A.	15	2	—

The number of guns captured from the enemy was no less than 151, besides 415 caissons. Of gun ammunition 14,249 rounds were taken, besides 40,668 lbs. of gunpowder and 1,973,400 musket ball-cartridges. The other spoils were countless; and it is difficult to conceive a more complete defeat. (MS. Official Return to D. A. Gen.)

Lord Wellington's account of the battle contains the following short, but satisfactory, allusion to the services of the artillery:—

The artillery was most judiciously placed by Lieut.-Colonel Dickson, and was well served; and the army is particularly indebted to that corps. (To Lord Bathurst dated 22 June, 1813.)

During the pursuit of the enemy after the battle, Colonel Dickson kept the artillery well up—and was rewarded, as will be seen from the following anecdote:—

In the pursuit after Vittoria, in the bad roads, Lord Wellington saw a French column making a stand, as if to halt for the night. 'Now Dickson,' said he, 'if we had but some artillery up!' 'They are close by, my Lord.' And in ten minutes, from a hill on the right, Lieut.-Colonel Ross's Light Division guns began; and away went the French two leagues farther off. (Extract from the private *Journal* of F. S. Larpent, Esq., Judge-Advocate-General to the British Forces in the Peninsula. Published by Sir G. Larpent.)

The same author from whom this quotation is made says:

Dickson, though only a captain in the Royal Regiment of artillery, now conducts the whole department here, *because he makes no difficulties*.

During the pursuit, the only remaining guns—two in number—taken away by the French from the field, were captured—one being disabled by the fire of the Chestnut Troop, and the other being taken within a league of Pampeluna, in which direction the French had retreated. (Lord Wellington's *Despatch*, dated 24 June, 1813; *Memoirs of Sir Hew Ross*.)

The results which followed the Battle of Vittoria are summarised by Napier in his description of the campaign, in which that battle was the chief incident.

In this campaign of six weeks, Wellington, with 100,000 men, marched 600 miles, passed six great rivers, gained one decisive battle, invested two fortresses, and drove 120,000 veteran troops from Spain.

The fortresses referred to were Pampeluna and San Sebastian; and it is now proposed to treat of the double siege of the latter, as an episode of essential importance in the history of the regiment, and one concerning which Sir Alexander Dickson left much valuable information, yet unpublished. Before doing so, however, there are two incidents which deserve to be mentioned.

In the *brevet* which followed Vittoria, Majors Frazer and Ross were made lieut.-colonels, and 2nd Captain Jenkinson (of the Chestnut Troop) was made major. Captain Jenkinson's brevet promotion was the first which had been received by a 2nd captain of artillery. In the beginning of the year 1813, the 2nd captains serving in the Peninsula had memorialised Lord Wellington on the subject. The memorial having been referred to England, a favourable reply was given, and Captain Jenkinson's promotion was the first fruits. (Sir Henry Torrens to Lord Wellington, 3 March, 1813.)

In addition to the somewhat scanty recognition of the artillery in this *brevet*, a boon was granted, which is described in the following extract from a letter written by the Master-General of the Ordnance, Lord Mulgrave, dated 16 July, 1813, to Colonel Dickson:—

> On receipt of your letter, addressed to Major-General Macleod, I did not fail to bring under the consideration of the Prince Regent the very striking and unexampled circumstance of the

whole of the British artillery having been brought into action at the Battle of Vittoria, and the whole of the enemy's artillery having been captured in the glorious victory which crowned the exertions of the Allies on that ever-memorable occasion. His Royal Highness has been graciously pleased—in consideration of the peculiar circumstances above stated—to mark His Royal Highness's approbation of the particular and successful activity of the corps of Royal Artillery under your orders, by granting severally to the officers entrusted with the command of divisions or brigades an allowance for good service in the following proportions:—To the officers commanding divisions, each 10*s. per diem*; to the officers commanding brigades, each 5*s per diem*; and to yourself a similar allowance for good service of 20*s. per diem*.

Better, far better, that these words had never been penned, and that the generous thought had died in its conception! For the day was to come when a reference to this precedent after Vittoria should call forth from him under whom the representatives of the corps had so often and so bravely fought, a letter as cruel and unjust to those of whom it treated, as it was unworthy of him who penned it. (*Vide* Appendix A.)

The other incident is one which has become a household word in the regiment. If there is one name more familiar than another to the artilleryman, it is that of Norman Ramsay. From public orders and the pages of history his gallantry and professional skill may be learnt; but it is from the pages of private correspondence that one ascertains how lovable he was. He joined the regiment in 1798, and he fell at Waterloo; and yet in that short space of seventeen years he had gained the love of his brother officers without exception, the devotion of his men, and the admiration of all. A man *sans peur et sans reproche*, he reminds one of the knights of Arthur, whose pleasure was to—

> *Live pure, speak true, right wrong, follow the king.*

A thorough master of his profession, he earned the respect as well as the love of those whom he commanded: and let all remember that the love of men for their commander must have that element in it to make the gift worth having. The personal qualities of an officer may attract the affection of his men; but if he is deficient in knowledge of his profession, there will be in their love an element approaching pity, which will be fatal to their confidence in the hour of trial. It will be like the love for a child—pure, warm, and sincere—but not such as will demand from the soldier, in the day of battle, blind confidence and unhesitating obedience. In Norman Ramsay were combined all the virtues which compel affection, and all the skill which demands respect. But there was more: he possessed that professional enthusiasm, which hallows the dullest tasks, and gilds the severest hardship. His pride in his troop made its men strive to be worthy of his good opinion; and it is in this way that a commander can with certainty generate *esprit de corps* among his men. Let him but place before them a standard of perfection, even although unattainable, and, in their voluntary efforts to reach it, they will rise far higher, than if driven by order, or goaded by fear of punishment.

Successful in all his aims, Norman Ramsay was yet so fortunate as to escape jealousy. The letters of his brother-officers—written for private eye alone, but subsequently published—show this to a singular extent. Sir Alexander Dickson, Sir Augustus Frazer, Sir Hew Ross, Major Cairnes, and others—all men of different characters and disposition—rarely wrote without a loving word or kind inquiry about Ramsay. If his troop distinguished itself, they all rejoiced as if it had been their own; if he met with any grief, they longed to share it; and if sorrow came upon themselves, their first instinct was to confide it to him. In October, 1813, a distinguished artilleryman, Sir Howard Douglas, lost in action a brother whom he deeply loved. Older than Ramsay, one yet finds without surprise that it was to him he went, "bitterly lamenting his loss." (Sir A. Frazer's *Letters*.) So also when any of them came within his reach at any time, the letters always speak alike—as if everyone would readily understand the writers' longings—"I *must* go and see Ramsay."

In these pages, later on, the story will have to be told how, in the midst of the din of battle, there seemed to fall a silence like a pall, as he, the brave and much-loved, met with a soldier's death; but the grief was then that of his friends. The incident now to be told tells of a grief which was his own—which never quitted him while he lived, and which was said by many who knew him to have led him to court unnecessary exposure on the day in which he died. At Vittoria, Bull's troop, commanded by Ramsay, had done special service. On the following day, during the pursuit, "Lord Wellington spoke to Ramsay as he passed; desired him to take his troop for the night to a village near, adding that if there were orders for the troop in the course of the night, *he would send them*." (Sir A. Frazer's *Letters*.) No orders came; but

Sir Augustus Frazer

at 6 a.m. an assistant quartermaster-general arrived, and ordered him to join the brigade to which he belonged. The troop at once marched, but was shortly afterwards overtaken by a written order from General Murray, the quartermaster-general of the army, directing "Captain Ramsay's troop to rejoin General Anson's brigade." (Sir A. Frazer's *Letters*.) The troop halted, while Ramsay rode on to discover the road; and at this moment Lord Wellington rode up, and called repeatedly for him. Sir Augustus Frazer wrote:

> His Lordship then called for Dickson, whose horse being unable at the instant to clear a wide ditch over which we had just passed, I rode up to mention the circumstance to Lord Wellington, who ordered me to put Captain Ramsay in arrest, and to give the command of the troop to Captain Cator. This I accordingly did. . . . It appears that Lord Wellington had intended that Ramsay's troop should not have moved that morning till he himself sent orders, and his Lordship declared that he had told Ramsay so. This Ramsay affirms he never heard or understood; and his Lordship's words, repeated by Ramsay, young Macleod, and a sergeant and corporal, all at hand when his Lordship spoke to Ramsay, are precisely the same, and do not convey such a meaning. I spoke instantly to Lord Fitzroy Somerset on the subject, who, together with every other individual about headquarters, was, and is, much concerned at the circumstance.
>
> Nay, two days afterwards, when the despatches were making out, every friendly suggestion was used by several that Ramsay might be mentioned as he deserved; but I have reason to believe that he is not. There is not, among the many good and gallant officers who are here, one of superior zeal or devotion to the service to Ramsay, who has given repeated proofs of spirit and good conduct. Admitting, contrary to all evidence, that he had mistaken the verbal orders he received, this surely is a venial offence, and one for which long-tried and faithful services should not be forgotten. . . . Few circumstances have engaged more general attention, or occasioned more regret. It has naturally been expected that after the first moment was over, a deserving officer would, at least, have been released from a situation most galling to a gallant spirit. . . . I trust this will soon be the case; but . . . I am at a loss to account for the delay in a point so easily set-

tled. In the meanwhile, Ramsay bears up with great fortitude, although he deeply feels.

Writing on the same subject, some weeks later, Sir Hew Ross, (*Memoir*), said:

Norman Ramsay is at present with his troop in this neighbourhood, and we are much together. He is quite well, and bears his unjust treatment, and consequent disappointment, in the manly and proper way that might be expected of him.

For a considerable time, he was kept under arrest; and the numerous applications on his behalf, including a very urgent one from Sir Thomas Graham, seemed to have the effect of irritating Lord Wellington. The consciousness of having done an unjust act is rendered more difficult to bear, when the victim has been one for whom affection has been entertained; and it was believed in the army that, as far as his undemonstrative nature would allow, Lord Wellington had a strong liking for Norman Ramsay. There was no doubt of the devotion of the latter for his great chief; and the keen suffering caused by injustice from a person whom one loves must be realised to be fully understood. He was happily released from arrest in time to carry his brave troop through the many actions, with which the war concluded; and he received a *brevet* promotion for these services; but he was never the same man.

At Waterloo, on the morning of the battle, as the duke rode along the line, he saw Ramsay at the head of his troop for the first time since his arrival Flanders. He accosted him cheerfully as he passed. Ramsay merely bowed his head sadly, until it nearly touched his horse's mane, but could not speak. In a few hours he was where sorrow and injustice are unknown. (Communicated by Sir J. Bloomfield, R.H.A.)

It is necessary now to turn to the siege of San Sebastian. Pampeluna was blockaded and ultimately starved into submission; but stronger measures were adopted with San Sebastian, into which place Marshal Jourdan had thrown a garrison of between 3000 and 4000 men. On the land side, it was invested by the left wing of the Allied army, under Sir Thomas Graham; and on the sea side it was blockaded by a squadron under Sir George Collyer. (Jones's *Sieges* vol. 2.)

On the 4th July, 1813, Lord Wellington wrote as follows to Colonel Dickson, dated Lanz, 4 July, 1813:

From what I have heard of San Sebastian, I am inclined to form the siege of that place, and I shall be very much obliged to you if you will send an officer to Bilbao to the train from thence to Passages. (Passages de la Calçada.)

The order was immediately obeyed, (Colonel Dickson to D.-A.-G. dated 10 July, 1813) and Captain Morrison's 18-pounder brigade was also directed to proceed to Passages for the same purpose. On the 12th, Lord Wellington reconnoitred San Sebastian, and on the 14th, he departed to join the army on the field, leaving Colonel Dickson to conduct the artillery part of the siege. Lord Wellington's operations in the field were at this time of a very delicate nature. The Allied army in the east of Spain had failed, and had raised the siege of Tarragona; while, in his front and on his right, there were menacing French armies. French garrisons in Pampeluna and San Sebastian also weakened his available force, by demanding troops to watch them.

Before entering on the details of the double siege, the following list of artillery officers, who were present, may be interesting.

MS. Returns dated 12 Sept. 1813.

LIST OF OFFICERS of the ROYAL ARTILLERY employed in the SIEGES of ST. SEBASTIAN under LIEUT.-COLONEL DICKSON, commanding the Artillery under the MARQUIS OF WELLINGTON.

	First Operation.	Second Operation.
Lieut.-Colonel May, A. A. General..	1	0
„ Frazer, R. H. Artillery	1	1
Major Buckner	0	1
„ Dyer	0	1
„ Webber Smith, R. H. Artillery	1	1
Captain Morrison	1	1
„ Douglas	0	1
„ Dubourdieu (killed)	1	0
„ W. Power	1	1
„ Green	0	1
„ J. B. Parker	1	1
„ Deacon	1	1
Captain Dansey	1	0
„ C. Gordon	0	1
„ A. Macdonald, R. H. Artillery	1	0
Lieutenant J. W. Johnstone	1	1
„ Henry Blachley, R. H. Artillery	1	1
„ R. H. Ord	1	1
„ W. Brereton, R. H. Artillery	1	0
„ J. Wood	0	1
„ Basil Heron	1	1
„ G. Mainwaring	0	1
„ R. Hardinge	1	0
„ R. Harding, R. H. Artillery	1	1

,,	R. F. Phillips					0	1
,,	J. Pascoe					1	1
,,	R. Manners					0	1
,,	W. Dennis					0	1
,,	Hugh Morgan					0	1
,,	C. Shaw					1	1
,,	H. Stanway					1	1
,,	R. Story					1	1
,,	H. Slade					0	1
,,	H. Hough					0	1
,,	F. Monro					1	0
,,	H. Hutchins					0	1
,,	John Bloomfield					1	1
,,	H. Palliser					0	1
,,	T. G. Williams					1	1
,,	A. Macbean					1	1
						25	33

Lieut. England's name also appears in some of the Journals of the First Operation, and in Jones's 'Sieges,' and should be included above.

Total, exclusive of King's German Artillery, present at St. Sebastian:

First Operation.—Colonel Dickson and 25 officers of the Royal Artillery.
Second Operation.—Colonel Dickson and 33 officers of the Royal Artillery.

Extract from a letter dated Passages de la Calçada, 12 Sept. 1813:

"These officers vied with each other in their endeavours to forward the "object in view in the most indefatigable manner."—COLONEL DICKSON to GENERAL MACLEOD.

The story of San Sebastian divides itself into three parts,—*viz*.: the first siege, terminating in an unsuccessful assault; the blockade; and the second and successful siege. The *matériel* at the disposal of the artillery at the first siege was inadequate, even when supplemented by field guns, and guns borrowed from the navy; but during the second siege the supply was ample, and the fire most efficient. In sieges, the association of the artillery with the breach made by them ceases when the assault commences; but this was not so in the second siege of San Sebastian, when the assault would certainly have failed but for the powerful fire maintained by the artillery over the heads of the assailants. Of this, however, more hereafter.

San Sebastian is built on a neck of land jutting out into the sea; and the first point which it was necessary to secure on the land side was a place which had been fortified—the convent of St. Bartholomew. (Colonel Dickson to D.-A.-G.) This was taken, after four days' vigorous cannonade, by assault, on the 17th July, 1813. The guns employed against the convent and the adjoining redoubt were placed in the batteries of the left attack, numbered 1 and 2, and were four 18-pounders and two 8-inch howitzers. (Colonel Dickson's *Diary*; Jones's *Sieges*.) Before the assault, however, Sir Thomas Graham, who had been left by Lord Wellington in command, directed as many field guns as possible to be brought into play in support. (Sir Thomas Graham to Colonel Dickson dated 15 July, 1813.) This was done; and they were found to be of material assistance, and were served with great effect during the assault. The number of rounds expended against the convent and redoubt was 3000: a quantity of hot shot was employed; and in his despatch announcing the success of the assault, (*Sieges*), Sir Thomas Graham said to Lord Wellington, dated 18 July, 1813:

> I cannot conclude this report without expressing my perfect satisfaction with all the officers and men of the Royal Artillery, both in the four-gun battery employed for three days against the convent, and on the opposite bank of the river, whence several field-pieces were served with great effect.

The batteries against the town had been in course of preparation during the bombardment of the convent; and the following tables extracted from Sir A. Dickson's letters and returns will show at a glance much that would otherwise occupy much space in description. The numbering of the batteries differs from that of the Engineers; but where possible, *both* have been shown.

The batteries were divided into those of the right and left attacks. Lieut.-Colonel May assisted, during the first siege, under Colonel Dickson; the left or detached attack was under Colonel Hartmann, K.G.A., and the batteries were armed, manned, and superintended as follows:—

RIGHT ATTACK.

Battery	Guns	Purpose
No. 1 Battery (No. 11 in Jones's 'Sieges')	2 24-pr. guns / 4 8-in. hows.	Against the Mirador and castle, and to enfilade the land fronts.
No. 2 Battery (No. 12 in Jones's 'Sieges')	2 24-pr. guns	Against defences: only used two days.
No. 3 Battery (No. 13 in Jones's 'Sieges')	4 24-pr. guns	For breaching.
No. 4 Battery (No. 14 in Jones's 'Sieges'[1])	12 24-pr. guns	For breaching.

[1] Jones's 'Peninsular Sieges' would appear to err here :—and to show one gun less than the real number in No. 4 Battery.

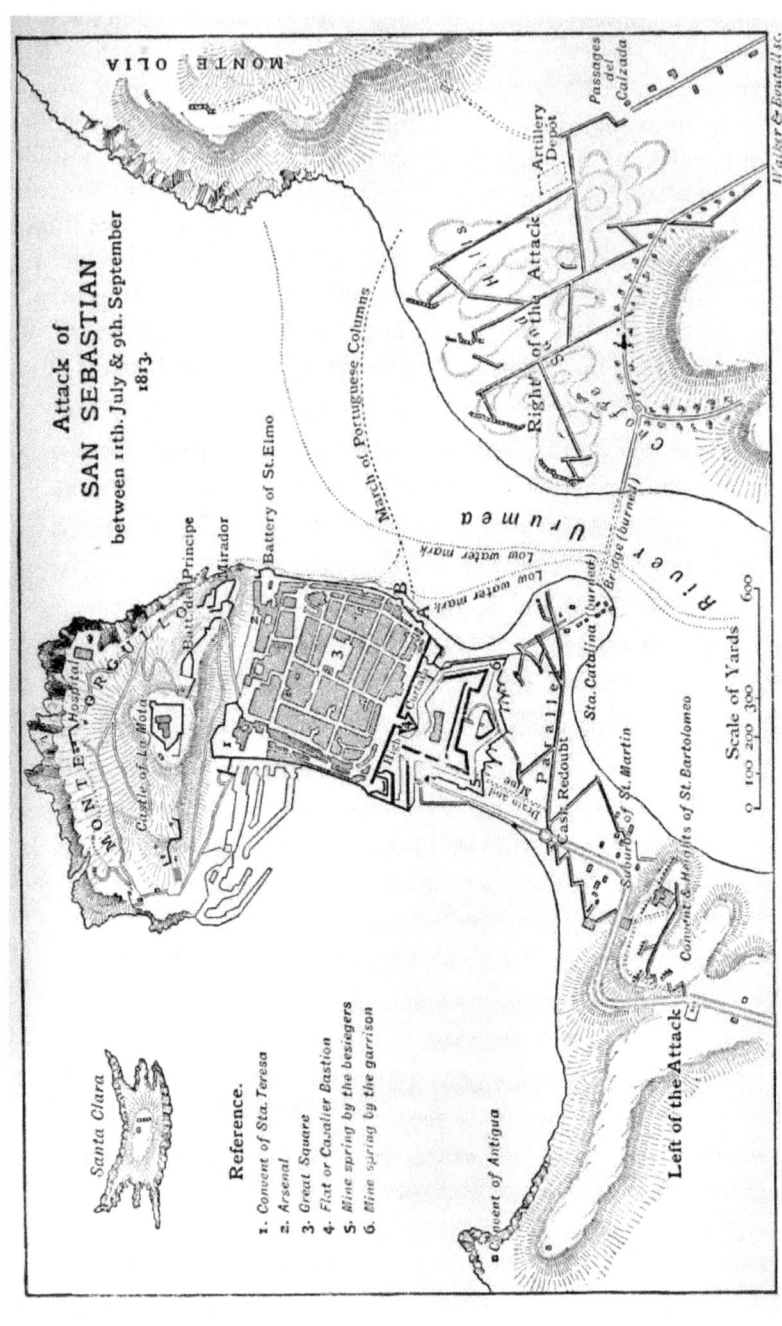

No. 5 Battery (No. 15 in Jones's 'Sieges')	4 68-pr. carronades	Against breach, and to annoy defences.
No. 6 Battery (No. 16 in Jones's 'Sieges')	4 10-inch mortars	Against land front and castle.
Total	32 pieces.	

Major Webber Smith, R.H.A., was in charge of Nos. 1, 2, and 6 Batteries.

Lieut.-Colonel Frazer, R.H.A., was in charge of Nos. 4 and 5 (the breaching) Batteries.

Major Arriaga, Portuguese Artillery, was in charge of No. 3.

The officers in the various batteries were as follows:—

No. 1 Battery.—Captain Macdonald, and Lieutenants Brereton, Heron, and Williams.

No. 2 Battery.—Captain Deacon and Lieutenant England.

No. 3 Battery.—Captain Rosières and Lieutenant Costa (Portuguese).

No. 4 Battery.—Captains Dubourdieu and Parker, and Lieutenants Hardinge and Bloomfield of the Royal Artillery, and Lieutenants Silva and Judice of the Portuguese Artillery.

No. 5 Battery.—Captain Dansey and Lieutenant Johnstone.

No. 6 Battery.—This was not manned at first.

LEFT ATTACK.

No. 1 Battery	4 18-prs.	Against the convent up to 17 July, 1813.
No. 2 Battery	2 8-inch hows.	Ditto. ditto.
No. 3 Battery	6 18-prs.	To annoy defences of land front, and support attack. Doubtless these included the guns from Nos. 1 and 2 Batteries.
No. 4 Battery	2 8-inch hows.	

The officers of the Royal Artillery engaged in the left attack, were—

Captains Morrison and Power

Lieutenants Shaw, Oldham, Story and Stanway.

The strength of the companies of artillery before San Sebastian, on the 18th July, 1813, was as follows:—

Captain Morrison's (18-pr. Brigade)	162	of all ranks
Major Lawson's	57	" "
Captain Dubourdieu's	66	" "
Captain Parker's	68	" "
Detachment	17	" "
Portuguese Artillery	107	" "
Total	476	

The ammunition expended during the first siege amounted to 27,719 rounds, and, as the batteries did not open until the 20th July, and the assault took place on the morning of the 25th, the rapidity of fire must have been excessive. In alluding to this, General Jones says:

> The expenditure from the breaching battery alone, on the 22nd July, amounted to 350 rounds a gun, expended in about 15 hours of daylight. Such a rate of firing was probably never equalled at any siege, great accuracy of range being at the same time observed.

Captain Dubourdieu of the Royal Artillery was mortally wounded in the batteries on the first day; and the total loss of the corps and the Portuguese artillery during the first operation was 12 *killed*, and 44 *wounded*.

On the morning of the 24th July, two breaches were deemed quite practicable, but the assault which was first intended to take place on that day was postponed until the 25th at 5 a.m. It completely failed: a certain amount of gallantry was shown by the attacking troops, but there was a feeling of depression among them, which seemed to have arisen from exaggerated ideas of the difficulty of the task. Sir Thomas Graham, while giving due credit for the courage which was shown, and which was proved by the list of casualties, felt that his troops were not in the same mood as those who stormed Badajoz. In a letter to Colonel Dickson on the night of the assault, dated 8 p.m. 25 July, 1813, he said:

> It is evident to me that *the troops here* never will carry this breach, unless every annoyance but the castle fire (which is not come-at-able at present) be removed....The approach to the breach is certainly very unfavourable, and does not admit of attempting to feed or renew the attack, as all must go in one narrow col-

umn over rough, slippery stones,—and *that*, with an enfilading and flanking fire, occasioned the complete failure; nor would it have been possible at last to get any other fresh men from the trenches to have advanced.

Further than keeping up a fire which would not interfere with the attacking party, the artillery had nothing to do with the assault; but Sir Thomas Graham in reporting the failure to Lord Wellington, dated 27 July, 1813, took the opportunity of referring to their services on the preceding days, in the following gratifying terms:—

> The conduct, throughout the whole of the operations of the siege hitherto, of the officers and men of the Royal Artillery and Engineers, never was exceeded in indefatigable zeal, activity, and gallantry; and I beg to mention particularly to your Lordship Lieut.-Colonels Dickson, Frazer, and May, and Major Webber Smith, of the Royal Artillery.

Lord Wellington came in person to look at the state of affairs, and as it was not deemed prudent to repeat the assault, and the ammunition of the artillery was nearly expended, the operations against the place were brought to a close;—greatly to the disappointment of many. (Colonel Dickson to D.-A.-Gen. dated 12 Aug. 1813.) After the failure of the assault, Lord Wellington ordered, for security, that all the guns, with the exception of a few pieces, should be removed from the batteries, and a blockade substituted for a siege. The forward movement of Soult's army, which will be discussed hereafter, produced a further order to embark the guns and stores.

On the French being driven back, Colonel Dickson received orders to land them again; the batteries also were repaired, new ones constructed, and everything put in readiness for a second siege as soon as ammunition should arrive from England. The arrival of this was, however, delayed beyond the endurance of Sir Thomas Graham, who was not so familiar with the dilatory habits of the Civil branch of the Ordnance, as Colonel Dickson was. In one of his numerous letters, dated 7 Aug. 1813, to the latter during this period, he wrote:

> It is too provoking to think of such mistakes and delays at home, where they have nothing else to do or think of, but the execution of demands made at an early enough period to give full time for preparation.

Sir Thomas Graham's correspondence shows at this time a feverish, almost fretful, anxiety about the preparations for the second siege, which was not unnatural in a general anxious to wipe out the recollection of failure. The reader of his letters cannot resist a wish to have seen his face when the incident occurred, described by Napier:

> With characteristic negligence, this enormous armament (*i.e.* two new battering trains) had been sent out from England with no more shot and shells than would suffice for one day's consumption.

At length, everything was in readiness, and the batteries opened on the 26th August, 1813. Before entering on the narrative of the siege, a list of the batteries with their respective armaments will be given, extracted not merely from Sir A. Dickson's official returns, but also from private letters written at the time, with all the necessary information at his hand.

To commence with the *Left Attack*. The only batteries used before the storming of the city on the 31st August were those numbered 5 and 6—containing 7 24-pounders, 2 8-inch howitzers, and Captain Morrison's brigade of six 18-pounders. Others will be given, hereafter, which were used at the bombardment of the castle. The object of the fire of the left attack was to breach the right face of the left demi-bastion, and the curtain over it; also, the face of the left demi-bastion of the hornwork, and generally to annoy the defences. Lieut.-Colonel Hartmann, K.G.A., again commanded the left attack.

The *Right Attack* was under the command of Lieut.-Colonel Frazer, and consisted of the following batteries, according to Colonel Dickson's numbering:—

No. 1 (evidently No. 11 in Jones's 'Sieges') containing 2 8-inch howitzers.
No. 3 (evidently No. 13 in Jones's 'Sieges') containing 1 12-inch Spanish mortar, and 5 10-inch mortars.
No. 4 (evidently No. 14 in Jones's 'Sieges') containing 5 8-inch howitzers, 4 68-pr. carronades, 6 24-pr. guns.
No. 5 (evidently No. 15 in Jones's 'Sieges') containing 15 24-pr. guns.
No. 6 (evidently No. 16 in Jones's 'Sieges') containing 4 10-inch mortars.
No. 7 (evidently No. 17 in Jones's 'Sieges') containing 6 10-inch mortars.

The breaching batteries were Nos. 4 and 5, but more especially the latter. Field officers were detailed for duty alternately in these two batteries, while the firing was going on: Majors Dyer and Webber Smith being in No. 4, and Majors Buckner and Sympher, K.G.A., in No. 5.

According to Sir J. Jones, the batteries opened with a general salvo from 57 guns;—according, however, to Colonel Dickson, only 48 were in action. The whole commenced by signal, and as Sir Thomas Graham wrote to Colonel Dickson, dated 26 Aug. 1813:

> Nothing could be more imposing than the opening of your fire this morning.

The guns in the left attack were found to be too distant for the effect required; but the fire from the batteries of the right attack was so destructive, that in the course of five days, from the 26th to the 30th, the demi-bastion was demolished, a breach made in the curtain behind it, the towers on each side of the former breach laid down, and the wall laid open which connected the curtain with the left of the first breach. (Colonel Dickson to D.-A.-Gen. 1 Sept. 1813.) The batteries of the left attack laid open a hornwork; and four guns having been brought forward into a battery (No. 7) which was much nearer the works, they breached the right face of the demi-bastion, and greatly assisted in bringing down the end of the curtain.

About 11 o'clock a.m. on the 31st August, the column for the assault, which had now been ordered, moved forward, and arrived at the breach with comparatively little loss. The defence of the French was such, however, that no lodgement could be effected—more than one attempt having been repulsed; and as the enemy occupied a higher position than his assailants, he was able to fire down upon them and inflict great loss. It was at this time that Sir Thomas Graham ordered the artillery to commence a fire, which has received the greatest praise at the hands of historians, and of which the following graphic description, from Colonel Dickson's pen, cannot fail to interest the reader:—

> The great body of our cannon, howitzers, and carronades fired upon the great curtain and behind it—over the heads of our own men (*only a few feet perpendicular lower down*), with a vigour and accuracy probably unprecedented in the annals of artillery. It was the admiration and surprise of Sir Thomas Graham, and Marshal Beresford, and all who beheld it. No one could say there was a single error to the disadvantage of our own people; and the force of the fire entirely prevented the enemy making any effort along the rampart to drive us from the breach. I must say the enemy stood with great firmness, firing over the parapet as well as they could, notwithstanding numbers had their heads taken off by our round shot. In short, on this occasion, our artil-

lery was served in such a manner that I would not have believed it, had I not seen it.

Sir J. Jones says of the artillery fire at this time, that it was admirable, and occasioned no casualties among the assailants; and Napier describes the stream of missiles, like a horrid tempest, in its fearful course strewing the rampart with the mangled limbs of the defenders. It was a critical time; and a want of precision on the part of the artillery would have produced a fatal panic among the assailants. In his despatch to Lord Wellington, dated Oyarzun, 1 Sept. 1813, announcing the success of the assault, Sir Thomas Graham admitted that, prior to the artillery coming into action on this occasion, the state of the attack was desperate; and he described the fire (which after consultation with Colonel Dickson he ventured to order) as having been "kept up with a precision of practice beyond all example." The ultimate success was almost accidental. A large number of shells and combustible materials had been accumulated above the breach to throw down on the storming party.

This was fortunately ignited by the fire of the Allied artillery, and a great explosion followed, killing many of the French, and producing a disorder which enabled the troops to establish themselves on the curtain, which they fought from traverse to traverse. Some additional troops having entered the town by another breach near the Towers, the curtain was abandoned, and the fighting confined to the streets; but very soon the French were driven into the castle, which alone remained in their hands at the end of the day. The Allies lost 500 killed, and 1500 wounded in this assault.

To ensure the surrender of the castle, a bombardment from mortars was kept up, until two batteries were made ready in the left attack (Nos. 9 and 10), which were armed with 17 24-pounders—and 2 24-pounders with 1 8-inch howitzer, respectively. No. 9 was to breach the Mirador and Battery de la Reyna, and No. 10 to operate against the lower defences of the castle, and to enfilade the back of the hill. On the morning of the 8th September, the preparations being complete, the whole of the batteries opened on the castle. Colonel Dickson (to D.-A.-Gen. dated 12 Sept. 1813.) describes the bombardment as having been conducted in beautiful style, and carried on so vigorously, that in two hours the enemy hoisted a flag of truce.

Sir J. Jones says that the fire was so extremely rapid and well directed, and of so overpowering a nature, that the castle scarcely returned a single shot. The terms of the capitulation having been agreed to, two batteries of the castle were delivered up the same evening, and on the next day the garrison marched out with the honours of war, and laid down their arms. Colonel Dickson was one of the three officers detailed to arrange the terms of the capitulation.

The sufferings of the garrison, and of the prisoners in the castle, during the bombardment, were excessive, as may readily be imagined when one learns that "they had not a bomb-proof in it except for powder." (Colonel Dickson to D.-A.-Gen. 12 Sept. 1813.)

✶✶✶✶✶✶

The number of rounds expended during the second operation was 43,112. The strength of the artillery (including 187 Portuguese) was 681. The casualties amounted to 7 *killed* and 31 *wounded*.—Jones's *Peninsular Sieges*.

✶✶✶✶✶✶

The siege of San Sebastian has an especial interest for the Royal Artillery—more especially for that part of the Regiment, the duties of which are confined to the use of heavy ordnance. This episode was selected by an able and dispassionate historian, (Gleig), as one reflecting especial honour on the corps.

It offers an example of precision of aim, and absolute coolness on the part of the gunners, never surpassed.... Such services as these were rendered thirty years ago by no other artillery in the world; and as the same spirit still prevails, which prevailed then, in the magnificent corps of which we are speaking, it cannot be doubted but that when the opportunity offers again, they will prove themselves worthy of the renown that attaches to them. (Gleig's *Military History*.)

These words corroborate what has been so frequently urged in this work, that a regimental history differs essentially in its aim from all others. The glow, which it endeavours to throw over past events, is not meant to conceal defects, or to distort facts, but to awaken the spirit of emulation;—the boastful way in which special honours are recounted, and distinctive triumphs sung, is not egotistical pride, or aggressive conceit, but merely the fond treasuring of a glory which has been gained by others, and transmitted to their successors for safe keeping;—and the anxious gleaning among the fields of former action is but to find herbs, which in times of peace shall brace the gleaner for coming days of work or danger. The more truly a soldier knows and values the deeds and honours of those who have gone before him in his corps—the more certain will he be to emulate them.

There is no jealousy of the dead. Admiration of their qualities passes unconsciously into a love for their memories; and this love inspires a longing not to be unworthy. It may seem to some but a poor ambition, to use the weapons well which have been given to us—to sacrifice one's will unmeaningly—and never to be downcast by discomfort or failure; but it is the highest ambition to which a soldier can aspire. Nor is it easy for him to conceive a higher.

Cheerful obedience and conscientious zeal imply most of the higher qualities of humanity; and a perfect soldier must possess both. The great poet of England in these days has been the noblest preacher, to whom her army has ever listened. As he places before his readers the ideal of a true knight, the soldier sees a standard which he should never cease to gaze upon. He sees, it may be for the first time, that opposite virtues should not rebel, but mingle; and that such should be found in himself as—

Utter hardihood, utter gentleness,
And loving, utter faithfulness in love,
And uttermost obedience to the king.

And, once realising this,—with the knowledge, possibly, in his heart that there have been in his corps before him men who approached even the standard of Arthur's knights,—he must, as he reads of their deeds, long—

To sweep
In ever-highering eagle-circles up
To the great sun of glory, and thence swoop
Down upon all things base, and dash them dead.

CHAPTER 10

Conclusion of the Peninsular War

The absence of Colonel Dickson from the headquarters of the army during the sieges of San Sebastian has had the effect of leaving the artillery share in the operations known as the Battle of the Pyrenees, unwritten. He did not rejoin headquarters until the 17th September, 1813: the period, therefore, between the Battle of Vittoria and that date is, as far as the operations of Lord Wellington's army are concerned, almost ignored in his correspondence. (Colonel Dickson to D.-A.-Gen. dated 18 Sept. 1813.) Soult had been sent to take command of the army of Spain, with orders to assume the offensive at once; which he did, with the ostensible view of relieving the blockade of Pampeluna.

This he failed to do, and that city ultimately surrendered on the 31st October, 1813, relieving Lord Wellington of a great drag on his movements. (Lord Wellington to Lord Bathurst, 1 Nov. 1813.) The mountainous country, in which the combats which constituted the Battle of the Pyrenees were fought, was unsuited to the movements of artillery; and the Chestnut Troop, which may be taken as a sample of those engaged, had its carriages completely shaken to pieces. Soult, having failed to relieve Pampeluna, made an attempt to raise the siege of San Sebastian (*Memoirs of Sir Hew Ross*); and, on the very day when the city was stormed, the 31st August, he attacked the Spanish forces on San Marcial for this purpose, but was defeated with loss.

The conduct of the Spanish on this occasion was much commended by Lord Wellington; and it was a singular and happy coincidence that this engagement, so creditable to the Spanish troops, was the last fought on Spanish soil. (To Lord Bathurst, 2 Sept. 1813.) Soult withdrew his forces across the frontier, and assumed the defensive. For six weeks Lord Wellington remained inactive, pending intelligence from the Allies in the north, who were then concentrating their forces against Napoleon, and would shortly demand from Lord Wellington a diversion in the south.

During these six weeks, much was done to render the equipment of the artillery suitable for a rough and winter campaign; measures were taken to expedite the arrival, from Lisbon, of some additional horses which had been sent from England; and, in the meantime, the troops and brigades were, as Colonel Dickson wrote to D.-A.-G. dated 3 Oct. 1813. Bathurst, 1 Nov. 1813), "kept above water" by the purchase of mules and French horses.

On the 7th October, Lord Wellington made a forward movement into France by crossing the Bidassoa. This has always been considered one of the ablest movements made by the great English general. The passage was effected as follows. (Colonel Dickson to D.-A.-G. dated 10 Oct. 1813.) The 5th Division and two 9-pounder brigades forded at Fuentarabia. The 1st Division, and General Wilson's brigade, with one 9-pounder brigade, and Webber Smith's Troop of Horse Artillery, crossed at Irun; the artillery of this column being commanded by Major Dyer. The passage of the 1st Division column was covered by the 18-pounder brigade and a troop of Horse Artillery.

General Freire's Galician Army passed at two fords higher up, covered by a 9-pounder brigade, Bull's troop of Horse Artillery, and a brigade of Spanish artillery. The passage of the river was effected, and the French position carried with great ease. The most difficult duty fell upon the Spaniards, who behaved well. The French, on the other hand, behaved ill. The 18-pounder brigade was especially useful in covering the passage of the troops. The attack upon the Puerto de Vera was made by the Light Division and General Giron's Spanish reserve army, supported by the 4th Division, who were successful in getting possession of the pass and adjoining heights; but not until the 9th October did the French quit the Montagne de la Rhune.

The night prior to the crossing of the Bidassoa had been very stormy, and aided in concealing the movements of the Allies. But Soult never imagined such a thing possible as "the astonishing hardihood of passing columns by fords where the tide rose 16 feet, and where the sands were half a mile broad, to force such a river as the Bidassoa at its mouth." (Cust.) In his description of the crossing of the Bidassoa, Sir Augustus Frazer mentions that, when he reached Irun with Ramsay's troop and Michell's (late Parker's) brigade, he found 400 Infantry waiting to pull the guns over the mountain to the places from which they were to cover the crossing of the army. "But," he adds with pride, "*Bull's (Ramsay's) horses never want assistance*; they were soon posted on a height with some Spanish Horse Artillery." (Frazer's *Letters*.) From a subsequent official return to the master-general, dated Vera, 10 Oct. 1813, it appears that the 9-pounder brigade which accompanied the 1st Division was Captain Dansey's; and that the 9-pounder brigade which accompanied the 5th Division was Lawson's, commanded by the 2nd Captain—Mosse. Captain Morrison still commanded the 18-pounder brigade; and Lieut.-Colonel Ross's troop of Horse Artillery was held in reserve, moving from one point to another as most required.

Including Major Arriaga's Portuguese brigade, and the other troops and brigade already mentioned, there were 48 British and Portuguese guns engaged at the passage of the Bidassoa; and the master-general was informed that the fire of the artillery on the occasion was well directed, and that the exertions made by the officers in bringing forward their respective brigades to the point of attack were most satisfactory. Lieut.-Colonel May was Assistant Adjutant-General to the artillery, Lieutenant Ord was Brigade-Major, and Lieutenant Pascoe Adjutant. Lieut.-Colonel Hartmann was in charge of the artillery in position, and Lieut.-Colonel Frazer and Major Dyer superintended the bringing forward of the guns.

Further inaction followed the passage of the Bidassoa, until the fall of Pampeluna, already mentioned, set Lord Wellington free for a further advance. During this time, attempts were made to supply mountain batteries for the coming service. Marshal Beresford brought a few 3-pounders from Lisbon; but it was found almost impossible to procure mules for them. Three guns of the same calibre, which had been taken from the French, had been temporarily equipped for single draught, and placed under the command of Lieutenant Robe, the son of the gallant officer who commanded at Roliça and Vimiera. (Colonel Dickson to D.-A.-G. dated 17 Oct. 1813.)

This young officer subsequently fell at Waterloo, having seen more battles than years. (Colonel Dickson to D.-A.-G. dated 24 Oct. 1813.) A medley equipment was found for the guns brought from Lisbon,— the artillerymen being Portuguese, but the drivers and mules being British. These guns were carried on the backs of the mules, and three of them were added to Lieutenant Robe's command. A detachment for rocket-service was also sent from England, but received by Lord Wellington with very mixed feelings, as he had rather a horror of the rocket as a weapon of war. (Colonel Dickson to D.-A.-G. dated 31 Oct. 1813.) The Chestnut Troop and Douglas's and Sympher's field brigades were also got over the mountains to Vera, for outpost duty, and to be in readiness to support the attack on the enemy's position, which Lord Wellington had decided to make as soon as Pampeluna should surrender.

The difficulty in getting these guns over was very great, and was aggravated by the tempestuous weather which prevailed; but it was effected without accident. When the news arrived from Pampeluna, which should have set the army free for forward movement into France, the weather had become such that movement was impossible. At Roncesvalles, the fall of snow was so heavy and unexpected, that three of Captain Maxwell's guns had to be abandoned in a redoubt—the guns being buried under ground and the carriages concealed under the snow. (Colonel Dickson to D.-A.-G. 7 Nov. 1813.)

Ross's, Douglas's, and Sympher's guns had, however, been advanced still farther to support in the meditated attack on the position of Sarre; Robe's mountain guns were attached to the 6th Division, and the Portuguese 3-pounders to the Light Division and Giron's army; while no fewer than 54 guns had been attached to the left of the army under Sir John Hope,—Colonel Hartmann being in command. It will thus be seen that all necessary arrangements had been made, as far as the artillery department was concerned.

(Official Report to master-general, dated St. Pé, 14 Nov. 1813, and letter from Colonel Dickson to D.-A.-G. of same date.)

The attack—which is known as the Battle of La Nivelle—took place on the 10th November, and resulted in the enemy's entrenched position being carried at every point, from St. Jean de Luz to the front of the Puerto de Maia; and in the capture of 51 French pieces of ordnance, and 1500 prisoners. The following was the distribution of the artillery during the battle; and it will be seen that the greater part remained on the left of the army—the nature of the country rendering it extremely difficult to move artillery, except by the high road from Irun:—

With Sir Rowland Hill's corps—
    Lieut.-Col. Tulloh's Portuguese brigades { One of 9-prs.
                                                                      { One of 6-prs.

With the 6th Division : Lieutenant Robe's mountain guns.

To support the attack of the 4th and ⎰Lieut.-Col. Ross's troop, R.H.A.
7th Divisions on the redoubts and ⎨Major Sympher's brigade of 9-prs.
position of Sarre.' ⎱Captain Douglas's brigade of 9-prs.

With General Giron's Spanish reserve: a half brigade of Portuguese 3-prs.

With the Light Division : a half brigade of Portuguese 3-prs.

With Lieut.-General Sir John Hope's corps—
    Lieut.-Col. Webber Smith's troop, R.H.A.
    Captain Ramsay's troop, R.H.A.
        „   Carmichael's brigade of 9-pounders.
        „   Mosse's brigade of heavy 6-pounders.
        „   Greene's brigade of 9-pounders.
        „   Cairnes' brigade of 9-pounders.
        „   Michell's brigade of 9-pounders.
    Major Arriaga's Portuguese 9-pounders.
        „   Morrison's 18-pounders.

There was also a brigade of Spanish artillery with General Freire's army.

The artillery with Sir John Hope's column was but little engaged, as its advance depended on the success of the right; but it kept up a heavy and successful cannonade, and met with a few casualties. The artillery on the right, in support of the attack on the redoubts, was, however, of essential service; and was skilfully handled by the field officers in charge, Lieut.-Colonels Frazer and Buckner. They opened a vigorous fire on the first redoubt, while the 4th Division was moving forward to assault it, and the effect of the fire was such as to compel the enemy to abandon the redoubt without waiting for the assault. At this time the Chestnut Troop distinguished itself especially. Colonel Dickson wrote:

> I must particularly notice the gallant manner in which Lieut.-Colonel Ross's troop was moved to an advanced position, when it reopened its fire at the distance of 350 yards from the work, and covered the approach of the others. In this operation Lieutenant Day was severely wounded.

As soon as the enemy quitted the first redoubt, the guns moved forward to support the 7th Division in the attack of the second, but after a few rounds it also was abandoned. In the subsequent operations on the right, the artillery were unable to take much part, on account of the difficulty in moving the guns. (Cust.) The frightful state of the roads also aided the ultimate escape of the enemy without pursuit. To use Sir Augustus Frazer's words, (*Letters*), the ground over which the

Battle of La Nivelle was fought was:

> So rugged, that it would be difficult to attempt a sketch of it. You must fancy rocks, and hills, and woods, and mountains, interspersed with rough heaths and rivers, and everything but plain ground.

The casualties in the artillery were as follows:—

> Lieut.-Col. Ross's troop—
> Killed: 1 man, and 1 horse.
> Wounded: 1 officer, 10 non-commissioned officers and men, and 4 horses.
> Lieut.-Col. Smith's troop—
> Killed: 1 man, and 2 horses.
> Wounded: 6 non-commissioned officers and men, and 7 horses.
> Major Bull's (Ramsay's) troop—
> Killed: 1 man, and 1 horse.
> Wounded: 2 non-commissioned officers and men.
> Captain Michell's brigade—Wounded: 3 gunners.
> Captain Carmichael's brigade—Wounded: No officers or men. 1 horse.
> Lieutenant Robe's brigade—Killed: 1 mule.
> Total—Killed: 3 men, 4 horses, 1 mule.
> Wounded: 1 officer, 21 non-commissioned officers and men, 12 horses.

The entire losses of the Allies at La Nivelle amounted to 2694 killed and wounded. The conduct of the artillery during the battle was such as to excite the following comments:

> Flattering compliments were paid by all on the undoubted service of the three batteries of artillery on this occasion, i.e. the attack on the redoubts. (*Letters*.)

Colonel Dickson wrote (Official Despatch 14 Nov. 1813):

> I beg you will further state to the master-general, that I have every reason to be satisfied with the conduct of all the field officers, officers, non-commissioned officers, and men, employed on this occasion; as also of Lieut.-Colonel May, and the officers of the Artillery Staff.

In his private letter to General Macleod, Colonel Dickson wrote:

The attack of the first redoubt at Sarre it was expected would be a very obstinate operation, and for that reason all the eighteen guns were brought up against it; however, their fire was so active and well directed, and Frazer pushed the guns up so close that the enemy could not stand it.

In another report, dated St. Jean de Luz, 21 Nov. 1813, Colonel Dickson said that the mountain guns under Lieutenant Robe, and the Portuguese guns of similar calibre, were most active and useful, accompanying their respective corps during the day, and supporting the advance of their light troops.

Captain Ramsay's troop and Captain Carmichael's brigade, with Sir J. Hope's force, were especially mentioned;—the former for having repeatedly silenced the guns opposed to him, and dismounted one in the redoubt in front of the 12th and 16th Dragoons; and the latter for having repeatedly driven back the enemy's skirmishers, silenced their guns, and dismounted one in the redoubt opposite the 1st German Regiment of Infantry. (Major Dyer to Lieut.-Col. Hartmann, 12 Nov. 1813.)

Lord Wellington, to Lord Bathurst, in his despatch, dated St. Pé, 13 Nov. 1813, said:

> The artillery which was in the field was of great use to us; and I cannot sufficiently acknowledge the intelligence and activity with which it was brought to the point of attack, under the direction of Colonel Dickson, over the bad roads through the mountains, at this season of the year.

The success of the Allies on the right obliged the enemy to abandon the works at St. Jean de Luz, but any further immediate advance was forbidden to Lord Wellington by the incessant rain which fell for some days. (Colonel Dickson to D.-A.-G. dated 28 Nov. 1813.) During this period of compulsory inactivity, every endeavour was made to generate confidence among the French inhabitants, and although rendered difficult by the irregularities committed by the Allied troops, the attempts were ultimately successful. Writing on the 5th December, 1813, Colonel Dickson, after his usual announcement that it had never ceased raining, and that the country was quite impassable, went on to say:

> The inhabitants continue to return to their homes, and we are the best friends possible.

The dullness of the weather at St. Jean de Luz, and the inactivity which Colonel Dickson abhorred, were cheered by an announcement that the Portuguese Government had been pleased to promote him to the rank of colonel in their service, in recognition of his recent services.

The weather having at length sufficiently moderated to admit of further operations in the field, Lord Wellington forced the passage of the Nive at Ustaritz and Cambo, on the 9th December, with the view of extending his right towards the Adour. (Lord Wellington to Lord Bathurst, dated 14 Dec. 1813.)

On the 10th, Soult made an attack on the Allies' left, near Biarritz, and on the Light Division near Arcangues; but he failed in both. The services on this occasion of Captain Ramsay's troop, and of a division of Captain Mosse's brigade, were very conspicuous. (MS. Return to the master-general, dated 15 Dec. 1813.) A similar attempt was made on the 11th, in which the French were again repulsed; Captain Ramsay's troop, and the whole of Captain Mosse's brigade, again rendering most valuable assistance in the defence of the position. (Colonel Dickson to General Macleod, dated 15 Dec. 1813.)

Marshal Soult, being thus disappointed in his hopes of making an impression on the Allied left, drew the greater part of his force back to Bayonne on the night of the 12th December, and in the early morning of the 13th, made a determined attack with great force on Sir Rowland Hill's corps, which was in position on the right of the Nive. His attempts were, however, vigorously repulsed, and he had eventually to retire into his entrenched camp, with great loss.

The artillery with Sir Rowland Hill consisted of the Chestnut Troop and Colonel Tulloh's Portuguese brigades. With reference to their conduct, Colonel Dickson wrote:

> Nothing could be stronger than the manner in which Sir Rowland expressed to me his satisfaction at the conduct of both these corps.

Colonel Tulloh was wounded on this occasion. At the same time as the passage of the Nive was forced, Sir John Hope's corps on the left reconnoitred Bayonne. General Hay, who commanded the 5th Division with this corps, wrote to Colonel Dickson, dated 12 Dec. 1813, as follows with reference to two guns of Captain Ramsay's troop, which were attached to him:

> I take the first spare moment to mention to you how much I was pleased, on the 9th instant, with the very gallant, zealous, and skilful conduct of Captain Cator, who commanded two

guns of Captain Ramsay's troop of Horse Artillery attached to me on that day, which were of the greatest use in assisting me to dislodge a very superior body of the enemy opposed to me.

The attacks made on the 13th by Soult were admirably planned, but the dogged courage of the five infantry brigades, which was the whole force which Sir Rowland Hill had at first to oppose to him, was invincible. Although driven back into his intrenchments, his position was one which was most objectionable to the Allies. His attacks were like *sorties* from a fortress—which he could make in great force upon any point, and if he failed, his retreat was short and easy. (Colonel Dickson to D.-A.-G. 15 Dec. 1813.)

It was resolved, therefore, to strengthen the position occupied by the Allies—to fortify one or two salient points—and to place some guns of position. The army then went into cantonments—the Spaniards recrossing the Bidassoa for that purpose—but, as may be imagined, winter quarters in front of an enemy, known to be very active, did not conduce to any sense of repose among the commanders. The conduct of the artillery at the action of the 13th December was thus noticed by Lord Wellington (to Lord Bathurst, 14 Dec. 1813):

> The British artillery under Lieut.-Colonel Ross, and the Portuguese artillery under Colonel Tulloh, distinguished themselves.

In the same despatch, the name of Norman Ramsay appears, as having been favourably mentioned by Sir John Hope. Like that brave general, Ramsay had also been twice wounded during the operations on the Nive.

During the few weeks which preceded the resumption of hostilities in 1814, the mortality among the artillery horses exceeded anything that had yet been witnessed. (In the end of January 1814, after giving over the horses to the pontoons, 460 were deficient for the artillery, and 200 others were sick or worn out. To meet this deficiency, 500 had been promised, and were to leave England in February.)

An accident, which occurred to a supply sent from England to reinforce them, by which many were killed on board the transports during a storm, was particularly ill-timed. And, to crown the evil, Lord Wellington, having decided on the passage of the Adour, ordered the pontoon train to be increased, and horsed without delay. There was no alternative but to take the horses from one of the artillery brigades; and the unfortunate Captain Cairnes was again the victim. Luckily for him, the promotions consequent on the formation of the Rocket troops had just been notified from England; and as Norman Ramsay received his promotion to the rank of 1st Captain, and returned to England, the command of his troop was given to Captain Cairnes.

The movements in the spring of 1814 were important, and on a considerable scale. In the end of January, the enemy showed considerable activity on the Adour, and fitted out several gun-boats to keep the navigation open, and to annoy the posts of the Allies. (Colonel Dickson to D.-A.-G. 30 Jan. 1814.) Against these Lieutenant Robe's mountain brigade was first employed, but it was soon found necessary to supplement it with guns of a heavier calibre. But in the following month, a change in the weather—from rain to frost—induced Lord Wellington to commence the execution of operations, which he had been quietly designing for some weeks. These included the passage of the Adour near its mouth—a feat deemed by Soult impossible—and a simultaneous attack on the left of the French Army to conceal his real intention from Soult.

Colonel Dickson was sent to assist Sir John Hope in the former operation, which the reader knows was well and skilfully executed. While the covering fire of the artillery at the passage of the Adour was generally effective, that of the now famous 18-pounder brigade was especially so. Lord Wellington superintended the operations on the right; and as his numbers were now superior to his enemy's, he was able without risk to carry out both parts of his scheme at the same time, and to drive Soult's forces back from their position. The various operations, which culminated in the Battle of Orthes, are too long to reproduce in a work of this description; suffice it to give an account of the services of the artillery at that great battle. Colonel Dickson being away, the command of the artillery with the right of the army fell to Major Carncross.

Colonel Frazer had been ordered to go with Sir John Hope's army to the Adour, in charge of Captain Lane's rocket detachments, which did good service during the passage of the river. It may here be mentioned, that during the operations prior to the investment of Bayonne, which followed the passage of the Adour, Colonel Frazer was wounded. Although, however, Major Carncross was senior officer of artillery on the field, yet, being with Sir Howland Hill's column, he did not participate in the action so much as Major Dyer, who was with Marshal Beresford's column, and from whose reports the services of the various batteries can more readily be traced.

On the morning of the 27th February, the 3rd, 4th, 6th, 7th, and light divisions of Infantry, Colonel Vivian's and Lord Edward Somerset's brigades of cavalry, Ross's and Gardiner's troops of Horse Artillery, and Maxwell's, Sympher's, Turner's (late Douglas's), and Michell's brigades of Field Artillery, had crossed the River Pau, over which a pontoon bridge had been placed during the night. (Major Jenkinson R.H.A. to Colonel Frazer, dated 4 March, 1814.)

Colonel Ross was no longer with the Chestnut Troop, he having returned to England on leave, and given the command to his 2nd Captain, Major Jenkinson. (*Memoirs.*) The enemy was found to be in full force on a strong height near the villages of St. Marie and St. Boe's, and his left covering Orthes, and the fords between Depart and Biron. (Major Jenkinson, 4 March, 1814.)

The battle commenced early in the day, and ended after severe fighting, and a loss to the Allies of 2200 killed and wounded, in the total defeat of the French, with a loss, which—if the numerous deserters be included, who came over afterwards—has been estimated at no fewer than 14,000. (Cust's *Annals.*) Although the verdict of Lord Wellington might satisfy the most fastidious artilleryman, (Despatch to Lord Bathurst, dated 1 March, 1814), "The conduct of the artillery throughout the day deserved my entire approbation,"—a few extracts from the correspondence of the officers present at the battle cannot fail to be interesting;—and the opinions of generals of division must be deemed valuable.

Taking the latter first, it is recorded that Sir Thomas Picton expressed himself in terms of the highest praise with reference to Captain Turner's brigade; and Sir Lowry Cole did the same in regard to Major Sympher's. (Colonel Dickson to D.-A.-G. dated 4 March, 1814.) The last-named officer, who had done such good and continuous service in the Peninsular War, was killed at Orthes, at the very commencement of the action. Major Jenkinson wrote in general terms, that "all the general officers speak in high terms of the services of Ross's and Gardiner's troops, as also of poor Sympher's brigade." Major Dyer, in his report, wrote to Colonel Dickson, dated 3 March, 1814:

> I had the satisfaction about one o'clock to get Lieut.-Colonel Ross's and Gardiner's troops of Horse Artillery, and the German brigade of artillery attached to the 4th Division, into position opposite the enemy's strongest columns: the fire from their guns was tremendous, and, being admirably served, soon caused the enemy to retire. The brigades then took up separate posi-

tions and annoyed the enemy. About 4 o'clock the guns ceased firing, the enemy retreating in great confusion, leaving some pieces of cannon on the field. I have to regret the loss of Major Sympher and many valuable artillerymen.

In his official report to Marshal Beresford, dated 3 March, 1814, Major Dyer wrote:

> I should really feel that I omitted a duty imposed upon me if I did not recommend to your Excellency's notice the conduct of Major Sympher, Major Gardiner, and Major Jenkinson on that brilliant day.
>
> Captain Beane's troop of Horse Artillery was with Sir Rowland Hill's force, under Major Carncross; and that officer was able to speak with pride of the steady, well-directed, and destructive fire kept up by it, although exposed to a very severe fire of musketry. On the 2nd March, Sir Rowland Hill's force came up with the enemy, and Captain Beane's troop performed services for which it was specially mentioned in orders. (Major Carncross to Colonel Dickson, dated 10 March,1814.)
>
> Four guns belonging to it were brought into action with great effect; and one of them, under Lieutenant Brereton, after a few rounds, silenced two of the enemy's, and forced them to retire. On this day, Captain Macdonald, of Captain Beane's troop, distinguished himself in leading on the Portuguese troops, who had been forced back; and received Sir Rowland Hill's thanks in public orders on the following day. Sir Rowland took the opportunity of assuring Major Carncross that, on the several occasions on which the troop had been recently engaged, he had been much satisfied with the officers, non-commissioned officers, and men composing it.

A period of inactivity followed the Battle of Orthes; and not until April did Wellington resume active operations; but in the meantime, Marshal Beresford, with a considerable force, proceeded to Bordeaux, and was received with great delight. Louis XVIII. was proclaimed, and the badges of the Empire were doffed by the magistrates. During this time Colonel Dickson's life had become a burden to him. Innumerable accidents and delays occurred to the horses which were on the way to reinforce his brigades; and at the same time the drain on his resources to meet the wants of the pontoon train daily increased. He wrote to D.-A.-G. dated 2 April,1814:

The pontoon equipment has become such a *sink* of horses under the stupidity, inability, and inactivity of the driver officers, that I have been obliged, in consequence of the continued observations of Lord Wellington, to place artillery officers to superintend the care of the horses, until the arrival of the Alicante army, when officers and men of the Royal Artillery are to be posted to the pontoon train, by which the bridge department will revert to the corps it always belonged to. The bad state of the concern in its mode of organisation enabled me to convince his Lordship of the benefit that would arise by having it under one head and managed by the same officers *He was ignorant of its having formerly been an artillery concern; and he added that he did not know how it had got into the hands of the engineers at first.*

To return, however, to the movements of the army. Marshal Soult, having learnt what had taken place at Bayonne, commenced to retire upon Toulouse, and Wellington followed in pursuit, but very leisurely. (Cust.) The Allies had 40,000 bayonets and 60 guns to oppose to Soult's 28,000 and 38 guns; but a reinforcement was expected by the latter in the shape of Suchet's army from the east of Spain; and the position at Toulouse, on which he was retreating had been strengthened by gradual intrenchments during the past few weeks.

In the commencement of Soult's retreat, one or two smart actions had taken place between divisions of the Allies and the French, but without any result other than perhaps increasing the rapidity of Soult's movements. Toulouse was an important strategic post for the French; it commanded the passage of the Garonne; a number of roads met there, which would enable Soult to carry out many different schemes; and it was the chief military arsenal in the south of France. Here, if ever, something might be done to benefit the fast-failing fortunes of the French Emperor, whom the Allies in the north were hunting relentlessly to his doom.

(Colonel Dickson to D.-A.-Gen. 13 April, 1814.) When Wellington reached the Garonne, his first intention was to cross it above Toulouse; but this was found so difficult that the idea was given up, and a flank march having been made on the 3rd April to a convenient situation about a mile above Grenade, and below Toulouse, the pontoon bridge was laid early in the morning of the 4th, and three divisions (the 3rd, 4th, and 6th) with their artillery, as also six regiments of cavalry with Major Gardiner's troop of Horse Artillery, crossed without opposition.

During this operation, however, the river rose considerably, owing to the rains which had fallen during the previous night; and at last the further passage of troops was suspended. Heavy rain fell again on the night of the 4th, and the river increased so much that the pontoons were obliged to be drawn into the banks, and the army was thus divided into two parts. Strangely enough, Marshal Soult did not avail himself of this circumstance, although it was the morning of the 8th before the river was sufficiently low to admit of the bridge being relaid. The Spanish corps, Colonel Arentschild's Portuguese artillery, and the headquarters staff passed over on that day. The bridge was then moved a little farther up the river, and early on the morning of the 10th April the Light Division crossed.

On this day was fought the Battle of Toulouse. The offensive was taken by Lord Wellington, who attacked a strong position which the enemy had fortified to cover the city of Toulouse, and succeeded in obtaining entire possession of it after an obstinate resistance. (MS. Official Despatch to the master-general, dated Toulouse, 13 April, 1814.)

In consequence of this defeat, Soult evacuated Toulouse during the night of the 11th, retiring by the route to Carcassone. The distribution and services of the artillery of the Allies were as follows. The Portuguese artillery, consisting of ten 9-pounder guns, under Colonel Arentschild, covered the attack made by the Spaniards on the left of the enemy's position. This artillery was warmly engaged during the best part of the day, and distinguished itself greatly by its firmness and correct firing.

A German brigade, under Captain Daniel, and Captain Brandreth's 9-pounder brigade, both under Major Dyer, were for some time employed in covering the movements of Marshal Beresford's column in its attack on the right of the position; and on that being carried, they moved up to higher ground, and assisted in taking the remainder of the position, and also in moderating the fire of the enemy from the opposite side of the canal, across which the French were ultimately driven. The enemy's fire from that point had greatly annoyed the Allies; and Colonel Dickson expressed himself highly satisfied with the counter-effect produced by the fire of Captain Brandreth's and Captain Daniel's guns.

Major Gardiner's troop of Horse Artillery was at first employed in supporting the left of the Spanish attack, and afterwards moved to the ridge carried by Marshal Beresford, where Colonel Dickson reported that it was "of infinite service." While these operations were going on,

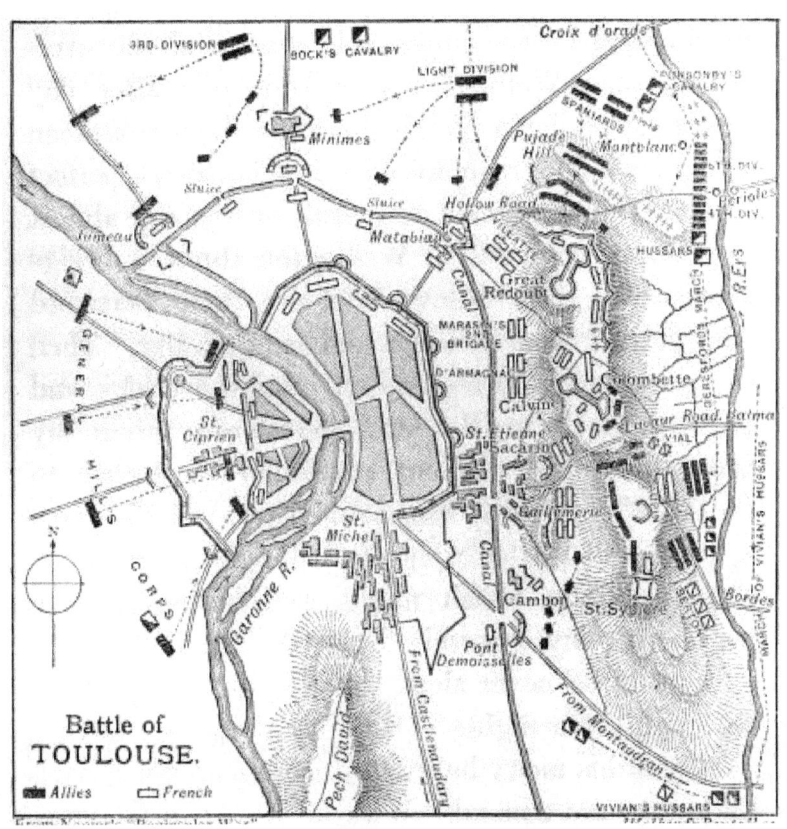

the 3rd and Light Divisions were employed in threatening the enemy's position along the canal, towards the point where it joined the Garonne. In this service, Captain Turner's (late Douglas's) brigade was engaged. Captain Bean's troop and Captain Maxwell's brigade (now No. 4 Battery, 7th Brigade) were on the opposite side of the river with Sir Rowland Hill's corps, engaged in the attack made upon the *tête de pont*. The officers on the staff of the artillery at the Battle of Toulouse were Lieut.-Colonel May, Lieut.-Colonel Frazer, and Lieutenants Ord and Bell. From these officers Colonel Dickson reported that he had received every assistance.

The casualties among the artillery engaged amounted to 1 officer (Lieutenant Blumenbach, K.G.A., killed) and 58 non-commissioned officers and men killed and wounded. Among the horses, 28 were killed and 13 wounded. The casualties among the Royal Horse Artillery engaged amounted to 8 men and 4 horses; and among the Royal Artillery brigades to 29 men and 23 horses. The remaining casualties occurred among the Germans and Portuguese. (MS. Return to B.O.)

Early in the morning of the 12th, the Allies took possession of Toulouse, and the white flag was hoisted. (Colonel Dickson to D.-A.-G. 13 April, 1814.) Lord Wellington was received by the corporation at the Town Hall, and addressed them, pointing out the necessity of weighing well the step which they were about to take at a moment when a congress was possibly sitting, for the purpose of making peace with Napoleon. *Vive le Roi!* however, was heard from every lip, and every one mounted a white cockade. In the evening of the 12th, a messenger arrived from Paris with the intelligence of Napoleon's abdication, and the restoration of the Bourbons. The intelligence was very welcome to the inhabitants of Toulouse, who could not but feel rather nervous after the step which they had taken. The same messengers carried to Marshal Soult the news of the Allies entering Paris, and of the official dethronement of Napoleon by the Senate; but he would give them no credence.

How faithfully Napoleon was served by his lieutenants, and how devotedly they clung to his cause, must be apparent to the most superficial reader of his history. In him, who has been called the incarnation of war in all its bad as well as good attributes, they saw but one who was *facile princeps* in the profession which they loved;—seeing this, they clung to his cause to the bitter end; and with a hungering in their hearts for his leadership, even while serving another prince, they turned to him, after his escape from Elba, with an enthusiasm more like the love of a woman than the cold, reasoning affection of a man.

Soldiers, indeed, have many of the qualities of the other sex. Once let them believe in a leader, and no disasters, no slanders will upset their creed; and from a leader, whom they love, even many harsh words will be forgotten in the presence of one word of kindness. There are those who think that a soldier's mind is like a blank page, on which their own views and wishes may with ease be inscribed.

And in one sense they are right. Let skill and courage once be visible in a commander, and the obedience and enthusiasm of his men will be his; but let him supplement these qualities by thoughtful consideration, by kind words, by ready participation in hardships, and he will earn from them a love which shall pass even the love of women. But the kind words will not win it without the skill, nor the consideration without the courage.

On Soult's refusing to credit the intelligence from Paris, Lord Wellington made arrangements for moving forward with the army. On the 16th, however, a French officer arrived from Paris with despatches for Marshal Soult; and this was followed by an officer arriving from the French Army to treat with Lord Wellington. (Colonel Dickson to D.-A.-G. dated Toulouse, 18 April, 1814.)

Had the despatches but arrived a little sooner, a loss of life would have been saved at Bayonne. A *sortie* was made from the city, on the 14th April, which, although unsuccessful, resulted in the death of General Hay and not a few brave officers, and in the capture of that most brave and chivalrous leader, Sir John Hope.

The war was now over; but, before closing this chapter, let a word be said with reference to the services of an officer of the corps who commanded with distinction the rocket detachments attached to the Allied army at Leipsic in 1813, and who met a soldier's death many years after, at the Battle of Inkermann—Thomas Fox Strangways. At Leipsic he commanded, from the circumstance that his Captain, Bogue, fell early in the day. He was then but a subaltern; but ere he left the field, at the head of his brigade he received the personal thanks of the Allied sovereigns; and the Emperor of Russia, taking from his breast the order of St. Anne, placed it upon that of the young officer whose services had been so eminent on that day. (From a letter written by Lady Fox Strangways.)

In recounting the story of the battle, Sir Edward Cust says that such was the fearful effect of the rockets, that a whole brigade surrendered after enduring their fire for a few minutes; and it has also been recorded, on the best evidence, that, at a most critical time of the battle, the Crown Prince of Sweden rode up to him, and implored him to advance his brigade, as nothing else would save the day. To his exertions at Leipsic was the subsequent organisation of regular rocket troops due; and on this taking place the command of the brave men, who had distinguished themselves at Leipsic, passed into the hands of one both able and brave,—one who had done noble service in the Peninsula, which he was to repeat at Waterloo,—gentle and yet enthusiastic,—the late Sir E. C. Whinyates.

In closing this narrative of the services of the artillery in the Peninsula, it is impossible to avoid feeling that it has fallen immeasurably short of the narrative to which these services are justly entitled. It is felt that the attempt to place before the reader the chivalry, courage, and endurance of those who represented the corps in the great wars with France, has been defeated by considerations of space, as well as by the writer's inexperience. To realise these qualities thoroughly, it will be necessary for the reader to clothe these skeleton pages with the noble drapery of Napier.

But if these qualities, which are matter of history, have failed to receive adequate description, how much greater has been the shortcoming in endeavouring to picture those virtues, which can only be detected in the intimacy of private friendship, or the study of private correspondence! It is only from the latter that the student is now able to see how almost brotherly was the relationship between the officers of the corps in Lord Wellington's army. For example:—on hearing of Colonel Dickson's promotion by the Portuguese Government, in the winter of 1813, what were the words of the man whom he had superseded, and who was as able as himself? Sir Augustus Frazer wrote:

> I wish that he were a general; he fully deserves all that can be given him either as honour or reward.

And as he felt, so did all. In the letters, also, announcing the artillery losses at the various battles in that war, of which it has been said that the Allies "left 40,000 of their own number dead on the plains and mountains of the Peninsula," (Cust.) how fervently does the loving, brotherly spirit appear! Each good quality in the dead is fondly dwelt upon; and as one gazes on the loving words, written on pages now so faded by hands so long still, there rises a picture of a Regimental unity which it were a sacrilege now to disturb by internal differences. It is, indeed, well at times to close our eyes to the present, and to look back at the past;—a standard is often to be found there which shall dwarf that which we may have set up in our self-esteem, and thought colossal.

Possibly, never in the whole history of the regiment has there been a time of such intellectual life among its members, as at the present day; but as the great school of experience, which in the beginning of this century made giants of our artillerymen, is not now open, it may be that there is almost a danger in this mental activity, unless it be tempered by the study of comrades, who in days gone by were the embodiments of duty, courage, and hardihood. Thus, history may furnish to the student a stability, which shall allay present restlessness.

CHAPTER 11

Waterloo

The year, with which this narrative must for the present be brought to an end, was an eventful one. The same year which witnessed the great Battle of Waterloo was the hundredth of the regiment's existence. How marvellous was the development of England's artillery between 1716 and 1815, cannot be better seen than in contrasting the two struggling companies of the former year with the magnificent force of artillery collected in Belgium in 1815, of which its commander, Sir George Wood, wrote to D.-A.-G. dated Brussels, 16 May, 1815:

> I do believe there never was in the world such a proportion of artillery so well equipped. The result must be felt by Europe.

The growing importance of the arm is apparent from the following statistics. The proportion of guns per 1000 men in the British armies at Marlborough's three famous battles was as follows: Blenheim, 1·2; Ramilies, 2; and Malplaquet, 1·1. In the Peninsula, the proportion was somewhat higher: at Corunna, 3; Talavera, 1·2; Albuera, 1·2; Salamanca, 2; Vittoria, 1·3; Nivelle, 1·3; Orthes, 1·3; and Toulouse, 1·2. But during the whole of the Peninsular War, the Duke of Wellington complained that he was inadequately supplied with artillery; and as soon as war was inevitable in 1815, he urged upon the Government at home to send him a large proportion of that arm. The result was that in the British army at the Battle of Waterloo the proportion of guns per 1000 men was no less than 3·7.

The circumstances, which led to this great battle, must first be briefly stated. It will be in the reader's recollection that in February 1815, Napoleon quitted Elba; and on the 20th March entered the Tuileries.

As he had foreseen, the army rallied round him; but to his mortification he found coldness and even mistrust on the part of the Chambers, and a decided apathy on the part of the civil population. He beheld also the whole of continental Europe resolving to arm against him,—to stamp out the man, who had so audaciously violated the solemn Convention of Paris; while England—to compensate for the weakness of her military contingent—furnished money to the other powers, and a general whose name was in itself a host.

No uncertain sound came from the European council, which sat at Vienna; and Napoleon saw before him a stern and growing resolution for war to the bitter end. He was not sorry. If he could win battles, he knew that he would have found a cure for all coldness at home:—the army, which had again placed him on the throne, would, if victorious, consolidate his power, and make him independent of all who distrusted him. He commenced, therefore, to reorganise and equip a force which should sweep all before it. He hastened his preparations, in the hope of encountering his enemies in detail, before they should have effected that concentration of their armies along the entire eastern frontier of France, which he knew they contemplated. It will be seen, hereafter, that on more than one occasion during this last of Napoleon's campaigns, he was guilty of unaccountable lack of energy; but no one can fail to admire the spirit and ability with which in the short spring of that fatal year he organised the army, which was to ensure his complete success, or witness his utter ruin.

To realise his difficulties, one must bear in mind the state of the country which he governed. "France had exhausted her vigour in the unrestrained indulgence of her passion for military glory. Her blood was impoverished—her muscles relaxed, her nerves unstrung, her moral force debilitated by twenty-three years of almost uninterrupted warfare. The laurels gathered in a hundred battles were poor compensation for a paralyzed industry and a crippled commerce,—for desolate cornfields and half-cultured vineyards. She was *la belle France* no longer;—she had used her prime in the debauch of war!" (Hooper.)

And yet from this country, Napoleon, before the middle of June, had raised the effective force of the regular army to no less than 276,000 men; besides having 200,000 other and inferior troops.

He determined to carry the war first into Belgium. For concentrating an army with this view, the line of fortresses on the French frontier to the north-east offered special advantages. And, on crossing it in force, he hoped to defeat the Prussians and English separately—to make by this means the war and the government unpopular in Eng-

Artillery at Waterloo

land—and to detach from the Allies some whom he believed to be but half-hearted in their opposition to him. Another and important reason for selecting Belgium as the theatre of his operations, was the undoubted presence in that country of many who on his first success would flock to his standard.

On the night of the 14th June, Napoleon had collected on the French side of the frontier an army ready to march on the following morning, consisting of 128,000 men, and 344 guns. Of this number, 22,000 were cavalry; and the whole force was divided into five *corps d'armée*, besides the Imperial Guard, and four corps of reserve cavalry. On that night he slept at Avesnes, which he made his headquarters, and from which he issued a characteristic address to his troops. Leaving him there,—with the great mass of his army "gathered, so to speak, to a head at Beaumont," (Hooper), and pointing directly upon Charleroi,—the reader is invited to turn to the English Army, and examine its constitution and disposition.

A force of artillery had been in Holland for some time with Sir T. Graham—under the command of Sir G. A. Wood; and this formed the nucleus of the contingent of that arm in the Duke of Wellington's army in Belgium. Many names familiar to the reader re-appear in the lists of those who fought at Waterloo. Colonel—now Sir Alexander—Dickson was still in America; but arrived in time for the battle. Others, who had received honours for their Peninsular services, were also there: Sir Augustus Frazer, Sir John May, Sir Hew Ross, and Sir Robert Gardiner. Norman Ramsay, transferred to another troop in order to be present, had also joined; and was already, as Sir Augustus Frazer wrote, "adored by his men:—kind, generous, and manly, he is more than the friend of his soldiers." (*Letters.*) Other names will appear, as the narrative proceeds; suffice it at present to say that it is doubtful if ever in one field, or even in one generation, the Regiment has had so many able men gathered together.

Sir George Wood was enthusiastic, and revelled in his command. His enthusiasm, while not forbidding him to point out his wants, aided him in remedying or bearing them. They were at first but two in number; but they were rather important to a force, for they were officers and men. Fortunately for him and the corps, General Macleod was still Deputy Adjutant-General of the Royal Artillery, and was indefatigable in supplying Sir George Wood's demands. As fast as the companies and drivers arrived from America, they were sent to Belgium; but the demand still exceeded the supply. Only six days before the battle, it is recorded that no fewer than 1000 drivers were wanting.

This had been partly caused by the Duke of Wellington insisting on the formation of three brigades of 18-pounders, to be placed under the command of Sir Alexander Dickson; and partly by the demands of the small-arm ammunition trains. He would neither hire nor enlist Belgian drivers, saying that he placed too much consequence on his artillery to trust it to such a crew; and he ordered Sir George Wood to write to General Macleod, 9 June, 1815, requesting that four companies of foot artillery might be sent out to act as drivers.

It was not often that the duke tried to coax the board, or honoured it with his reasons; but on this occasion he did. He said that he was well aware that it was not the particular duty of artillery soldiers to take care of horses, but he was confident that should the master-general be pleased to allow that duty to be performed by gunners for the present, the service would receive much greater benefit,—"the artillery officers having more power over their own men, than any given number from the Line;" and that in the case of a siege they might do their artillery duties in the trenches, as at Antwerp in 1814.

It was on the 4th April, 1815, that the Duke of Wellington reached Brussels. Less fortunate than Sir George Wood, he found that his demands, at first, were merely made excuses by the authorities at home for the exercise of official patronage. He at last ironically suggested to them that it would be well, before sending him any more generals, to send him some men for them to command. The local arrangements, as far as the artillery was concerned, are graphically described in Sir A. Frazer's letters, and in General Mercer's journal of the Waterloo campaign.

The historian must, however, draw his information from a less sparkling stream—the official letters of Sir George Wood and others. From these it is ascertained that Ostend was the principal port of disembarkation for artillery and stores: that Sir George Wood himself, and afterwards Sir A. Frazer and Lieutenant-Colonel S. G. Adye, superintended the arrival of these at Ostend, and their removal to various places; and that in these matters they were assisted by a man whom all united to pronounce marvellously able, Mr. Commissary Stace.

It appears that the urgent demands for more Horse Artillery came from Sir A. Frazer, who was appointed to the command of that branch; whereas the duke himself at first seemed more anxious to get drivers for the brigades, and foot artillerymen for the garrisons of Mons, Oudenarde, Ghent, and Ath. (Sir G. Wood to D.-A.-G. Ostend, 1 May, 1815.) As early as the beginning of May, the duke almost broke Captain Whinyates's heart by deciding on changing his rocket troop into an ordinary troop: nor was it without much difficulty and pleading, that Sir G. Wood succeeded in obtaining permission for him to carry a proportion of 12-pounder rockets with his guns. (Mercer's *Journal*, vol. 1.)

The duke's prejudice against rockets was unmistakable; and his unofficial language on this occasion was somewhat unfeeling; but the official reason he gave was that when he had a proper proportion of artillery attached to his army, as all other nations had, then he would bring the Rocket Corps into play, (Sir G. A. Wood to D.-A.-G. 1 May, 1815); but that he thought, situated as he was, the gun a superior weapon. The argument, which had most weight in support of the request to retain a proportion of rockets, was thus stated by Sir G. Wood to D.-A.-G. 8 May, 1815:

> The duke was determined at first to place the rockets in depot, but after the good appearance of our friend Whinyates's troop, and the plan and mode he suggested to his Grace, he has permitted him to take into the field eight hundred rounds of rockets with his six guns, which makes him very complete.

The horsing of the Horse and Field Batteries during the Waterloo campaign was admirable; but the Field Artillery excelled in this particular to such an extent, that Sir George Wood wrote to D.-A.-G. 8 May, 1815: "the Horse Artillery are really jealous of their appearance." The duke had inspected the 9-pounder Field Brigade, commanded by Captain C. F. Sandham, and had been so pleased that he desired General Maitland to write to that officer as follows:

> The Duke of Wellington has desired me to communicate to you (and I have to request you will do so to the officers, non-commissioned officers, and soldiers under your command), his *unqualified approbation* of the appearance of the brigade. I feel gratified in being able to assure you that he commented on the horses, appointments, and every part of it, with peculiar approbation.

This company, which was No. 9 of the 3rd Battalion, and fired the first shot at Waterloo, was—alas!—reduced in 1819. In forwarding a copy of the above complimentary letter to the Ordnance, Sir G. Wood said: "All the other brigades are equal, if not better, in horses." What a contrast to the Field Brigades of Egypt, and the first years of the

Peninsula!—how staunchly had the lessons taught by the experience of the latter been studied and accepted!

On the 12th May, the duke desired Sir G. Wood to write to the Ordnance, D.-A.-G. Brussels, 12 May, 1815, requesting that two troops of Horse Artillery, in addition to the six already in Belgium, should be sent out; stating, as his reason, the deficiency of Field Brigades, and the impossibility of getting drivers in sufficient numbers. He would gladly have taken 1000 drivers over his actual artillery wants, for service with the small-arm ammunition waggons, which he had succeeded in horsing in the country. Sir H. Ross's, the Chestnut Troop, and Major Beane's, were accordingly despatched; and arrived, the former, at Ghent, on the 9th June, and the latter on the 10th, at Ostend. Frazer's *Letters*.)

Constant changes in the armament of the troops of Horse Artillery in Belgium had been suggested with a view to increasing the weight of metal, and some of a tentative description were made in the beginning of May. On the 16th of that month, the following armament was finally decided upon:—

M.S. Return to D.-A.-G. with Letter from Col. Adye, 30 May, 1815, and Sir G. Wood, to D.-A.-G. 2 June, 1815.

	Guns.				Ammunition Carriages.				
	9-prs.	Light 6-prs.	Hvy. 5½-in. how^s.	Total.	9-prs.	Light 6-prs.	Hvy. 5½-in. how^s.	Caissons.	Total.
Sir H. D. Ross's Troop	5	..	1	6	7	..	2	..	9
Sir R. Gardiner's ,,	..	5	1	6	..	7	2	..	9
Lt.-Col. Webber Smith's ,,	..	5	1	6	..	7	2	..	9
Captain Mercer's (G) ,,	5	..	1	6	7	..	2	..	9
Major Ramsay's ,,	5	..	1	6	7	..	2	..	9
Major Bull's ,,	..	..	6	6	..	..	9	..	9
Captain Whinyates's ,,	..	5	1	6	..	5	1	6	12
	15	15	12	42	21	19	20	6	66

N.B.—Major Beane's Troop, when it arrived, was armed like Sir H. Ross's.

This change of armament proved very beneficial at Waterloo; but the credit of introducing it seems to have been ascribed, without reason, to the Duke of Wellington. Writing two days after the battle, Sir A. Frazer (*Letters*) said:

> I must be allowed to express my satisfaction, that, *contrary to the opinion of most, I ventured to change (and under discouraging circumstances of partial want of means) the ordnance of the Horse Artillery.*

And again:

> I bless my stars that I had obstinacy enough to persist in changing the guns of the Horse Artillery.

The forethought was certainly more consistent in one who was an able and enthusiastic Horse-Artilleryman, than in one who, like the Duke of Wellington, knew little of artillery details or tactics.

The arrangement and constitution of a troop of Horse Artillery at Waterloo are given with minuteness by General Mercer in his *Diary*, vol.1. Taking the troop, which he commanded, although only its 2nd Captain, as a sample of those more heavily armed, it appears that each gun, and the howitzer, were drawn by 8 horses, and each waggon by 6. Each of the six mounted detachments required 8 horses; 5 were required for the staff-sergeants and farriers; 18 for the spare-wheel carriage, forge, curricle-cart, baggage-waggon, &c.; 17 horses for officers, and 6 mules, and 30 spare, additional horses. This gave a total of 226 per troop. There were 23 non-commissioned officers, artificers, and trumpeters; 80 gunners, and 84 drivers. On parade, the 5½-inch howitzer was the right of the centre division of the troop.

★★★★★★

> Sir A. Dickson, being only *regimentally* a 1st Captain, had been appointed to the command of G Troop, on Sir A. Frazer's promotion; and in his absence in America, Captain Mercer held the command. At Waterloo, Sir A. Dickson was otherwise employed.

★★★★★★

It was of this troop that Blücher said, at the review near Grammont on the 29th May, that "he had never seen anything so superb in his life;" (Mercer's *Diary* vol. 1), concluding by exclaiming, "*Mein Gott! dere is not von orse in dies batterie wich is not goot for Veldt-Marshal!*"

There is in the official correspondence of May and June 1815, a collection of quaintly amusing letters from various 2nd Captains of

Artillery in Belgium, who, prior to the war, had been left in undisturbed command of their batteries,—their 1st Captains being specially employed—and who now wrote begging that the latter should not be allowed to join, and thus rob them of their chances of distinction and preferment. One of these—Captain Napier—wrote direct to the master-general, protesting against the appointment of Captain Bolton to command his battery; which, he wrote, "hurt him much." Little did he think as he wrote that a mightier hand than the master-general's was in a very few days to cancel the appointment, and that ere the first battle should be over, he should resume the command, vacant by his senior's death! Pages might be filled with instances of this resentment at the presence of a 1st Captain; nor were they confined to attempts to prevent the seniors from joining. One 2nd Captain, whose commanding officer was wounded at Quatre Bras, wrote off immediately, begging the master-general to appoint no one in his place, but to leave the command in his hands.

When the Allies were ready, as far as equipment was concerned, Brussels remained the headquarters of the Duke of Wellington, and the army was scattered through the country, in a way which has excited much criticism among continental writers. Napoleon, when he fought the battles of Ligny and Quatre Bras, had hoped to find the English Army still in its cantonments; but he was disappointed, for it had quitted them, and commenced to concentrate on the 13th and 14th June.

His intention had been to defeat the Prussians, and compel them to retire on the base of their communications and supplies, and to compel the advanced part of the Anglo-Allied Army to retire from Quatre Bras on Brussels. In neither particular were his hopes fulfilled. He certainly compelled the Prussians, after their defeat at Ligny on the 16th June, to retire; but they quitted the main road to Namur, along which Napoleon expected that they would continue their retreat, and marched to Wavre by a road parallel to that occupied by Wellington between Quatre Bras and Brussels.

This brilliant movement was unsuspected by Napoleon, whose remissness after Ligny and during the early part of the 17th was unaccountable. Disappointed in his plans with regard to the Prussians, he failed also in his purpose against the English. (Sir G. Wood to D.-A.-G. 24 June, 1815.) Marshal Ney with two corps attacked part of the Allied force at Quatre Bras, a place in front of the village of Genappe, where two main roads—from Genappe to Charleroi, and Namur to Nivelle—cross one another. The endurance of the Allies was tried to the utmost by having to wait the arrival of reinforcements, and to fight against superior numbers, but it was rewarded by a complete, although costly, victory. The first attack was received by the Belgians; but Picton's English division, over 7000 strong, soon came up, followed by over 6,500 Brunswickers and Germans.

The battle commenced at 2 p.m. on the 16th; and at 4 o'clock the Duke of Wellington came on the field with a brigade of foreign cavalry, and assumed the command. (Cust.) Later in the evening, the 1st British division, under Generals Cook and Maitland, with its artillery, arrived from Enghien, having marched for a period of fifteen hours; and with the approaching darkness came the retreat of the French on Frasnes.

★★★★★★

Communicated by Sir D. E. Wood, K.C.B., &c. &c.:—

In later times, the most remarkable march made by artillery was on one occasion during the Indian Mutiny, when a battery of R.H.A. marched 78 miles in 24 hours, and continued marching, elephants carrying the forage.

★★★★★★

This defeat ruined the French Emperor's plans, and paved the way for the greater defeat of the 18th.

The following field-officers, troops, and brigades of artillery were present at the Battle of Quatre Bras (Sir G. Wood to D.-A.-G. 24 June, 1815):—

Lieut.-Colonel S. G. Adye, commanding the Artillery of the 1st Division.
„ Sir A. Frazer, commanding Royal Horse Artillery.
„ Sir J. Hartmann, commanding King's German Artillery.
„ Sir J. May, Assist. Adjutant-General.
„ Sir A. Dickson.

Captain Sandham's Brigade, R.A. } Attached to the 1st Division.
Major Kuhlmann's Troop, K. G. L. }
Major Lloyd's Brigade, R.A. }
Capt. Cleeve's „ K. G. L. } „ 3rd Division.
Major Roger's „ R.A. „ 5th Division.

Major Heise, with Captain Rettberg's brigade of Hanoverian artillery, was also engaged.

The Horse Artillery and British cavalry did not come up until after the battle; and the want of the latter was severely felt during the day, the French being very strong in that arm.

Major Lloyd's and Major Rogers' batteries were warmly engaged at Quatre Bras. Two guns belonging to the former were lost, but were

The Duke of Wellington with the R.H.A. at Waterloo

afterwards recovered. (*Letters.*) The troop of German Horse Artillery was of great service, sustaining the reputation which that corps had earned in the Peninsula. But the losses among the artillerymen were small in proportion to those among the regiments of infantry. (*Letters.*) Of 3750 British killed and wounded at Quatre Bras, only 28 belonged to the Royal Artillery. The losses were, however, very severe among the horses, and crippled the batteries very much. In Sir George Wood's despatch to D.-A.-G. 24 June, 1815, announcing the battle, he wrote:

> I beg you will be pleased to mention to his Lordship, the Master-General, the good conduct of that part of the artillery which was engaged on the 16th. They were warmly engaged, being several times charged by the French cavalry—and tended much to the success of the day.

The merits of Quatre Bras, as a scene on which English courage and endurance were nobly displayed, are too often forgotten in the recollections of the greater battle, by which it was so speedily followed.

In consequence of the Prussians moving on Wavre, it became necessary for the Duke of Wellington to fall back also; and orders were given on the 17th for the army to retire to Mont St. Jean, not far from the village of Waterloo. This position had been carefully selected and examined by the duke, with a view to the event which was now at hand.

The retreat through Genappe was effected with the greatest order, and was covered by the Horse Artillery and cavalry. Captain Mercer's (*Diary*) and Captain Whinyates's troops were the last to retire, the former officer having been detailed for that duty—the latter having exceeded his orders, and remained behind, hoping to come in for some fighting.

******

This statement is based on Mercer's *Diary*, but it seems possible that he refers to the retreat of the centre of the army, to which he was attached. Sir Robert Gardiner, who was on the extreme left, always believed that his troop was the last to retire. Certainly, the army retreated from the right, and Sir Robert's troop, on the left, had to make a very hurried retreat through the fields to the east of the Brussels road.

******

For the Horse Artillery and cavalry, the retreat was no bed of roses. The heavy rains had made the roads and fields almost impassable. Genappe is in a hollow; and as the Horse Artillery mounted the slopes towards La Belle Alliance, pursued by the French cavalry, they had to move at a gallop through fields, which would have tried them even at a walk. Sir Robert Gardiner's troop was especially taxed in this way; and he used frequently to say that it was fortunate that his 6-pounder armament had not been exchanged for the heavier nature; for his guns would certainly have been captured had this been done.

The nature of the ground which was traversed may be gathered from the fact that not a horse in Sir Robert's troop reached Mont St. Jean without losing at least one shoe. The whole night of the 17th was spent in shoeing the horses, and getting the troop ready for the work of the following day. (Communicated by Colonel L. Gardiner, R.-H.-A.)

On the morning of the 18th June, the French Army was drawn up on the south side, and the Allies on the Brussels side, of a long hollow, which common *parlance* has inaccurately named the "field of Waterloo." The strength of the French Army, according to the industrious Siborne—checked by later writers—was, in round numbers, 72,000; that of the Allies, about 68,000.

The French had, in addition, Marshal Grouchy's force of 33,000 men, fourteen miles away, on a blind chase after the Prussians, who were already six miles nearer Waterloo than their pursuers; and Wellington had a division of 18,000 men on detachment to his right, towards Hal, at a distance of ten miles. This extra precaution—this strange nervousness about his right—has been much and justly condemned by critics.

When one reflects of what value that force would have been at different times during the 18th, one cannot but feel that if the Allied information to the right had been as carefully procured, as it had been to the left of the army, the whole of these 18,000 men might have been drawn in to the main body. However, even admitting this to be a blunder, the French were nevertheless utterly outmanoeuvred.

Napoleon's remissness on the night of the 16th, and his idleness on the morning of the 17th, were now to receive the punishment which such qualities in the face of an enemy always deserve, and generally get.

The artillery engaged on the side of the Allies was as follows (Sir George Wood to D.-A.-G. 24 June, 1815):—

                    Sir G. A. Wood commanding.
Lieut.-Colonel Sir A. Frazer, commanding R. H. A.
    „   S. G. Adye,   „   Artillery of 1st Division.
    „   Gold,   „   „   2nd Division.
    „   Williamson,   „   „   3rd Division.
    „   Sir J. Hartmann,   „   King's German Artillery.
    „   A. Macdonald,   „   { Six troops of H. A. attached
                                      to Cavalry.
  Major Drummond,   „   Reserve Artillery.
                    Lieut.-Colonel Sir A. Dickson.

The troops of Horse Artillery attached to the cavalry were those commanded by—

Lieut.-Colonel Webber Smith,
Lieut.-Colonel Sir R. Gardiner,
Major R. Bull,
Major N. Ramsay,
Captain Mercer, and
Captain Whinyates.

The divisional artillery was as follows:—

Captain Sandham's Brigade, R.A. } 1st Division.
Major Kuhlmann's Troop, K.G.A.
Captain Bolton's Brigade, R.A.   } 2nd Division.
Major Sympher's Troop, K.G.A.
Major Lloyd's Brigade, R.A.   } 3rd Division.
Captain Cleve's Brigade, R.A.
Major Rogers' Brigade, R.A.   5th Division.

The reserve artillery—the whole of which came into action early in the day—consisted of—

Lieut.-Colonel Sir H. D. Ross's Troop, R.H.A.
Major Beane's Troop, R.H.A.
Captain Sinclair's Brigade, R.A.

Major Heise, and two brigades of Hanoverian artillery, were also engaged.

It will thus be seen that the number of troops and brigades of the Royal Artillery engaged at the Battle of Waterloo was thirteen, or a force of 78 guns, exclusive of the German and Hanoverian artillery. Some companies of the regiment were also present with the small-arm ammunition for the army.

Captain Baynes acted as Brigade-Major to the artillery; and Captain Pakenham, Lieutenants Coles, J. Bloomfield, and W. Bell, acted as staff officers.

The description of the battle which will now be given will be brief; as it will be necessary subsequently to enter with more detail into the services and conduct of the artillery during the day. (*Vide* Appendix.)

The Battle of Waterloo was—as Sir James Shaw Kennedy expresses it—a drama in five acts. The first was the attack on Hougomont at 11.30 a.m., many precious hours having been wasted by Napoleon; the second was the attack by the French on La Haye Sainte, at half-past 1; the third was the celebrated succession of cavalry attacks on the Allied line between Hougomont and La Haye Sainte, commencing at 4 o'clock; the fourth was the successful attack by Marshal Ney on La Haye Sainte, at 6 o'clock,—an event which if properly used by Napoleon might have had a very grave effect on the result of the battle, for it caused a great gap in the very centre of the Allied line; and the fifth was the celebrated attack on the Allied centre made by 12 battalions of the Imperial Guard, strengthened by the co-operation of other divisions, and supported "by a powerful artillery, and what remained of the cavalry." (Kennedy.)

In the attack on Hougomont, the battery which most distinguished itself was the famous old I Troop—later D Battery, B Brigade, R.H.A.—under Major R. Bull, whose Peninsular history rivals that of the Chestnut Troop. It was armed with howitzers; and cleared the wood in front of Hougomont of the French troops,—firing shell with wonderful accuracy over the heads of the English Infantry; an operation so delicate, as to make the duke remark to Sir Augustus Frazer, who ordered it, that he hoped he was not undertaking too much. (*Letters*.) But Sir Augustus said that he could depend on the troop; and the event proved that he was right: for after ten minutes' firing, the French were driven out of the wood. Webber Smith's troop was also hotly engaged during this first attack, and suffered during the day very severely, not merely—as all did—from the French skirmishers, but also from having been on one occasion enfiladed by one of Prince Jerome's batteries.

Captain Bolton's field brigade, which was to have so great glory at a critical period in the day, was in action at the first attack on Hougomont; and when subsequently moved more to the centre of the Allied line, its place to the left of Hougomont was taken by Norman Ramsay's troop. It has already been mentioned that the first shot fired by the Allied artillery at Waterloo was fired by Captain Sandham's brigade. This was in reply to the first attack on Hougomont; and during the day no fewer than 1100 rounds of ammunition were fired by this single brigade. (Many of the guns at Waterloo actually became unserviceable *from incessant firing*.)

Although beyond the province of this work to enter into the Infantry details of the battle, it must yet be said that, even in a day when the British Infantry showed a valour and endurance which have never been surpassed, their defence of Hougomont shines with especial lustre. Knowing its value, as strengthening the right of his line, the duke had taken precautions on the previous night by loopholing the walls to render its defence more practicable. Although set on fire, and attacked repeatedly by superior numbers, it was never lost; its defenders showing a tenacity and courage, unexampled almost in the annals of war.

In the second act of the drama—the first attack on La Haye Sainte—Captain Whinyates's troop and Major Rogers' field brigade were first engaged; and it is important to remember, with a view to the argument, which is to come, that it was during this act that the artillery of the reserve was brought up. (*Vide* Appendix A.) Sir Hew Ross's and Major Beane's troops suffered at this time great loss. Among the officers alone, Major Beane was killed, and both 2nd captains and two subalterns wounded.

The third act, the charges of the French cavalry, will be fully discussed in the argument, which will be found in the Appendix. Suffice it to say, at present, that they were preceded by clouds of skirmishers, and by a tremendous artillery fire; and that at no period of the day were the losses among the artillery more severe. Among those who fell then was Norman Ramsay; and it was the lot of his dearest friend to witness and to tell the circumstances. Sir Augustus Frazer wrote:

> In a momentary lull of the fire, I buried my friend Ramsay, from whose body I took the portrait of his wife, which he always carried next his heart. Not a man assisted at the funeral who did not shed tears. Hardly had I cut from his head the hair which I enclose, and laid his yet warm body in the grave, when our convulsive sobs were stifled by the necessity of returning to renew the struggle. (*Letters*.)

Two days later, (Nivelle, 20 June, 1815) the same hand wrote:

> Now that the stern feelings of the day have given way to the return of better ones, I feel with the bitterness of anguish not to be described, the loss of my friend Ramsay. Nor for this friend alone, but for many others, though less dear than poor Norman.

And yet again, writing from Paris, dated 6 July, 1815, Sir A. Frazer said:

> I cannot get Ramsay out of my head; such generosity, such romantic self-devotion as his, are not common.

It was written of Ramsay, "*Sibi satis vixit,—non patriæ;*" and it is difficult to conceive a nobler eulogy. A man who never tampered with temptation, but trampled on it instead—he left behind him the story of a life, which is a model for his successors in the corps to imitate. There is a Waterloo going on daily in a soldier's life: his enemies are more skilled than Napoleon—they are as relentless as death: they come dressed in many garbs, but their names are sloth, ignorance, and vice; and the weapon by which alone they can be overcome is an earnest and conscientious performance of duty. This weapon must be grasped most firmly, and wielded most mercilessly, when the duties to be performed are monotonous or uninviting; but its unfailing use, even through a life of uninteresting routine, will earn for the soldier, when the night comes, the same words as were spoken of Norman Ramsay, "*Satis sibi vixit,—non patriæ.*"

The fourth act of the drama witnessed, at 6 o'clock, the capture of La Haye Sainte by the French, after a magnificent defence by Major Baring and part of the King's German Legion, which only failed from want of ammunition. There seems little doubt that the Duke of Wellington had underrated the importance of this position; indeed, he is said in later years to have admitted it. Fortunately, Napoleon did not sufficiently note the advantage he had gained; and contented himself with using its now friendly cover in preparation for his great final effort.

The Prussians had by this time arrived, and were in force on the French right. At the village of Planchenoit, they were already in such numbers that the French general, Lobau, required 16,000 men to keep them in check. On the extreme left of the English, at Papillote, the advanced parties of another Prussian column had also arrived; and, all fear for his left being now at an end, the Duke of Wellington was enabled to strengthen his centre, and his right centre, by moving Vivian's and Vaudeleur's cavalry brigades from the left, accompanied by Sir Robert Gardiner's troop of Horse Artillery.

The necessity of a great final effort was now apparent to Napoleon; and the curtain rose on the fifth act of the drama at half-past 7 o'clock. It is a point which the artilleryman should never forget, that, in this majestic advance of the Imperial Guard, its head was broken and thrown into confusion by the fire of Captain Bolton's guns, before the 52nd Regiment, and the Guards, did their celebrated work. It was at this time that Captain Bolton was killed, and that the duke personally gave his orders to Captain Napier—the 2nd Captain—as the French approached, to load with canister.

While the advancing columns of the enemy were in the hollow, their artillery carried on a cannonade over their heads, more terrible than had been witnessed during the day. The following description of Mercer's battery at the end of the day will give the reader an idea of the murderous fire to which the Allies were exposed. He wrote (*Diary* vol. 1):

> Of 200 fine horses, with which we had entered the battle, upwards of 140 lay dead, dying, or severely wounded. Of the men, scarcely two-thirds of those necessary for *four* guns remained; and those so completely exhausted, as to be totally incapable of further exertion. Lieutenant Breton had had three horses killed under him; Lieutenant Hincks was wounded in the breast by a spent ball; Lieutenant Leathes on the hip by a splinter; and although untouched myself, my horse had no less than eight wounds. Our guns and carriages were all together in a confused heap, intermingled with dead and wounded horses, which it had not been possible to disengage from them.

And this was but typical of most of the batteries engaged.

As for the infantry, words cannot paint too highly their endurance on that long day. One regiment had 400 men killed or wounded, before they were allowed to fire a trigger; and all suffered heavily. Yet there was not a word of distrust as regarded their great commander. They pined with all their hearts for permission to attack, instead of lying where they often were—being shot by scores; but discipline was stronger than desire.

Even at the worst times, a word from the duke, or a report that he was coming, sufficed to produce a silence and a steadiness, as perfect as if on parade in a barrack-square. For those who were present, Waterloo was thus a double victory—over their enemies, and over themselves. True discipline is a succession of such victories.

With the noble charge of the 52nd, followed by the general advance of the whole line, the French retreat became a rout—the most disastrous, as has been said, on record to that date.: The Prussians took

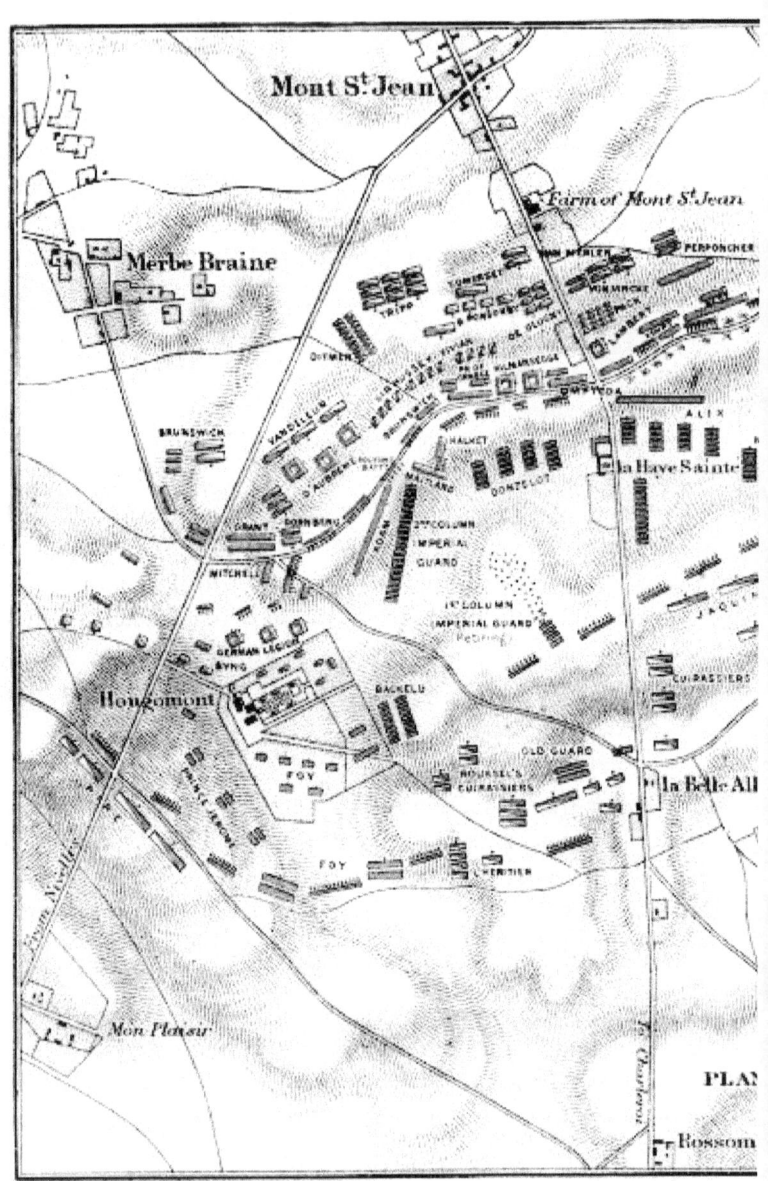

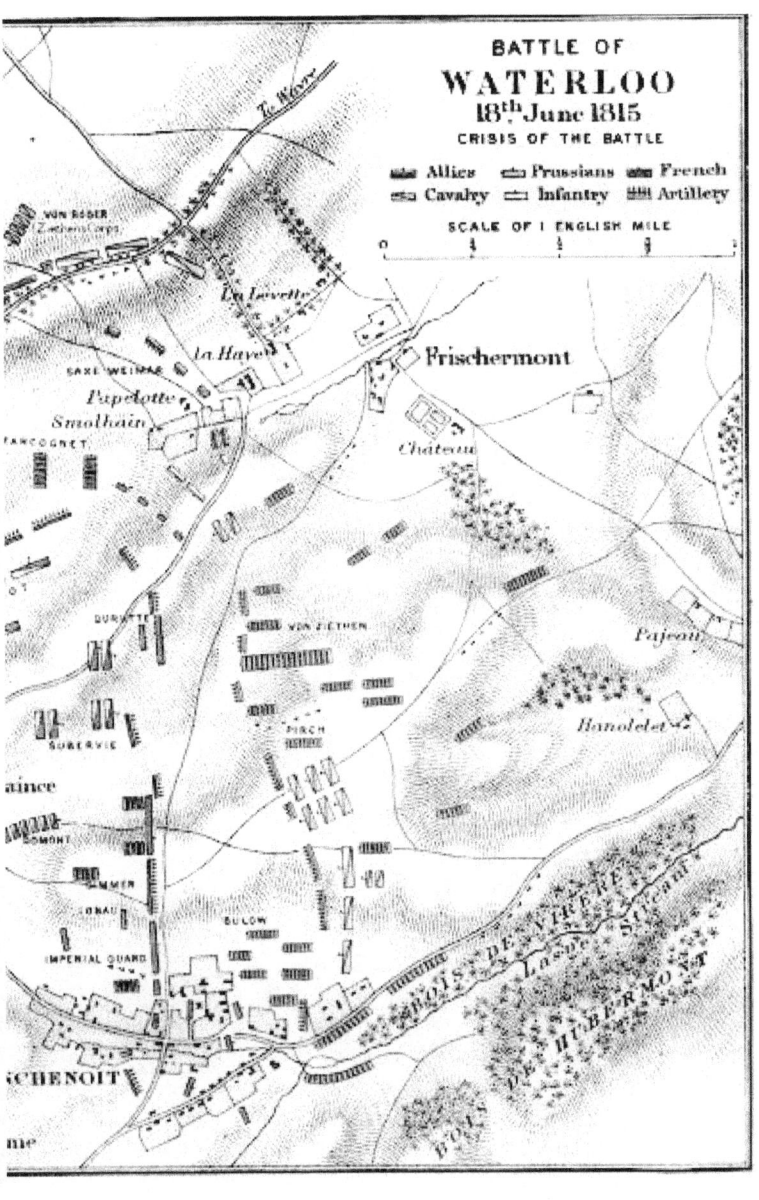

up the pursuit, and the Allied Army bivouacked on the field of battle.

So much detail connected with the services of the artillery at Waterloo must of necessity be given in the Appendix, that it has not been thought advisable to anticipate it here. But there are several interesting Regimental matters connected with the battle, for the insertion of which this seems the most suitable place.

In the first place, the names of the officers belonging to the troops and brigades, which were present, may be given.

TOTAL NUMBER OF ALL RANKS of the following TROOPS and BRIGADES present at WATERLOO, according to MS. RETURNS to BOARD OF ORDNANCE, dated Paris, 18th September, 1815.

R.H.A.

Major R. Bull's Troop, now "D" Battery, B Brigade.

	No.
2nd Captain Brevet-Major R. M. Cairnes	
Lieutenant Louis	168
„ Smith	
„ Townsend	

Lieutenant Colonel Webber Smith's Troop, now "B" Battery, B Brigade.

2nd Captain E. T. Walcott	
Lieutenant Edwards	167
„ Forster	
„ Crawford	

Lieutenant-Colonel Sir Robert Gardiner's Troop, now "A" Battery, B Brigade

2nd Captain T. Dyneley	
Lieutenant Harding	174
„ Swabey	
„ Ingilby	

Captain Whinyates's Troop (reduced in 1816).

2nd Captain Dansey	
Lieutenant Strangways	194
„ Wright	
„ Ward	
„ Ord	

2nd Captain Mercer's Troop, now "C" Battery, B Brigade.

2nd Captain Newland	
Lieutenant Leathes	164
„ Hinks	
„ Breton	

Major Ramsay's Troop, now "D" Battery, A Brigade.

2nd Captain A. Macdonald	
Lieutenant Brereton	173
„ Sandilands	
„ Robe	

Lieutenant-Colonel Sir H. D. Ross's Troop, now "A" Battery, A Brigade.

2nd Captain and Brevet-Major Parker
Lieutenant Hardinge
„ Day
„ Warde
„ Onslow
} 159

R.H.A.

Major Beane's Troop (reduced in 1816).   No.

2nd Captain Webber..
Lieutenant Maunsell
„ Bruce
„ Cromie
} 169

R.A.

Captain C. F. Sandham's Brigade (reduced in 1819).

2nd Captain Stopford
Lieutenant Foot
„ Baynes
„ Jago
} 105

This and all the other Field Brigades were armed, each with five 9-pounders and one 5½-inch howitzer.

Captain Bolton's Brigade, now "E" Battery, 8th Brigade.

MS. Returns, dated 30 May, 1815.

2nd Captain Napier..
Lieutenant Pringle ..
„ Anderson
„ Spearman
„ Sharpin ..
„ B. Cuppage
} 101

Major Lloyd's Brigade (reduced in April, 1817).

2nd Captain S. Rudyerd
Lieutenant Phelps
„ Harvey
} 97

Captain Sinclair's Brigade, now "4" Battery, 3rd Brigade (Captain Gordon being absent).

2nd Captain F. Macbean
Lieutenant Wilson
„ Poole
„ Burnaby
} 104

Major Roger's Brigade, now "7" Battery, 13th Brigade.

Lieutenant R. Manners
(*Other officers' names not given.*)
} 94

These were the only troops and brigades which were engaged. There were others, which were in the vicinity, but not present at the battle; and there were also detachments of other brigades present with small-arm ammunition. Lieutenants E. Trevor, W. Lemoine, J. Bloomfield, and others already named, were present on staff or unattached duty.

Of the officers named above, the following were killed or wounded at the Battle of Waterloo (Sir George A. Wood to master-general, 24 June, 1815):—

Major W. N. Ramsay, R.H.A.,		..	Killed.	
„ R. M. Cairnes	„	..	„	
„ G. Beane	„	..	„	
„ J. B. Parker	„	..	Severely wounded: leg amputated.	
„ R. Bull	„	..	Slightly wounded.	
Captain Whinyates	„	..	„	
„ Dansey	„	..	„	
„ Macdonald	„	..	„	
„ Webber	„	..	„	
Lieutenant Strangways	„	..	„	
„ Brereton	„	..	Severely, not dangerously.	
„ Robe	„	..	„ (since dead).	
„ Smith	„	..	Slightly wounded.	
„ Cromie	„	..	Severely: both legs amputated.	
„ Forster	„	..	„ not dangerously.	
„ Crawford	„	..	Slightly wounded.	
„ Day	„	..	„	
Major H. Baynes	R.A.	..	Slightly wounded.	
Captain Bolton	„	..	Killed.	
Major Lloyd	„	..	Severely wounded (died).	
Captain Napier	„	..	Severely wounded.	
Lieutenant Spearman	„	..	„	
„ R. Manners	„	..	Severely (since dead).	
„ Harvey	„	..	„ right arm amputated.	
„ Poole	„	..	„ not dangerously.	

The numerical losses, as shown by Sir George Wood in his official return (dated 24 June, 1815) to the Ordnance, were as follows:—

	Officers.	Sergeants.	Rank and File.	Horses.
Royal Horse Artillery—				
Killed	3	1	31	229
Wounded	14	8	107	59
Missing	0	0	7	21
Total	17	9	145	309
Royal Artillery—				
Killed	1	0	19	80
Wounded	7	4	61	34
Missing	0	0	2	12
Total	8	4	82	126

	Officers.	Sergeants.	Rank and File.	Horses.
King's German Legion Artillery—				
Killed	1	1	10	47
Wounded	6	1	47	44
Missing	0	0	1	3
Total	7	2	58	94
General Total	32	15	285	529

There were two field brigades, which formed part of the Duke of Wellington's army, but which were not brought up in time for the battle, although they were of great importance during the subsequent siege operations against the fortresses. Their armament was the same as that of the others; and one of them, Captain Brome's, would appear to have been in position, although not engaged;—possibly detached at Hal. The officers with these, and their numbers, were as follows:—

Captain Brome's Brigade, now 2 Battery, 13th Brigade, R.A.

	Total of all Ranks.
2nd Captain J. E. G. Parker	
Lieutenant Saunders	
„ Cater	106
„ Molesworth	

Major G. W. Unett, now 3 Battery, 7th Brigade, R.A.

2nd Captain Browne	
Lieutenant Lawson	106
„ Montagu	

These brigades received the boon service granted for the Battle of Waterloo under a Horse Guards' decision, which was promulgated in Paris on the 5th September, 1815, including among Waterloo men all troops, which had on the 18th June been employed either in the village of Waterloo, or had been detached to the right to prevent the advance of the enemy towards Brussels by Hal.

The commendations passed on the corps generally for its services at Waterloo will be found in the Appendix, in support of the argument therein contained. But it may be interesting to the friends or descendants of individual officers, who were present, and who specially distinguished themselves, to read extracts from the reports sent to the Ordnance. These will be given without comment. Sir George Wood wrote, dated Le Cateau, 24 June, 1815:

> I feel that I should particularly mention that I wish Lieutenant-Colonel Sir John May may succeed to one of the vacant troops;

and I do assure you the conduct of Major Lloyd was conspicuous to the whole army. This officer and Captain Mercer are candidates for the other vacant troop. (The casualties at Waterloo promoted Captain Mercer to the rank of 1st Captain.) Captain Mercer was the senior second captain in the field, and behaved nobly. I must also mention that Lieutenant Louis commanded Major Bull's troop for some time. Lieutenant Sandilands was the only officer left with the command of poor Major Ramsay's troop, the rest of the officers being wounded.

I beg to mention him to your protection, as well as Lieutenants Coles and Wells, whom I have appointed to do duty with the Horse Artillery, and I beg you will use your interest with the master-general that they may be confirmed. . . . I shall certainly give in the name of Captain Macdonald for brevet promotion; it was with great difficulty that he could be made quit the field when severely wounded,—as well as Lieutenant Brereton, who remained in the field of battle until Lieutenant-Colonel Macdonald ordered him to the rear, to have his wounds dressed. . . . Although Lieutenant-Colonel Gold was in command of a Division of artillery in the field, I beg you will mention to the master-general that I have received great benefit from his advice and zeal, during the time I have commanded the artillery in the Pays-Bas. . . . I beg leave to mention that Lieutenant Bloomfield was both days in the field with me; and should he wish at some future time to be posted to the Horse Brigade, I hope he will not be forgot.

In another despatch to General Macleod, Sir George Wood wrote as follows:

I must call your particular attention to the officers who attended me personally in the field, whose merits I beg to recommend to the consideration of His Lordship the Master-General.

These officers were Lieutenant-Colonel Sir A. Frazer, Lieutenant-Colonel Sir J. Hartmann, Lieutenant-Colonel Sir A. Dickson, Lieutenant-Colonel Sir J. May, Captain Baynes, Brigade Major, Lieutenants Coles, Bloomfield, Bell, and Meëlmann—all of whom were mentioned by name. Lieutenant-Colonel Macdonald thus described the services of his adjutant:

In justice to the conduct of Captain Pakenham, who acted as

> my adjutant in the battle of the 18th, I feel it a duty I owe this most promising officer to state to you that he made himself equally conspicuous by his coolness and bravery, and the precision with which he conveyed my orders to the troops of Horse Artillery I had the honour to command on that occasion. (To Sir G. A. Wood, 24 June, 1815.)

Sir Augustus Frazer spoke in equally favourable terms of his adjutant to Sir G. A. Wood, 23 June, 1815.

> I beg to submit my hope that, in the promotion which may be expected, the Horse Artillery may not lose the services of Lieutenant Bell, who, both here and in the Peninsula, has acted as Adjutant of Horse Artillery, and is an officer of much professional merit, whose judgment, intelligence, and unceasing application to the duties of his office, have rendered him very valuable.

Major Bull thus described the conduct of his gallant troop, later D Battery, B Brigade, Royal Horse Artillery to Sir A. Frazer, 19 June, 1815:

> I consider it a duty I owe equally to the officers, non-commissioned officers, gunners, and drivers, to say that, throughout the day, and in every situation, nothing could exceed their coolness, intrepidity, and strict attention to orders; and as a proof of their zeal in the service, at one period of the evening when we were short of ammunition, and H Troop (Major Ramsay's) on our left rather short of gunners, on an application for assistance, several of my men volunteered joining their guns, until our ammunition came up; and as far as was prudent or necessary, I granted their request.
> I must also beg leave to say that, from Major Cairnes having unfortunately fallen very early in the action, I received the greatest assistance throughout the day from Lieutenant Louis's activity; and it is but justice to this officer to add, that, when I was under the necessity of quitting the field for half an hour, in consequence of my being wounded, he commanded the troop during my absence in a manner that did himself great credit, and gave me perfect satisfaction at a very arduous period of the action.

General Colquhoun Grant, in writing of Captain Walcott, to Sir G.

A. Wood, 15 July, 1815, said:

> I beg to recommend this gallant and meritorious officer to your attention. I have great pleasure in embracing this opportunity to mention my entire and full approbation of the conduct of Lieut.-Colonel Webber Smith, and the officers and men of his troop (later B Battery, B Brigade, Royal Horse Artillery), during the whole of the period they have been attached to the brigade under my command.

Lieutenant-Colonel Macdonald—an enthusiastic Horse Artilleryman—in addition to the letter quoted above, wrote to Sir G. A. Wood, dated 16 July, 1815, as follows:

> In addition to the names of the various officers belonging to the six troops of Royal Horse Artillery, attached to the cavalry, whose lot it was to command troops on the memorable day of the 18th June, it has occurred to me to be no less my duty to express to you my admiration of the cool and determined conduct of Captain Walcott, who was some time detached from his troop on that day; and who, in the handsomest manner, after the whole of his ammunition was expended, volunteered to take charge of some of the guns of Major Ramsay's troop, after it had suffered much by the loss of officers. It is also highly satisfactory to me to report to you the equally gallant conduct of Captain Dansey, of Captain Whinyates's Rocket Troop, which I also had an opportunity of witnessing; and who was wounded when detached with rockets in the *chaussée*, which crossed the centre of the position.
>
> You are already aware, from your own observation, how much all the officers of these troops distinguished themselves on the occasion, and what a noble example they set to the non-commissioned officers and men by whom it was so gallantly initiated. Words are indeed inadequate to express my sense of the conduct of all, where the reputation, which the Horse Artillery had before obtained, was so nobly sustained, if not even surpassed; and which I must plead as my excuse for extending the limits of this communication beyond my original intention, *viz.*, that of drawing your attention to the merits of Captains Walcott and Dansey.
>
> In reporting the death of Major Lloyd, from his wounds, Sir George

Wood wrote, dated Paris, 3 Aug. 1815:

> I can, without hesitation, affirm that a braver, or more zealous officer, never entered a field of battle; and who did his duty on the 16th and 18th to the satisfaction of every general officer.

A few days later, 17 Aug. 1815, in enclosing a letter from Lieutenant Brereton, Sir George said:

> I have received from every commanding officer the handsomest testimony of the conduct of Lieutenant Brereton, both in the Peninsula, and at the Battle of Waterloo; and I have it from General Byng to say that, on the battle of the 16th (the Horse Artillery not being engaged on that day), he proffered his service to act as *aide-de-camp*, which service he performed to the great satisfaction of the general.

At a subsequent date, 8 Oct. 1815, in forwarding an application from Major Percy Drummond, Sir George Wood said:

> I have ever found Major Drummond a most active, zealous, and attentive officer, having been under my command on several occasions, particularly in the Battle of Waterloo.

In acknowledging a letter from Major Rogers, Sir George said, 28 Jan. 1816:

> Your company at all times did you every justice, and proved it under your command at the Battle of Waterloo, in which your brigade bore a distinguished feature."

Almost every officer who served in the artillery at Waterloo, received from his gallant commander some official commendation; and, by this means, many Regimental incidents connected with the battle have been handed down. In writing, for example, about an officer who lived to be a revered general in the corps, Sir George Wood said, dated Valenciennes, 29 Feb. 1816:

> Lieutenant William Anderson has conducted himself in every situation as a good and zealous officer. On the 18th June—on many occasions during that day—he carried my orders, and brought off some disabled guns under a severe fire. Having my horses shot, I was forced to dismount him.

At the Battle of Waterloo, the artillery expended 10,400 rounds of ammunition. The amount fired by one battery, Captain Sandham's, has already been stated; and it may be mentioned here that Captain Whinyates's troop fired 309 shot, 236 spherical case, 15 common case, and 52 rockets. (Sir G. A. Wood to Gen. Macleod, dated 3 July, 1815; *Memoir* of Sir E. C. Whinyates.)

The subsequent operations of the English Army during the year, in which this history comes, for the present, to an end, will merely be glanced at. The main body of the army marched at once towards Paris; and the damage suffered by the artillery during the battle was so quickly repaired, that Sir George Wood was able to take every gun with him that had been on the field, with four 18-pounders in addition; making a total of 123 pieces of ordnance, and over 20,000 rounds of ammunition, with which the army marched on Paris. (Sir G. A. Wood to Gen. Macleod, dated 3 July, 1815.) The collapse of any opposition, and the ultimate occupation of that city by the Allies, are facts well known to the reader. There were, however, some artillery operations against the French fortresses, in which some brigades of artillery, under Sir Alexander Dickson, were engaged. Maubeuge surrendered on the 12th July, and was taken possession of on the 14th, after three days' open trenches, and firing.

Landrecy surrendered on the 21st, and was taken possession of on the 23rd July, after two day's open trenches, and about two hours' firing. Marienbourg surrendered on the 28th, and was taken possession of on the 30th July, after one day's open trenches and heavy bombardment. Philippeville was taken possession of on the 10th August, having surrendered on the 8th, after one day's open trenches and heavy bombardment. (Sir Alexander Dickson to D.-A.-G., dated 12 Aug. 1815.)

Sir Alexander Dickson spoke in the highest terms of the officers and men under his command; he attributed to their energy the fact that at every place he was able to collect, previous to commencing operations, sufficient ordnance and ammunition to have reduced it, as he said, by main force. At Maubeuge, he had 60 guns—30 of which were 24-pounders—20,000 round shot, and 26,000 shells. At Landrecy he had 60 guns, 24,000 round shot, and 22,000 shells. At Marienbourg, he had 15 mortars, with 3000 shells; and 6 24-pounders arrived, just as the place surrendered. At Philippeville, he had 66 pieces of ordnance, with 17,000 round shot, and 23,000 shells. During these operations, the artillery was attached to a corps of the Prussian Army, by which the sieges of the fortresses were conducted. The terms on which the duties were performed were somewhat peculiar.

Sir A. Dickson wrote to D.-A.-G., dated 12 Aug. 1815:

Our line of duty is to move the battering-train, keep it in order, fix the shells, fill the cartridges, and, in short, do every individual thing except fighting the guns: which my instructions neither authorise me to do, nor would it be pleasant to do, if they did; for we should not get the credit we ought, when working in competition with the Prussian artillery: whereas, as the duty is conducted now, every fair and just credit is allowed for our exertions, and the service goes on with the utmost cordiality. Prince Augustus of Prussia is chief of the artillery of that kingdom, and he takes into his own hand very much the application of the artillery; which is very pleasant for me, as I receive all the arrangements and instructions, direct from his Royal Highness. An application is given in every morning at the park during a siege, expressing the ordnance and ammunition required for the next day; and in the evening the Prussian artillery come to receive their demands. I have, however, a few officers and men of the Royal Artillery in the trenches, to afford any assistance when required; and also, to watch the practice, report about the fuses, &c.

After the fall of Philippeville, Major Carmichael's company, with the advanced division of the battering-train, consisting of thirty-three mortars and howitzers, reached a point near Rocroy, on the 15th August:—followed by Major Michell's and Major Wall's companies with ten 24-pounders, and a large supply of ammunition. (*Ibid* to D.-A.-G., dated 22 Aug. 1815.) The Prussians opened the trenches on the night of the 15th, and batteries were prepared for twenty-one mortars and howitzers. With such effect were these opened on the morning of the 16th, that before 9 a.m. Rocroy capitulated.

After this event, Prince Augustus expressed himself highly satisfied with the exertions of the British artillery attached to the battering-train; and orders reached Sir Alexander Dickson from the Duke of Wellington to bring the second battering-train, which was at Antwerp, to Brussels, and to land it forthwith. The next operation of any importance was against the town of Givet, against which no fewer than one hundred guns were collected. Before the bombardment commenced, however, the governor consented to give up the place, and retire into Charlemont; which he did on the 11th September.

A force under Sir Charles Colville had been sent against Cambray, immediately after Waterloo, and the place—after a short siege—was carried on the 25th June. Of the conduct of the artillery on this occasion, Sir Charles wrote to the Duke of Wellington, 26 June, 1815:

> The three brigades of artillery under Lieutenant-Colonel Webber Smith, and Majors Unett and Brome, under the direction of Lieutenant-Colonel Hawker, made particularly good practice.

The services of Major Unett's brigade (later 3 Battery, 7th Brigade) received special mention in a report from Sir Charles Colville to Sir George Wood, (Sir George Wood to D.-A.-G., Paris, 4 Sept. 1815); and the following extract is from a letter by Major Unett to Sir George Wood dated, 3 Aug. 1815

> My brigade, being in reserve, had not an opportunity of witnessing the late glorious Battle of Waterloo, but it afterwards proceeded with the 4th Division of the army for the purpose of reducing the fortress of Cambray; and, in justice to my officers, I must be permitted to say that my three subalterns, never having been under fire before, deserve much praise for their cool and steady behaviour at their guns (within four hundred yards of the curtain of the citadel, in an open field), and which was clearly evinced by the uncommon good practice made, which so completely silenced the enemy as to cause (by driving them from their guns and ramparts) a most trifling loss to our Infantry when they stormed the place.

The French king entered Cambray on the day after it was taken: and on the same day, Peronne was taken by General Maitland and the Guards.

Arrangements for concluding hostilities, and entering upon a treaty, were soon made in Paris. One of the conditions inflicted on the French people was that an army of occupation should be left in France for five—afterwards reduced to three—years; and considerable difficulty was found in apportioning the various arms in the English contingent of that army.

The Duke of Wellington decided on reducing the artillery share to a point far below what Sir George Wood thought desirable; and the latter urged his views very strongly, but, as he said, "What can a lieut.-colonel do against a field-marshal?" (Although a colonel in the army, Sir George Wood was only a regimental lieutenant-colonel in 1815.) However, his importunity succeeded in obtaining an addition of two companies to the artillery force which was at first intended to remain in France.

MS. Return to B. of Ordnance, dated Paris, 10 Dec. 1815.

The following was the number ultimately decided upon:—

1 colonel, 1 assistant adjutant-general and 1 brigade major all for duty as the Regimental Staff of the Royal Artillery in the Army of Occupation

Three troops of Royal Horse Artillery to be attached to the cavalry, and to amount to 542 of all ranks, with 516 horses.

Seven brigades of Foot Artillery, having a company of artillery to each; six of which were to be attached to the three divisions of the army, and one to be in reserve. The total of all ranks, with these brigades, amounted to 790; and there were in addition 599 officers and men of the Royal Artillery Drivers, and 770 horses.

For duty with the small-arm ammunition brigades for the three divisions of the army, there were three officers of Royal Artillery; 150 non-commissioned officers and men of the Royal Artillery Drivers; and 210 horses.

There was also a company of Royal Artillery in reserve, numbering 111 of all ranks.

One lieut.-colonel and one major were attached to the Royal Horse Artillery.

Two lieut.-colonels and one major were attached to the Royal Artillery.

And one lieut.-colonel was attached to the Royal Artillery Drivers.

The following were the five troops of Horse Artillery selected to return to England, when the above establishment was decided upon, (MS. Return to B. of Ord. dated Paris, 10 Dec. 1815):—

	Strength.	Horses.	R. A. Drivers attached.
Lieut.-Colonel Sir R. Gardiner's troop	179 of all ranks.	198	22
,, Webber Smith's ,,	176 ,,	197	20
,, Sir H. D. Ross's ,,	189 ,,	219	30
Major Whinyates's ,,	223 ,,	219	nil.
Captain Mercer's (late Beane's) ,,	176 ,,	196	26
Detachment R. H. A.	59 ,,	156	83

Orders for the shipment of the battering-train also arrived in the end of 1815, with a view to its return to England; and, as Sir Alexander Dickson's active duties on the continent then ceased, it seems but justice to the memory of one whose name has occupied so prominent a place in these pages, to quote a passage from a letter written by Sir George Wood, to D.-A.-G., R.A., dated Cambray, 2 April, 1816, proving that his exceptional Peninsular honours had not unfitted him for serving, when required, in a subordinate position:—

> You may expect Sir A. Dickson in the course of the next week at Woolwich. I have found him the same good officer and man, as you well know him.

The reductions, which followed the Battle of Waterloo have been frequently alluded to in these volumes. They would furnish but a gloomy topic for the historian, for the pruning-knife was used without regard to sentiment, and some of the best companies in the regiment were the victims.

It is more pleasant to close this story in 1815, when the corps was at the greatest strength attained since its birth—a hundred years before. Suffice it to say that from 114 troops and companies in that year, it fell to 79 before 1819, and even these were mere ghosts or skeletons of their former selves. (Kane's List.) For nearly thirty years, after 1819, the history of the Regiment was almost a blank page, and hopelessness and depression weighed heavily on its members.

But 1815 is the year in which this narrative ends; nor is it meant to close it with any gloomy foreshadowing of the years of inaction and despondency, which rolled on with dismal monotony, until the Regimental firmament was lit by the lurid fires of the Crimean struggle. In 1815 the military reputation of England was at a maximum. She possessed an army which had graduated with honours in the sternest school, and a general to whose words the sovereigns of Europe listened with deference. Determination, single-mindedness, and an exalted sense of duty were the qualities which had animated the Duke of Wellington through his whole career. Their reward was found in his successes; and his successes were crowned in Paris. Imperfections exist in the most able, and even in the most conscientious; and England's greatest general was certainly no exception to this rule.

But, if we allow for the irritation caused by frequent and injudicious interference,—and for occasional hastiness, which led him to speak without always testing the accuracy of his information,—we must admit the Duke of Wellington to have been the most perfect type of an English soldier ever presented in the pages of our history. When, however, the artilleryman seeks for something that is genial and lovable in the soldiers of that victorious age,—he turns from the cold and undemonstrative chief, and dwells fondly on the men who had by their exertions raised artillery, as a science, to an unprecedented point, and had elevated with it the corps they loved. The researches of a recent writer (Hime) have brought to light words spoken by a chivalrous enemy, (General Foy), which should be emblazoned in the records of every battery, and impressed on the mind of every artilleryman:—

> *Les canonniers Anglais se distinguent entre les autres soldats par le bon esprit qui les anime. En bataille leur activité est judicieuse, leur coup d'œil parfait, et leur bravoure stoïque.*

Of the latter three qualities, two may be ensured by diligence in peace, and the third is tested by the difficulties and dangers of war: but the history of the great and the good in the corps must indeed have been feebly written, if it do not strengthen among its living members that which exists now, as of old, *"le bon esprit qui les anime."*

Appendix

THE DUKE OF WELLINGTON, AND THE ARTILLERY AT WATERLOO.

In the first volume of Sir J. T. Jones's *Sieges in Spain*, edited by Lieutenant-Colonel H. D. Jones, the following passage occurs:

> It becomes the duty of the editor to remove the very injurious and unmerited censure cast upon the officers of engineers who were employed at the Siege of Badajoz, and which is contained in a letter from the Earl of Wellington to Major-General G. Murray, a copy of which is published in the collection of the despatches of the Duke of Wellington.

The editor then proceeds to prove, most clearly and successfully, that the hasty language used with reference to the Engineers was not only injurious, but also unmerited.

The same great general is also convicted by his admirer, Napier, of hasty inconsistency in his private correspondence. It was of the very same troops, and referring to precisely the same time, that the Duke of Wellington wrote in one letter: "The soldiers are detestable for everything but fighting; and the officers are as culpable as the men:" and in another, "that he thought he could go anywhere, and do anything with the army that fought on the Pyrenees." (Napier's *Peninsular War*, vol. 6.)

Well might Napier say that the vehemence of the censure in the former of the quotations is inconsistent with the latter, and now celebrated, observation.

It now becomes the painful, and yet necessary, task of the chronicler of the services of the Royal Artillery, as of the member of the sister corps already quoted, "to remove a very injurious and unmerited censure" cast upon the regiment, in a private letter, written by the Duke of Wellington, with reference to its conduct at the Battle of

Waterloo. Of this letter's existence the world was ignorant until the year 1872, when it made its appearance in a volume of *Supplementary Letters and Despatches of the Duke of Wellington,* published by his son. The sensation which it was certain to produce was foretold by one of the reviews, (*Athenaeum*) and was anticipated by the noble Editor.

As, however, his object was to tell the truth, the whole truth, and nothing but the truth, the present duke did not feel justified in withholding from publication any letter, which was found among his father's papers, merely because it might wound the feelings of its readers, or give a new interpretation of historical events. And although the indiscriminate publication of a man's private correspondence is a doubtful tribute to his memory, and a severe test of his reputation, it is, on the whole, fortunate for the Royal Artillery that this letter made its appearance, while officers were yet alive, who had taken a part in the battle referred to in its pages, and clearly remembered its details.

The original letter was written by the Duke of Wellington to Lord Mulgrave, then Master-General of the Ordnance, on the 21st December, 1815. The published letter was from a copy, or draft, of the original, which was found among the duke's papers. The hope that perhaps there may have been modifications in the original, which did not exist in the draft or copy, disappears before the fact that Lord Mulgrave's answer was also found among the duke's papers, expressing his amazement at the letter he had just received. The harsh statements in the published draft, or copy, were doubtless, therefore, left in the original when forwarded. The circumstances under which the letter were written were as follows. The field officers of the Royal Artillery, who had been present at Waterloo, applied to the Master-General of the Ordnance for the same pensions for service as had been given after Vittoria.

The indignation with which the Duke of Wellington had heard of the Vittoria pensions was well known in the regiment: nor can one avoid sympathising with him. Discipline must suffer if the power of rewarding, or recommending for reward, be independent of the commander of the forces as a channel. The special interference of the Ordnance on behalf of the corps, which was their *protégé*, was not merely a breach of discipline, to which a man like the Duke of Wellington was not likely tamely to submit, but must have had an irritating effect on the rest of the army.

When, therefore, the field officers of artillery present at Waterloo resolved to apply for the same reward as had been given after Vittoria, they had the alternative before them of making their request through the duke, basing it upon a precedent which was detestable in his eyes, or of availing themselves of the dual government, under which they served, by making a direct application to the ordnance. Of these alternatives, the former would have been the more soldierlike, but was not likely to succeed: the latter, therefore, was unfortunately adopted.

The application was not couched in a very official form, nor was it officially pressed by Sir George Wood. The only reference to it which can be traced in that officer's correspondence is in a letter, dated Paris, 3 Aug. 1815, announcing Major Lloyd's death, in which he writes:—

> Should Lord Mulgrave, in his goodness, be inclined to grant pensions to field officers and captains commanding brigades, similar to the Battle of Vittoria, I hope and trust that the late Major Lloyd's family may receive the benefit his service deserved.

The precedent of Vittoria was not quite a parallel case to that of Waterloo: in the former every brigade with the army had been in action; while, in the latter, some had been detached. It seems to have been on this distinction, mainly, that Lord Mulgrave based his refusal to grant the reward. To justify himself, he referred the matter to the Duke of Wellington, who approved of the refusal, as might have been expected, but did so in terms which reveal an inaccuracy, and a hastiness, unparalleled in his Grace's correspondence. He wrote as follows:—

> To the Earl of Mulgrave.
>
> Paris, 21st December, 1815.
>
> My dear Lord,
> I received yesterday your Lordship's letter of the 10th, regarding the claim of the field officers of the artillery, present in the Battle of Waterloo, to the same measure of favour granted to those in the Battle of Vittoria.
> In my opinion you have done quite right to refuse to grant this favour, and that you have founded your refusal on the best grounds. I cannot recommend that you should depart from the ground you have taken. To tell you the truth, I was not very well pleased with the artillery in the Battle of Waterloo.
> The army was formed in squares immediately on the slope of the rising ground, on the summit of which the artillery was placed, with orders not to engage with artillery, but to fire only when bodies of troops came under their fire. It was very diffi-

cult to get them to obey this order. The French cavalry charged, and were formed on the same ground with our artillery in general, within a few yards of our guns. In some instances, they were in actual possession of our guns. We could not expect the artillerymen to remain at their guns in such a case. But I had a right to expect that the officers and men of the artillery would do as I did, and as all the staff did, that is, to take shelter in the squares of the infantry till the French cavalry should be driven off the ground, either by our cavalry or infantry.

But they did no such thing; they ran off the field entirely, taking with them limbers, ammunition, and everything: and when, in a few minutes, we had driven off the French cavalry, and had regained our ground and our guns, and could have made good use of our artillery, we had no artillerymen to fire them; and, in point of fact, I should have had no artillery during the whole of the latter part of the action, if I had not kept a reserve in the commencement.

Mind, my dear Lord, I do not mean to complain; but what I have above mentioned is a fact known to many; and it would not do to reward a corps under such circumstances. The artillery, like others, behaved most gallantly; but when a misfortune of this kind has occurred, a corps must not be rewarded. It is on account of these little stories, which must come out, that I object to all the propositions to write what is called a history of the Battle of Waterloo.

If it is to be a history, it must be the truth, and the whole truth, or it will do more harm than good, and will give as many false notions of what a battle is, as other romances of the same description have. But if a true history is written, what will become of the reputation of half of those who have acquired reputation, and who deserve it for their gallantry, but who, if their mistakes and casual misconduct were made public, would not be so well thought of? I am certain that if I were to enter into a critical discussion of everything that occurred from the 14th to the 19th June, I could show ample reasons for not entering deeply into these subjects.

The fact is, that the army that gained the Battle of Waterloo was an entirely new one, with the exception of some of the old Spanish troops. Their inexperience occasioned the mistakes they committed, the rumours they circulated that all was

destroyed, because they themselves ran away, and the mischief which ensued; but they behaved gallantly, and I am convinced, if the thing was to be done again, they would show what it was to have the experience of even one battle.
Believe me, &c.,
(Signed) Wellington.
P.S.—I am very well pleased with the field officers for not liking to have their application referred to me. They know the reason I have not to recommend them for a favour.

In discussing this letter, it is proposed to examine what may be termed the internal and external evidences of its inaccuracy, commencing with the former.

In his despatch of the 19th June, 1815, announcing the victory, the duke wrote:

> The artillery and engineer departments were conducted *much to my satisfaction* by Colonel Sir George Wood and Colonel Smyth.

Evidently, then, the fact "known to many" of the artillerymen running off the ground had not been known to him when he wrote his despatch, or he could hardly have described the artillery department as having been conducted much to his satisfaction. Nor does the fact, even when made known to him, seem to have produced the effect upon his Grace's mind, which misconduct among the troops under his command, in the face of an enemy, would at any other time have instantly created. Were not the genuineness of the letter beyond all question, some of the contradictions and inconsistencies in it would have justified the reader in pronouncing it a forgery, invented to throw discredit on the reputation of England's greatest general.

Was it the Duke of Wellington who, after writing the words, "They ran off the field entirely, taking with them limbers, ammunition, and everything," proceeded to say, "The artillery, like others, behaved most gallantly"? Was it the Iron Duke who, after saying, "In point of fact, I should have had no artillery during the whole of the latter part of the action, if I had not kept a reserve in the commencement," went on, with the resignation of a martyr, to say, "Mind, my dear Lord, I do not mean to complain"? The inconsistency with his known character is astounding.

After describing the disappearance of his artillerymen, and the straits to which he was consequently reduced, he proceeds in this letter to say: "It would not do to reward a corps under such circumstances." If he were correctly informed as to these circumstances, there would not have been a single individual in the whole of his army who would have differed from him as to his conclusion. But, unfortunately for him, he endeavoured to prove too much. Not content with giving, as a reason for withholding rewards, an assertion which, if accurate, would have more than justified him, he must needs strengthen an already overwhelming case by a mysterious insinuation in the postscript of the letter, respecting some other unexpressed ground of his displeasure, with which the field officers must be familiar as a cause for his refusing to recommend them for reward. Was there not, in this piling of Pelion upon Ossa, some consciousness of the necessity of self-justification?

But these are merely striking self-contradictions and inconsistencies in style. It is when the truth of the statements made by the duke in this letter is inquired into, that one stands astounded at the inaccuracy of his informants, and the hasty assumptions of the writer himself. The letter is so involved—so confusing in its mixed references to the artillery and to the army generally—so laden with marvellous didactic sentences as to the propriety of writing a history of the Battle of Waterloo—that it is not always easy to ascertain the connection between argument and conclusion. So slovenly, indeed, is the style at the end of the letter, that it reads as if the whole army ran away! Let two sentences be reproduced:

> The fact is, that the army that gained the Battle of Waterloo was an entirely new one, with the exception of some of the old Spanish troops. Their inexperience occasioned the mistakes they committed, the rumours they circulated that all was destroyed, because they themselves ran away, and the mischiefs which ensued; but they behaved gallantly....

One rises from a perusal of these words with a bewildered feeling that gallant behaviour among troops is identical with running away;—and that the whole army, with the exception of some of the old Spanish troops, exhibited their gallantry in this singular manner. But, as the statement, that the army was entirely a new one, is used apparently in the first instance to account for the artillery running off the field, it may be interesting to glance at the troops and brigades, whose inexperience seemed—in the duke's mind as he wrote—to have made their flight almost natural.

Of the eight troops of Horse Artillery present at the Battle of Waterloo, five were the old tried troops of the Peninsula, whose gallant services had been recorded year after year by the duke's own hand: Sir Hew Ross's, Sir Robert Gardiner's, Colonel Webber Smith's, Major Beane's, and Major Bull's. A sixth, Captain Whinyates's, was the famous Rocket Troop of Leipsic; and of the other two, one had fought at Buenos Ayres, and the other in Walcheren. It was to one of these latter and more inexperienced troops, Captain Mercer's, that the victory at one period of the day was due.

With regard to the field brigades of this new army, it would seem that Major Rogers's company had been engaged for two years past in the operations in Holland, and had been in the Walcheren Expedition previously; that Captain Sinclair's brigade had been at Copenhagen, Corunna, and Walcheren; Captain Sandham's at Copenhagen and Walcheren; Major Lloyd's at Walcheren; and that Captain Bolton's, the only brigade without war service, happened to be the one whose effect in breaking the head of the columns of the Imperial Guard has become historical,—and whose inexperience would therefore hardly appear to have been very detrimental. (Battalion Records of the Royal Artillery.) From this statement it is evident that the artillery element in the duke's army at Waterloo was veteran, rather than new;—for, if the troops and brigades possessed such records as are given above, much more did the majority of the field and staff officers present deserve the title of veterans.

But the next inaccuracy is more unpardonable; and the informants of the duke on the subject were guilty of errors for which there was no excuse. The duke wrote:

> In point of fact, I should have had no artillery during the whole of the latter part of the action, if I had not kept a reserve at the commencement.

Fortunately for the exposure of this grave inaccuracy, there is no point on which there is more full and official information both in Sir George Wood's and other despatches, and more detailed notice in private correspondence, than on the subject of the artillery reserves at Waterloo. As stated in the last chapter of this volume, it was composed of Sir Hew Ross's and Major Beane's troops of Horse Artillery, and Captain Sinclair's Field Brigade.

So far was this force from being kept in reserve, and being brought forward providentially at the end of the action to replace the runaways, that it was actually in action—every gun—almost at the *commencement of the day*, and suffered the heaviest losses before half-past one. By a happy coincidence, the artillery, which must have been represented to the duke as his reserve, is mentioned by Sir Augustus Frazer (*Letters*):

> Some time before this—*i.e.*, the massing of the second line *during the cavalry attacks*—the duke ordered me to bring up all the reserve Horse Artillery, which at that moment were *Mercer's* and *Bull's troops*."

But, instead of these troops being a reserve kept, as the duke's letter says, "from the commencement,"—they also had both been in action from the beginning of the day, and Bull's troop had actually been sent to the centre of the second line "to refit and repair disabled carriages!" (*Letters*.)

The importance of this inaccuracy in the letter cannot be overrated. If the artillery, which the duke admits having had at the end of the day, was not the reserve, which he had kept in hand—and it certainly was not,—what was it? The asserted flight of the gunners with their limbers and ammunition hangs upon the truth, or otherwise, of there having been reserves in hand to replace them. But the fact of these reserves having been in action from the beginning of the day is incontestable; and is proved by the correspondence of Sir Hew Ross, who commanded one of the reserve troops, as well as by the official and semi-official correspondence of others.

It is possible that the arrival of Sir Robert Gardiner's troop, with Vivian's and Vandeleur's brigades, from the left of the line, at the end of the day, may have deceived the duke's informant, and led him to imagine that it was fresh artillery from the reserve. That it was not so, however, but merely moved with the division to which it was attached, is a matter of fact; and at no time in the day was this troop ever in reserve. Therefore, in a vital point, the duke's letter is unquestionably inaccurate.

The next statement in the letter, which demands scrutiny is the following:

> The artillery was placed with orders not to engage with artillery, but to fire only when bodies of troops came under their fire. It was very difficult to get them to obey this order.

Sir John Bloomfield, who was on Sir George Wood's staff, carried this order to all the troops and brigades, and is confident that, with one exception, it was rigidly obeyed. He remembers that the duke saw a French gun struck by a shot from one of the English batteries—and, under the impression that it came from Captain Sandham's brigade, he sent orders to have that officer placed in arrest. This was not done some satisfactory explanation having been given—relieving Captain Sandham of the disobedience. Singularly enough, the offender was never discovered, until, in 1870, with the publication of General Mercer's *Diary*, came the confession of the crime:

> About this time, being impatient of standing idle, and annoyed by the batteries on the Nivelle road, I ventured to commit a folly, for which I should have paid dearly had our duke chanced to be in our part of the field. I ventured to disobey orders, and open a slow, deliberate fire at the battery, thinking, with my 9-pounders, soon to silence his 4-pounders. (Vol.1.)

As Captain Mercer's troop was placed near Sandham's brigade at this time, it is evident that this occurrence, and that mentioned by Sir John Bloomfield, are identical. Sir John, whose duties carried him to all parts of the field, and whose recollection of the day is as clear as possible, asserts positively, that in no other instance was the order disobeyed; and it will be seen from accounts, both French and English, to be quoted hereafter, that the order to fire upon bodies of troops approaching was literally obeyed with the most marked results. Was it, then, quite worthy of the Duke of Wellington to reason from the particular to the general, and to visit the disobedience of one officer upon a whole corps? As has been well said by the son of one of the bravest artillery officers on the field, Sir Robert Gardiner, (Colonel Gardiner R.H.A.):

> If a regiment of infantry had run away, and all the others had behaved splendidly—would the whole arm have been similarly condemned? Would it not have been more just to reward those who deserved it?

The mention of reward suggests the next amazing inconsistency in the duke's letter—and makes it almost certain that it was written on receiving some subsequent information from another source—not from his personal observation. In this letter, dated six months after the battle, he wrote: "It would not do to reward a corps under such circumstances;" and again: "The field officers know the reason I have not to recommend them for a favour." How are these sentences to be reconciled with the following extract from the *London Gazette*, which immediately followed the battle, dated Whitehall, 22 June, 1815, and was issued while all its details must have been fresh in the duke's recollection?

> His Royal Highness the Prince Regent has further been pleased to nominate and appoint the undermentioned officers to be Companions of the said most Honourable Military Order of the Bath, *upon the recommendation of Field Marshal the Duke of Wellington, for their services in the battles fought upon the 16th and 18th of June last*:
>
> | | |
> |---|---|
> | Lieut.-Colonel S. G. Adye | Royal Artillery. |
> | Lieut.-Colonel R. Bull | "   " |
> | Lieut.-Colonel C. Gold | "   " |
> | Lieut.-Colonel A. Macdonald | "   " |
> | Lieut.-Colonel J. Parker | "   " |
> | Major T. Rogers | "   " |
> | Lieut.-Colonel J. W. Smith | "   " |
> | Lieut.-Colonel J. S. Williamson | "   " |
> | Colonel Sir G. A. Wood, Kt. | "   " |

This list includes the very field officers of whom the duke wrote afterwards,:

They know the reason I have not to recommend them for a favour.

Was it no favour to be recommended for the Order of the Bath? Again the duke in December, 1815, wrote:

> It would not do to recommend a corps under such circumstances.

Let the reader glance at the following picture of an unrewarded corps.

Out of thirteen troops and brigades, with the requisite staff, the following officers obtained rewards, in addition to the nine appointments to the Order of the Bath, quoted above. It must be remembered that the number eligible excluded subalterns, and was further reduced by the death of Majors Beane, Lloyd, Ramsay, Cairnes, and Captain Bolton.

Brevet promotion, for service at Waterloo:

> Major R. Bull to be Lieut.-Colonel, dated 18th June, 1815.
> Major J. Parker to be Lieut.-Colonel   "   "   "   "

Captain E. Whinyates to be Major " " " "
Captain T. Dynely to be Major " " " "
Captain A. Macdonald to be Major " " " "

Brevet promotion for services at Waterloo was also conferred in January 1819 on

Captain C. Napier
Captain W. Webber
Captain W. Brereton Subaltern at Waterloo
Captain R. H. Ord Subaltern at Waterloo

At the request, also, of the Duke of Wellington, (dated Paris, 2 Aug. 1815), Sir George Wood obtained permission to accept a knighthood of the Order of Maria Theresa, from the Emperor of Austria; and, a few days later, (21 Aug. 1815), the Order of St. Wladimir, from the Emperor of Russia.

Yet again, at the request of the Duke of Wellington, (8 Oct. 1815), the following officers obtained permission to accept from the Emperor of Russia the Order of St. Anne, "in testimony of His Majesty's approbation of their services and conduct, particularly in the late battles fought in the Netherlands:"

Lieut.-Colonel Sir J. May   K.C.B., R.H.A.
Lieut.-Colonel Sir H. Ross   "   "
Lieut.-Colonel Sir R. Gardiner "   "
Lieut.-Colonel R. Bull   "   "
Major A. Macdonald   "   "

It is unnecessary to add that the boon service granted for the Battle of Waterloo, and the Waterloo medals, were given to the artillery present, without exception. It would, therefore, appear that for a corps which did not deserve to be rewarded, it did not fare badly; and that its merits were only called in question when pensions based on an unpopular precedent were asked for. It is also impossible that the duke could have been so generous in his original recommendations, had he known of his own personal observation, that which he stated in his letter of the 21st December, and which must now receive grave consideration; the asserted flight from the field of Battle of many of the artillerymen with their limbers, &c.

In ascertaining the unmistakable inaccuracy of this cruel and hasty assertion, which must have been made by the Duke of Wellington on the most worthless evidence, the advantage of the late publication of the letter has become apparent. Much of the evidence, which will be adduced to rebut it, was not written with the view of meeting such an accusation, but is merely extracted from the simple narrative of a battle, in which the facts are stated without any idea of their being questioned. Had the duke's letter been published while the writers of many of the letters to be quoted were alive, their answers would not have had half the historical value they now possess, for they would have been regarded as the pleadings of interested defendants. The statements of disinterested historians will conclude this brief argument.

When the celebrated charges of the French cavalry at Waterloo took place, the English guns lined the crest of the position, and the Infantry was formed in squares in their rear. The order given by the duke was that the artillerymen should stand to their guns as long as possible, and then take refuge in the infantry squares; and that *the limbers should be sent behind the squares.* This order was carried to the various batteries by Sir John Bloomfield, and was obeyed to the letter. Colonel Gardiner writes:

> The idea of six limbers, with six horses in each limber, going into a square of Infantry, was of course an impossibility, and never contemplated. (Communicated by Sir. J. Bloomfield.)

The gunners had cartouche-bags slung round them, containing ammunition, and invariably, with the exception of those of Captain Mercer's troop, took refuge in the adjacent squares, or under the bayonets of the kneeling ranks. When the cavalry retired, on each occasion the gunners ran out, and, as a rule, the guns were in action against the retreating cavalry before they had gone sixty yards. The delay of a few moments occurred once or twice, while shot were being brought from the limbers; and Sir John Bloomfield remembers an expression of impatience escaping the duke on one of these occasions. Nor was it unnatural. Colonel Gardiner writes:

> To lose an opportunity of inflicting destruction on the French cavalry, directly they turned their backs, and before they could get out of the range of canister, must have been very tantalising.

But that the delay ever exceeded a few moments, or that a single limber ever left the ground, Sir John Bloomfield is confident is an utter delusion. Such an occurrence as is described in the duke's letter could not have happened without being well known. The duke himself said, "It is known to many;" and yet Sir John lived for three years with the headquarter staff in Paris, and never heard even an insinuation on the subject. Another Waterloo survivor (General B. Cuppage, R.A.), writes on this point to the Author:

> I never did hear, nor anyone else, of the artillery misbehaving at Waterloo. Sir Alexander Dickson took me with him into Brussels after the battle. We saw every officer who came in, and the action was in every part the constant theme of conversation, both in our private, as well as more general moments. Had anything bearing such a term taken place, it would certainly have been canvassed. I was in daily conversation with our wounded in the town. Surely, I may say, but that the Duke of Wellington says it, it is as cruel as it is unjust.

If known to many, it could hardly have escaped the commanding officer of the corps most interested. The fact that Sir George Wood did not write his despatches to the ordnance until the 24th June,—that during the six days' interval since the battle he had been constantly with the duke,—and yet that he could write as follows, proves most clearly that the duke himself cannot have been aware of what he afterwards wrote to Lord Mulgrave, and that his letter must have been based on subsequent malicious and worthless testimony. The wording of Sir George Wood's letters have an almost providential bearing on the point at issue; and could not have been used, had there been even a doubt as to the conduct of the corps.

He wrote, dated Le Cateau, 24 June, 1815:

> I beg leave to call the attention of His Lordship the Master-General to the skill and intrepidity so eminently displayed by the British and German artillery. The accompanying return of their loss will show how much they participated in the action, and I can assure His Lordship the Master-General, that, notwithstanding their being outnumbered by the artillery of the enemy, *their merits never shone more conspicuous* than on this occasion. It now remains for me to express with much pleasure and satisfaction that *every officer and man in the field of battle did their duty*.

With his despatch, Sir George wrote a private letter to General Macleod, (dated Le Cateau, 24 June, 1815) in which the following passage occurs:

> I do assure you, I have not words to express the extreme good

conduct of the corps. All exerted themselves, both officers and men, and such a conflict of guns never was in the memory of man.

But there are recorded, also, the opinions of the generals of other arms, under whose immediate command various troops and brigades served: and who would have known had any misconduct occurred among them, better than the duke himself, on account of the more limited field of their observation. General Colquhoun Grant's complimentary order with reference to Colonel Webber Smith's Troop has already been quoted in the last chapter. The following order was issued by Lord Hill, dated Nivelle, 20 June, 1815:

> The highly distinguished conduct of the 2nd Division, and Colonel Mitchell's Brigade of the 4th Division, who had the good fortune to be employed in the memorable action, merit His Lordship's highest approbation; and he begs that ... Colonel Gold, commanding Royal Artillery of the 2nd Corps, ...
> .... Major Sympher, commanding a troop of Horse Artillery, King's German Legion, Captain Napier (to whose lot it fell to command the 9-pounder Brigade, 2nd Division, on the death of Captain Bolton), will accept his best thanks for their exemplary conduct, and will be pleased to convey his sentiments to the officers, non-commissioned officers, and men under their command.

The following extract from the 5th Division orders, by Sir James Kempt, dated 19 June 1815, speaks equally favourably of another brigade:

> The British brigade of artillery commanded by Major Rogers, and the Hanoverian brigade commanded by Major Heisse, were most nobly served, and judiciously placed; and these officers and men will be pleased to accept of his—*i.e.* the major-general's—particular thanks for their service.

References to the services of other brigades, and of the Horse Artillery, by the officers of the corps under whom they served, have already been quoted; and in every case commendation of the warmest description was passed upon them. The following quotation from Sir Augustus Frazer's correspondence is interesting here, as asserting what was denied by the duke in his letter to Lord Mulgrave, that the men took shelter in the squares.

The repeated charges of the enemy's noble cavalry were similar to the first: each was fruitless. Not an infantry soldier moved; and, on each charge, abandoning their guns, our men sheltered themselves between the flanks of the squares. Twice, however, the enemy tried to charge in front; these attempts were entirely frustrated by the fire of the guns, wisely reserved till the hostile squadrons were within twenty yards of the muzzles. In this, the cool and quiet steadiness of the troops of Horse Artillery was very creditable. (*Letters*.)

This was written two days after the battle; and no man had better opportunity of seeing the conduct of his corps than the writer. Every historian of the battle endorses this version: and the testimony of an impartial historian always represents the carefully sifted testimony of many. Sir Edward Cust, the laborious military annalist, writes thus:

Suddenly some bugles were heard to sound, and all the artillerymen, abandoning their guns and tumbrils, ran back into the infantry squares. . . . In a moment, the artillery gunners quitted the protection of the squares, and running up to their guns, which were most of them ready loaded, opened heavily with grape and with every species of projectile. . . . The cavaliers again mounted the plateau; again, the gunners abandoned their guns, and took refuge within the squares.

Creasy writes:

As the French receded from each attack, the British artillerymen rushed forward from the centre of the squares, where they had taken refuge, and plied their guns on the retiring horsemen.

The same is the account given by every historian of the battle. Were they all dreaming? or were they in some conspiracy to conceal the truth? And if so, did the duke himself join it? In the thirty-seven years of his life after Waterloo, he never contradicted the numerous accounts of the battle, all of which agreed in their statement of the eminent services of the artillery. Was it consistent in one, who professed belief in an occurrence "known to many," and who gave that belief as a ground for the refusal of favours—to allow such passages as the following to be published without contradiction, unless indeed he had subsequently ascertained the worthlessness of his information? (This seems the most probable solution of the difficulty.) Chaplain-General G. R. Gleig wrote (*Battle of Waterloo*):

There, every arm did its duty; the artillery from the beginning to the close of the day.

Again:

In the course of the day every battery was brought into action; and not even the records of that noble corps can point to an occasion in which they better did their work.

Sir James Shaw Kennedy, (*Waterloo*), in summing up his description of the battle, says:

Full scope was thus given for the British cavalry and artillery to display their surpassing gallantry and excellence; and they did not fail to display these qualities in an eminent degree.

But it has been admitted that Captain Mercer's troop was an exception to the others; that his men did not take shelter within the Infantry squares. Let him tell his own story (*Diary*):

Sir Augustus, pointing out our position between two squares of Brunswick infantry, left us with injunctions to remember the duke's orders (to retire within the squares) and to economise our ammunition. The Brunswickers were falling fast . .. these were the very boys whom I had but yesterday seen throwing away their arms and fleeing, panic-stricken, from the very sound of our horses' feet.... Every moment I feared they would again throw down their arms and flee.... To have sought refuge amongst men in such a state were madness; the very moment our men ran from their guns, I was convinced, would be the signal for their disbanding. We had better, then, fall at our posts than in such a situation.

He accordingly made his men stand to the guns, until the cavalry were within a few feet of them; and on each occasion the havoc he wrought among them—as he drove them back—was frightful. The immense heap of dead, lying in front of Mercer's guns, was such that Sir Augustus Frazer said that, in riding over the field next day,:

He could plainly distinguish the position of C Troop from the opposite height by the dark mass, which, even from that distance, formed a remarkable feature in the field. (*Diary*.)

Captain Mercer's men, therefore, were those who did not obey the duke's order. It was a fortunate act of disobedience, and it saved the Brunswickers; but Captain Mercer was severely punished for it. He was not recommended for brevet rank; and, on his appointment by Lord Mulgrave to a vacant troop, he was deprived of it by the Duke of Wellington, who got it summarily reduced in 1816. (*Diary*.) Did, however, the limbers of Captain Mercer's battery ever leave the ground? That they did not, can be shown most clearly. In his diary, he describes the state of his troop after a heavy fire, to which it was exposed *after* the charges of the French cavalry. In the description, he says:

> The guns came together in a confused heap, the trails crossing each other, and the whole *dangerously near the limbers* and ammunition waggons.

The same description also proves that the frightful losses suffered by the troop took place during the very time when, according to the duke's letter, the men and limbers would have been off the field. In going to take up the position, they moved at a gallop, and in so compact a body, that the duke cried out: "Ah! that's the way I like to see Horse Artillery move!" In a short time, such was the havoc committed among men and horses, that Captain Mercer wrote:

> I sighed for my poor troop; it was already a wreck.

With regard to the insinuation as to the lack of artillery at the end of the battle, it is shown clearly by Siborne, in his model of the battle as it was at a quarter before 8 p.m., that thirteen troops and brigades of the Royal Artillery were in action, when the final attack took place; *this being the entire number with the army*. Of these, some were so crippled by losses—as Mercer's was—that they were unable to join in the pursuit; and possibly some recollection of this fact may have been in the duke's mind when he wrote. That the artillery fire, however, at the end of the day was slack from the cause stated in the duke's letter is an utter mistake; nor do the French seem to have found it very slack, as will be seen presently.

One word before appealing to a few other historians. If such conduct had taken place, as is described in the letter under consideration, it would have been bruited over the whole army. Concealment, or collusion, would have been impossible; enquiries would have been officially instituted. To believe that such an occurrence could have been kept quiet, requires a considerably greater stretch of credulity, than to believe that the Duke of Wellington was misinformed. In fact, that such unanimity of testimony to one version, and such a general agreement to be silent to another, should be possible, unless the former were true, and the latter imaginary, would be nothing short of a miracle. One or two miracles of this description would demolish all belief in history.

In the earliest and most detailed account of the Battle of Waterloo, the tenth edition of which was published in 1817, and which is called *The Battle of Waterloo, also of Ligny, and Quatre Bras, described by the series of accounts published by authority, by a near observer*, edited by Captain G. Jones, the following passage occurs:

> No account yet published of the battle, seen by the Editor, has mentioned in adequate terms the effect of our artillery at Waterloo—no *English* account at least. *The enemy felt* it, and in their manner of expressing themselves have passed the greatest compliments. A French account, given in our preceding pages, says: 'The English artillery made *dreadful* havoc in our ranks.'....
> 'The Imperial Guard made several charges, but was constantly repulsed, *crushed by a terrible artillery, that each minute seemed to multiply.'* (At this time, according to the duke's letter, he had nothing but his reserve artillery, the rest having quitted the field!) These invincible grenadiers *beheld the grape-shot make day through their ranks*; they closed promptly and coolly their shattered ranks.... In proportion as they ranged up the eminence, and darted forward on the squares, which occupied its summit, *the Artillery vomited death upon them, and killed them in masses*...
> ... In an account given by an officer of the *Northumberland*, of Napoleon's conversation on board that ship, he says: 'Bonaparte gives great credit to our infantry and artillery.'

Again:

> The artillery on both sides was well served, but Bonaparte had upwards of 250 pieces in the field. Notwithstanding our inferiority in this arm, which was still more apparent from the size of the enemy's guns (being 12-pounders, ours only 9 and 6), than from their numbers, ours were so well fought, that I believe it is allowed by all they did equal execution.... See also the account of Captain Bolton and Napier's Brigade of Foot Artillery, from which it appears the artillery had turned the enemy, previous to the advance of the Guards. The French displayed the greatest rage and fury; they cursed the English while they were fighting,

and cursed the precision with which the English grape-shot was fired, which 'was neither too high nor too low, but struck right in the middle.'

From the many writers who have done credit to the exertions and courage of the artillery at Waterloo, three more extracts will be made.

In proof of the activity of the corps at the end of the day, the following quotation, from an author (Gleig) already mentioned, is given. In describing the reception given to the French Imperial Guard, he says:

> The English gunners once more plied their trade. It was positively frightful to witness the havoc that was occasioned in that mass.

Sir James Shaw Kennedy also describes the strength of the British artillery fire at the end of the day.

In a Paper on 'The Campaign of Waterloo,' which appeared in the *United Service Journal*, in 1834, the following passage occurs:

> If we admit that, during this arduous and terrible day, the British Infantry acted up to the right standard of soldiership, which their long career of victory had established, it must be added that *the artillery actually surpassed all expectation*, high as, from their previous conduct, that expectation naturally was. In point of zeal and courage, the officers and men of the three arms were of course fully upon a par; but the circumstances of the battle were favourable to the artillery; and certainly, the skill, spirit, gallantry, and indefatigable exertion which they displayed, almost surpasses belief.

Only one more witness will be called from the ranks of historians. Hooper, in his work on Waterloo, to which he devoted eight years, and in the compilation of which he used every known authority on both sides, made use of words which appropriately close this argument:

> The artillery, so devoted and effective, gathered another branch from the tree of honour.

www.ingramcontent.com/pod-product-compliance
Lightning Source LLC
Chambersburg PA
CBHW031621160426
43196CB00006B/225